Days on the Family Farm

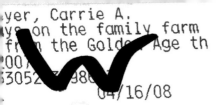

DAYS ON THE
FAMILY FARM

From the
GOLDEN AGE
through the
GREAT DEPRESSION

CARRIE A. MEYER

UNIVERSITY OF MINNESOTA PRESS
MINNEAPOLIS • LONDON

Published with assistance from the Margaret S. Harding Memorial Endowment honoring the first director of the University of Minnesota Press.

Maps were created by Gary Lauben at LilyPad Graphics. www.LilyPadGraphics.com.

Unless otherwise credited, photographs are from the author's family collection.

Published by the University of Minnesota Press
111 Third Avenue South, Suite 290
Minneapolis, MN 55401-2520
http://www.upress.umn.edu

Library of Congress Cataloging-in-Publication Data

Meyer, Carrie A.
    Days on the family farm : from the Golden Age through the Great Depression / Carrie A. Meyer.
        p. cm.
    Includes bibliographical references and index.
    ISBN-13: 978-0-8166-5032-3 (hc : alk. paper)
    ISBN-10: 0-8166-5032-2 (hc : alk. paper)
    ISBN-13: 978-0-8166-5033-0 (pb : alk. paper)
    ISBN-10: 0-8166-5033-0 (pb : alk. paper)
        1. Farm life—Illinois—Winnebago County—History—20th century.
    2. Rural families—Illinois—Winnebago County—Diaries. I. Title.
    S521.5.I3M49 2007
    630.9773'31—dc22
                                                    2007011937

Printed in the United States of America on acid-free paper

The University of Minnesota is an equal-opportunity educator and employer.

12 11 10 09 08 07   10 9 8 7 6 5 4 3 2 1

THIS BOOK IS DEDICATED TO
THOSE WHO MADE

Guilford Township

A COMMUNITY AND TO THOSE WHO
STILL HOLD THE BONDS DEAR

Contents

Acknowledgments

A project that spans as many years as this one involves many people who assisted either directly or with moral support along the way; they are too numerous to mention, but their contributions are nonetheless appreciated. Many others must be mentioned, for without their help this project could not have been accomplished.

I am particularly indebted to those who provided key research materials and permission to use them. Janice Lyford Leitz loaned her mother's diaries from 1930 to 1934. Stanley Wayne Lyford loaned several diaries that belonged to May Davis. The Guilford Hope Grange provided access to its secretarial records. Others provided photographs and are credited in the captions.

Many members of the Lyford, Davis, and Campbell families and of the Guilford community provided interviews, answered questions, and searched for information or pictures. I am grateful to JoAnne and Wilbur Reid, Carolyn and Gene Wheeler, John and Shirley Pearse, Sharon Waugh, Frances and Bob Green, Harold and Beulah McLarty, Sandy Lyford, Leslie Oswald, Jackie Otto, Warren and Helen Paulson, Jim and Harriet Reid, Bob Greene, Frank Lyford, David Lyford, and Bob and Ila Price.

The organizations in Winnebago and Boone counties that facilitated research include the Boone County Historical Society, the Cherry Valley Historical Society, the Winnebago County Farm Bureau, and the Winnebago County Association for Home and Community Education.

Many readers offered generous comments that helped shape the manuscript, including Jeremy Atack, Allan G. Bogue, Ernest Carlson, Bruce L. Gardner, Craig Heinecke, Laurie Hertzel, Mary Laschober, Rob Nicholson, Fred Peters, Debra Reid, Yesim Yilmaz, and two anonymous reviewers.

Gary Lauben created the maps and touched up photographs. Dan Snodderly helped trim this manuscript to a reasonable size; his editorial judgment was extremely valuable.

Other editors made critical suggestions, including Michael O'Malley, Jack Repcheck, Elizabeth Demers, Kathleen Courrier, and Todd Orjala at the University of Minnesota Press. Many colleagues at George Mason University and elsewhere gave me helpful advice or support. Several research assistants lightened my workload, including Adam Summers, James Plummer, Andrés Marroquín Gramajo, and Chloe Kissinger. Many librarians and information specialists have been instrumental. John Molyneaux from the Rockford Library, Mary Pryor from Rockford College, and Lee Grady from the Wisconsin Historical Society deserve special mention.

The Midway Village and Museum Center and the Rockford Historical Society facilitated research support. The efforts of Suzanne and John Crandall, David Byrnes, and my parents, Norman and Anne Meyer, are much appreciated. Walter Williams and the economics department at George Mason University provided summer research funding.

Finally, this research could not have been accomplished without the support of my family. My mother contributed tireless research assistance, and my father and older brother, Karl, answered my incessant questions that probed their farming knowledge. My younger brother, Eric, found the diaries, and he and my sister, Becky, encouraged my efforts throughout.

Diaries of a
Family Farm

As children, my siblings and I walked down Bell School Road, past Spring Creek Road, and over Keith Creek to Bell School. The school occupied a corner of the land my father farmed in Illinois. Before he farmed it, it had been Elmo's farm.

Elmo—E. M. Davis. His name still appeared in chalky white letters on the large rock out by the road in front of our house, despite an effort to scrub it off. Elmo was not my grandfather; he was my grandfather's elder cousin. Although he died before my parents were married, his memory was alive in the barns we played in.

May Lyford Davis was Elmo's wife; and it was she who kept the farm diaries, although he was the main character in them. May began keeping a diary in 1896 and continued with some gaps until shortly before her death in 1944. May and Elmo were married on January 1, 1901; from that date until her death, May also kept careful ledgers of farm income and expenses. I came upon the diaries and ledgers in November 2000, after my grand-mother died and the books were found in her attic.

As I read through the diaries searching for clues to the young life of my grandfather, I soon realized that the story unfolding before me had much more to offer. Although I had always known that most media images of farm life were sharply at odds with my personal experience and my sense of family history, I was astonished to read her descriptions of community life and farming activity. Community life was far more vibrant than I had imagined, and economic life was far more prosperous.

May and Elmo married during the Golden Age of Agriculture, but they spent their life together on a rather typical midwestern farm. It was about average in size for an Illinois farm, and they produced roughly the same crops and livestock that their neighbors did. The farm was located in a region with affluent roots in the old Guilford Township of Winnebago County, Illinois

Elmo M. Davis, ca. 1925.

(since incorporated into the city of Rockford), in the north-central part of the state, about eighty miles west of Chicago. Rockford was a prototypical midwestern industrial town. Surrounding smaller towns, such as Argyle, Cherry Valley, and Belvidere, had their counterparts all across the Midwest.

Like almost all midwestern family farms, May and Elmo's farm was a commercial enterprise; they sold most of their produce in the marketplace and depended on the cash income. Popular media often separate commercial farmers from family farmers. Commercial farmers are depicted as post–World War II phenomena with few roots in agricultural communities and few family ties; their success has come at the expense of family farmers. Family farmers, on the other hand, have trouble feeding their families and paying their debts; most are purported to have gone broke during the Great Depression and fled the land, after years of scratching out a meager existence with two mules and a plow. But such images belie the reality of midwestern family farming.

Commercial farming began in Winnebago County in 1836, as soon as the earliest settlers made it through the first year, and Chicago began to grow explosively as a wholesale market for commercial agriculture.[1] Although Guilford farmers benefited early on from proximity to Chicago, this advantage diminished by the late 1800s, when railroads linked almost all midwestern farming communities to large agricultural markets. Proximity to Rockford also benefited Guilford farmers, just as other midwestern cities and towns benefited nearby farmers with access to markets.

May's diaries and ledgers tell the story of midwestern farming through the Golden Age before World War I and through the trials of the 1920s and 1930s. It is an epic tale of family and community, prosperity and depression, and of automobiles, horses, gasoline engines, and tractors. The story ends with May's death in the midst of World War II, when farmers prospered once again. But by then the character of farming was changing irrevocably.

THE DIARIES AND LEDGERS

It was my brother who brought home the cardboard box of diaries from our grandmother's attic that Thanksgiving holiday of 2000; he set it on the kitchen table. The box was filled with little books of varying sizes—dozens of them. Eventually we discovered that while most of these diaries had belonged to May; others had belonged to her mother, Emily Lyford. The series of May's diaries was not entirely complete. It began in 1896, but many years were missing. Ultimately, with the help of family members, we found forty diaries that had belonged to May, eleven that had belonged to Emily, and another five that had belonged to Marian Lyford, May's niece by marriage.[2]

Farm diaries are not easy reading, however; I was fortunate to be related to the author. May's 1896 diary is a tiny book, only two by four inches, with thin delicate pages and seven entries to a two-page spread. That year May seldom wrote more than twenty words an entry. In some years the diaries were larger, so she had more room to write. The following entries appear for early January 1896:

> JAN 1—Fine day, S. wind. Opened new churn, leaked. Hauled up hickory wood from pasture.
>
> JAN 2—Windy. 7:40 AM ther. 29° above 0. Mrs. Geo Br & mama call on Mrs. Doolittle. Move hickory from pasture.
>
> JAN 3—7:00 AM 8° below 0. Very windy NW. Some plants frozen. Baked bread, cake, fried cakes. Churned.
>
> JAN 4—17° below 0. Mama & papa went to R. Starr & I went to singing school.

The diaries were intended to be a record of the weather and the accomplishments of the day. Births, deaths, illnesses, trips to town, and social events were recorded; so were the names of friends that stopped by. During her married life, May faithfully recorded Elmo's farming activity and that of

May Lyford, ca. 1896.

the hired man. She also recorded canning activity. Similar farm diaries have been mined for bits of information, but they have usually been dismissed as trivial. The unfamiliar people, places, and abbreviations make for awkward reading. Edited portions of only a few have been published.[3]

While May's notes might seem trivial, they were quite disciplined. I found that when I read through 365 entries similar to those above, clear images of seasons passing and powerful rhythms of farm life emerged. When I continued reading over the course of a decade or more, distinct patterns of social, economic, and technological change began to leap from the pages. There was nothing trivial about it; it was remarkable.

I was fortunate in that her brief descriptions of activity—often involving horses, buggies, and sleighs—took place on landscapes so familiar to me. And all the names, which might put off the average reader, pulled me in; their familiar sound echoed back across the memories of the generations, like the chords of an old hymn, connecting me to the time of my forebears. I was enchanted; before I knew what happened, I began to transcribe the diaries. With the help of modern software, I combed and reshuffled the diary entries to present May's story so that others might enjoy it.

The records in May's ledgers were even more disciplined. In these much larger books, May kept sections for general expenses (both farm and household), groceries, hired help, produce sold, and milk or cream sold. She created an index in the front, as a guide to the page where groceries for 1904 could be found, for example. May recorded each expenditure in chronological order, including each piece of candy, the stabling fee, the packet of garden seeds. She also recorded all produce sold chronologically—oats, hogs, hay, or corn—and often recorded the price and quantity in addition to the value. Frequently she noted the person or company the product was sold to. For hired help, both the wage rate and the length of contract were noted. Occasionally over the years, her accounting system changed; so I made adjustments for consistency. I transcribed the records of farm production and took careful notes on key expenditures. I added up figures to get monthly and yearly totals.

The ledgers provided an intimate economic record, and the diaries provided details on farming activity and family and community life. Archival family history and local historical resources helped to fill gaps and provide context; so did numerous interviews with members of the old Guilford community and extensive library and Internet research. When combined, the picture of life on the farm in Guilford Township from 1901 to 1944 was very nearly complete.

What was most missing, ironically, was May. She had little to say about herself. She almost never recorded private thoughts and rarely expressed emotion. May's mother revealed more of herself. Perhaps because rheumatoid arthritis left May unable to walk shortly after she married, she preferred to record her husband's activity. Still, May's words convey a quiet dignity and cheerful courage and determination in the face of her handicap. Her story includes women and children as well as men. The prominent place of family and community in her life is clear. And her command of the household financial information attests to the quality of her partnership with her husband, Elmo.

MAY AND ELMO IN THE LATE NINETEENTH CENTURY

May and Elmo grew up living on farms across the road from each other. Both were born in 1873. Elmo Davis was born on the farm in Guilford Township where he and May later spent their married life. May Lyford and her family came to live across the road from the Davis farm when May was a little girl. A letter, dated 1887 and addressed to Elmo, implied that he was sweet on her then, but May and Elmo married later in life than many of their contemporaries; they were twenty-seven years old at the time of their marriage.[4]

Elmo's father, Joseph Davis, died in 1892; Elmo took over the farm just in time to face the worst recession of the nineteenth century. That might explain why he was not ready to settle down earlier. Financial panic struck all around the country in 1893. Rockford industry was hit hard, and farm prices dropped sharply nationwide from 1893 to 1896, before the economy began to recover. Elmo had debts to pay off during those years.[5]

The parents and grandparents of May and Elmo were early pioneers to Winnebago County. They were among the enterprising New England Yankees who were the primary settlers of northern Illinois. Joseph Davis had arrived in 1839, when he was fourteen years old. His parents, Thaddeus and Catherine Davis, traveled six weeks on foot with their ten children, driving sheep, cattle, and teams of oxen hauling all their possessions to settle in the Guilford area. May's father, Joseph Lyford, came to Winnebago County as a child of three years in 1842. His parents settled in Roscoe, about fifteen miles north of Guilford. The family of Elmo's mother, Almina Campbell, was among the earliest pioneers. Her parents arrived in 1836 and settled in Durand, in the northwest corner of the county. May's mother, Emily Brown, came to Rockford in the mid-1850s when her father, the Reverend Brown, accepted a position at the Rockford Female Seminary.

Joseph Davis had seen firsthand dramatic transformations on the fertile Illinois prairie. Chicago was but a fur-trading settlement when Chief Black Hawk was defeated in 1832 and the settlement of northern Illinois began. But it grew frantically as it fed on the farm trade. Farmers traveled to Chicago in long lines of wagons with their livestock and grain; they bought lumber, nails, tools, and other goods to take back with them. Beginning in the 1850s, the building of railroads exploded in Illinois and farther west; virtually all major lines led to Chicago. By the time of the Civil War, Chicago was the most important livestock market in the United States. During the war, the Chicago Board of Trade began to establish formal rules for futures markets. It had already become one of the most important grain markets in the world.[6]

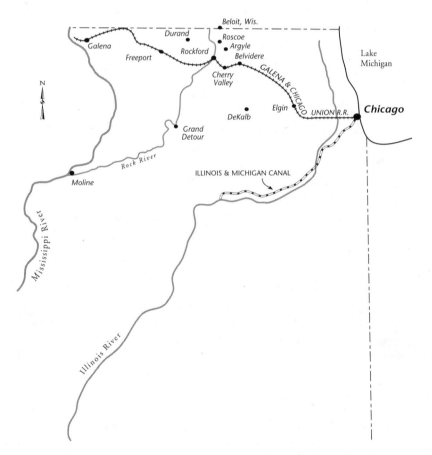

Towns and features significant to the settlement of northern Illinois in the early 1830s.

When the Davis family settled in Guilford in 1839, Rockford was little more than a site for a sawmill and a gristmill on the Rock River, midway between Chicago and Galena. (Galena was a lead-mining town on the Mississippi River, the only significant outpost of white settlement in northern Illinois before 1832.) But by the mid-1850s, Rockford was well known for its farm implements and flour mills. Shortly after the railroad came through in 1852, Rockford became known as the Reaper City. It was home to the Manny reaper, a successful competitor of Chicago's McCormick reaper. The company that produced the Manny became a cornerstone in Rockford industry for many decades. During the Civil War, Rockford flour mills supplied the Union army, and area farmers prospered when prices for wheat, other grains, and livestock shot up.

In the latter part of the nineteenth century, when May and Elmo were young, midwestern farmers lived well in many respects. They had large frame houses, teams of horses to power an increasing array of mechanical equipment, and large barns to hold their crops and shelter their animals. (Farmers west of Illinois adopted machinery even more readily and, once settled, caught up quickly to those in Illinois, Indiana, and Ohio.) The farms provided most of the food that families needed, but market produce also provided cash income to reinvest in the farm and to spend on consumer goods. Even though farm prices and consumer prices were falling during this time, Illinois farm values nearly doubled between 1870 and 1900.[7] (Farm values in Iowa, Minnesota, and Nebraska increased even more rapidly, though from a much lower base.)

Many farm families lived surrounded by other kin, although limited farmland forced some family members to look elsewhere for opportunities. Some of the nine siblings of Elmo's father had either died or moved away. But at least three families of Davis cousins still lived and farmed in Guilford Township in the early 1890s. Elmo's aunt Harriet Davis and cousins Aham and Florence were particularly close kin. Not only was Harriet the widow of his uncle Jacob Davis; she was also his mother's sister. Elmo's half sister, May Purdy, and her husband also farmed in Guilford Township. They had two daughters just a few years younger than Elmo. Elmo's full brother died, however, at the age of eighteen, and his half brother had also died before Elmo started school.[8]

May Lyford and her brother, Starr, moved to Guilford Township with their parents when May would have been ready to start school. They walked to school with Elmo and his brother, and many of their other schoolmates were Elmo's cousins. Many of their Lyford relatives lived farther north in

Winnebago County in Roscoe. May also had cousins on her mother's side that had moved out to Wichita, Kansas; May took the train out to stay with them for several weeks in 1896. Both May and Elmo had other relatives in Rockford, which was seven miles away.

While May and Elmo were young, Bell School was the center of social life in the northeast corner of the township. Originally named Enoch School after the first settler in Guilford Township, the school was rebuilt in 1869 with a new bell and a seating capacity for seventy students; all eight grades were in one room. Before the end of the century, Guilford residents built a town hall in the center of the township. It became the site for rallies, conventions, meetings, and larger social events than could take place at any of the five grade schools in the township.

Before the turn of the century most everyone in Guilford Township was either an early settler or the child or grandchild of an early settler. Although the bulk of them were New England Yankee stock, a few had come directly from England or Germany. And many others were Scottish; about five miles to the north of Guilford was the Scottish settlement of Argyle. These families had all come from Argyleshire, Scotland, beginning in 1836. The community had prospered, and the Scots were increasingly moving south into Guilford. By the turn of the century, all these groups had intermarried in the Guilford farming community.

Surrounding towns helped to define rural life for farming communities. Guilford Township itself had no town center beyond the town hall. Six miles to the north of the Davis and Lyford farms was Argyle, which had few businesses beyond the grain elevator and the creamery. Although Argyle had a train depot, it was not on a main line, and thus it hadn't fostered much growth. The Presbyterian church was the real core of the community. Cherry Valley was the closest town to the south, also about six miles from the Davis and Lyford farms. It was a bustling and diverse community of some eight hundred residents in the late nineteenth century. It had boomed when the railroad came through in 1852, headed northwest out of Chicago. It had many businesses to serve farmers, including grain elevators, livestock dealers, hotels, blacksmith shops, the flour and gristmill, and carriage makers, in addition to a variety of other shops. Cherry Valley also had a variety of churches and more recent immigrants than were found on the farms. Many of the Irish, for example, who came out to build the railroad had decided to stay in Cherry Valley. Belvidere was about six miles to the east, also on the main railroad line to Chicago. It was the Boone County seat and the site of a popular county fair. Belvidere had many more businesses

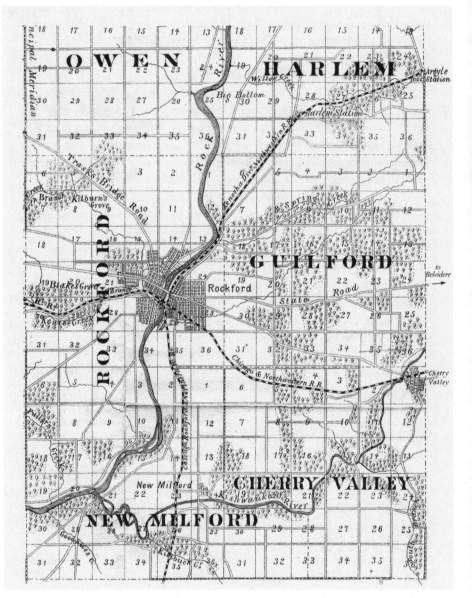

Guilford Township, Rockford, and Cherry Valley, Illinois, as depicted in an abstracter's map, ca. 1880.

and churches than Cherry Valley had; it was home to 6,750 people before the end of the century. Belvidere also had some heavy industry, but it had much less to offer than Rockford. In all three of these towns, the population was peaking and beginning to taper off at the turn of the century, as in other small towns across the Midwest.

CITY AND COUNTRYSIDE DIVERGE

In contrast with small midwestern towns, urban industrial areas, such as Chicago and Rockford, were growing rapidly, and a cultural divide had begun to open between rural and urban areas in the latter part of the nineteenth century. Industry diversified in Chicago and Rockford from its base in farm implements to include furniture, hardware, and machine tools in particular. Immigrants poured in to work in the factories. Yankees dominated the spirit of Rockford until after the Civil War, although many of the Irish immigrants that had built the railroad in the early 1850s stayed to build factories, and Swedish immigrants had also begun to arrive on the railroad, not long after it reached Rockford. After the Civil War, however, Swedish immigrants flooded into Rockford and soon became an important force in Rockford industry. By the turn of the century, Rockford's population had grown to over 31,000; the Swedes outnumbered the Yankees.[9] Hundreds of thousands of immigrants poured into Chicago; it grew to a city of 1.7 million people. Meanwhile, farmers became a minority in the nation's workforce for the first time in U.S. history.

By the turn of the century, midwestern cities boasted many modern conveniences that were absent on the farm. They had municipal water systems and electricity for factories, as well as good high schools, hospitals, libraries, and opera houses. Electric streetcars moved people, and telephone service was available to businesses.

As urban centers prospered, many farmers grew resentful of middlemen, some of whom were skimming off profits. Abuses in the late 1860s were real. Chicago grain elevators, in league with railroads, speculated in grain markets with inside knowledge about supply. The Chicago Board of Trade was also concerned and took action to initiate regulations.[10] About the time May and Elmo were born, the Granger movement was spreading rapidly, establishing cooperatives to purchase farm inputs and to market farm products. Illinois was the first state to pass what became known as Granger laws to break the arrangements between elevators and railroads and to give states the right to regulate railroads. The Grange had been established in 1867 with social and educational purposes in mind, but economic and political goals soon took over. The first grange in Illinois, Guilford Hope Grange, was chartered in Guilford Township in 1871; several other granges were also chartered in Winnebago County before 1875.[11] Most of the Grange cooperatives turned out to be financial failures, however, and the Grange died down just as suddenly as it had arisen.

Later in the nineteenth century, farming conditions in the Midwest were fairly prosperous, but farm prices were nevertheless falling, and they didn't turn around until 1897. Farm prices fell because production increased with the westward movement of the frontier. The total land in farms more than doubled between 1870 and 1900. Wheat production moved farther west, while Illinois farmers began to raise more corn and livestock and more oats for horses in urban markets. Because input prices and consumer prices were also falling, many farmers did well, although those with large debts suffered. Despite strong immigration, farm production outpaced population growth, so exports to Europe increased, which left farmers vulnerable to changing conditions in the world market. Other agrarian political movements, such as the Farmers' Alliance and the People's Party, flourished, especially on the Great Plains and in the South, throughout the late nineteenth century.[12] As the century ended, however, the farm situation was beginning to improve.

CHAPTER 1

THE NEW
CENTURY DAWNS
1901–1910

May and Elmo began their marriage on the first day of the new century, just weeks before the reign of Britain's queen Victoria came to an end. The new century would belong to America, whose industrial sector was now the largest and most innovative in the world. As U.S. corporations grew, many worried. Teddy Roosevelt was in the White House from 1901 to 1909 and gained a reputation as a "trust buster" for his efforts to reign in big business.

May and Elmo courted in 1900 with buggy rides and sleigh rides; then in 1901, the first gasoline-powered automobile, an Oldsmobile, arrived in Rockford. Within a few years, many area farmers, including Elmo, had bought stationary gasoline engines for power on the farm.

Farming prosperity had returned. What became known as the Golden Age of Agriculture had already begun by 1897, and it would last through World War I. With U.S. industry attracting European immigrants, urban areas continued to grow rapidly, and so did the demand for food. In the first decade of the century, thousands of Italians joined the Irish on Rockford's west side, and Swedish immigrants continued to settle on the east side of the river. Rockford's population increased by almost 50 percent over the decade, and Chicago grew to a city of two million people. The westward expansion of farmland was essentially ended, however; so now food prices moved higher and farm income increased.

Throughout 1900 while they courted, May and Elmo went to barn dances that followed barn raisings. Several of their close friends married that year; usually a barn raising or, in one case, a new house, preceded the wedding by several months. Elmo had built a new barn in 1898, and he built a new shed in 1900. Elmo's niece Bertha Purdy married Ely Breckenridge in 1900. Elmo helped Ely haul lumber for the raising of their barn. Before the end of the decade, however, Bertha and Ely moved to Tacoma, Washington.

May and Elmo Davis, January 1, 1901.

Other family members had already married and settled in the area. Elmo's cousin Aham Davis had married Carrie Whittle in 1891. Within a few years, they bought a 260-acre farm just north of Cherry Valley and built a beautiful multigabled house on it before their son, Fred (my grandfather), was born in 1894. Aham's sister, Florence, had married Ed Fitch in 1892, and they started a family the next year. Fred Whittle, Carrie's brother, also farmed in Guilford Township. He married Elmo's other niece, Belle Purdy, in 1903; their daughter, Marion, was born in 1904. Elmo's sister, May Purdy, also farmed with her husband over near the town hall.

When May and Elmo married, Elmo's mother, Almina, moved to Cherry Valley, so the newlyweds could set up housekeeping on the Davis farm. Almina lived with two sisters who were also widowed, Harriet Davis and Sophronia Post. These three elderly Campbell sisters were known throughout the Valley as Aunt Hat, Aunt Mina, and Aunt Phrone. Harriet was the mother of Aham, who lived just to the north. Elmo and May spent many a Sunday in Cherry Valley. During the winter months, Elmo brought wood to his mother and aunts, and on warm summer evenings, he and May came to call.

May's parents, Emily and Joseph, were still on their farm across the road and up the lane from Elmo and May, although they built a new house there in 1902. Shortly thereafter, May's brother, Starr, married Maggie McFarland, whose family also farmed nearby. The couple made their home about a mile to the southeast of Joseph and Emily's home, on a 160-acre farm that Joseph and Starr had bought some years earlier. A little more than a year into the marriage, children began arriving at regular intervals. First was Annetta in March 1904, and then came Joey; by 1910 Annetta had four brothers. Maggie's sister, Nettie, moved in with the family to help with the children.

New neighbors arrived by mid-decade, including Mat Ralston, from the Scottish community, who began farming the old Dan Davis place. Charles Kleckner was first mentioned in May's 1902 diary. He joined Joseph and Emily for dinner several times that year and was likely renting the farm he later owned, just to the west. The Peppers, an old-settler family, moved in 1902 to a farm south of Elmo and May on Bell School Road and just west of Starr's. Before long, Mary Pepper married Charles Kleckner, and they started a family. Across from the Peppers were the Molanders, one of the first Swedish families in the neighborhood.[1]

While others their age were busy raising children, no children were born to Elmo and May. Moreover, sometime between 1902 and 1907, May's rheumatoid arthritis overtook her, preventing her from walking ever again.

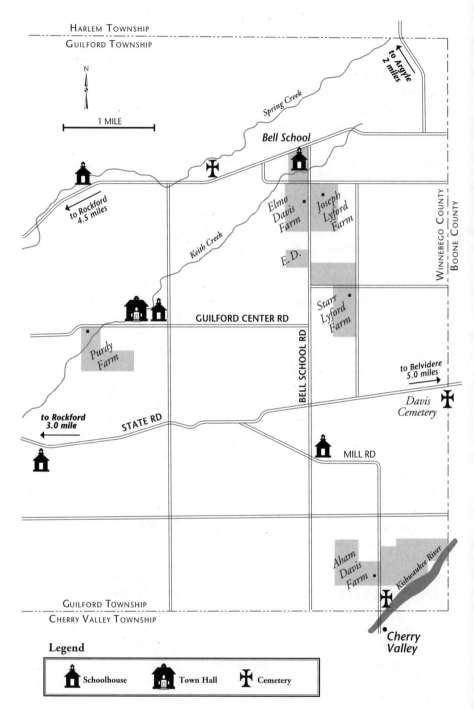

East side of Guilford Township, ca. 1905.

Her diaries for these painful years are absent, except for part of 1902; her ledgers record many doctor bills.

May's first year of marriage was not recorded in a diary either,[2] but many of the expenses in her 1901 accounts reflect changes as she settled in. Early in the year, a wedding present was exchanged for a carving set, and the silver was engraved. Lumber and brick were purchased for a new icehouse. There was also new carpet ($22.13), a mattress, a "refrigerator" (a $7 icebox), furniture, dresser scarves, a tablecloth, and other "household goods." Later in the spring, $63 was spent on lumber, and other expenditures were made for a sink, a pump, and pipe. Carpenters cost about $27. In June came "tin on porch roof," painting the carriage, wallpaper and white lead, and having pictures framed. A well drilled in November cost $67.50. All together, such expenses added up to more than $300 at a time when average factory wages in Rockford were about $470 a year.[3]

May did keep a diary for much of 1902, but she left many gaps. The diary fails to explain the weekly trips to Rockford, beginning in January, where

Carrie, Fred, and Aham Davis, ca. 1901.

she apparently saw a doctor, and other trips when Elmo went alone to Rockford and also apparently saw a doctor.

The doctor bills mounted in 1903 and 1904 and then stopped suddenly the next year. In 1903, on two separate occasions, expenses to Chicago and expenses at "Mudlavia" were recorded for about fifty dollars each time. In the late summer and fall of 1904, treatments with a Mrs. Van Anne added up to about a hundred dollars. Other payments to a Dr. Calkins were recorded regularly throughout both years until November 1904. Years earlier, in 1896, May had recorded a series of treatments for rheumatoid arthritis in Rockford.

Neither diaries nor ledgers clarify when May lost the ability to walk, but her mobility seems to have diminished around 1903. Judging from the activities in her diary, May was walking in 1902. She and Elmo hosted family dinners regularly for her parents and Starr and had other social dinners for family and friends. May had only weekly help with the wash that year, but beginning in mid-1903, a hired girl helped May with housework and cooking. In 1907 and 1908, social dinners at May's were rare; she and Elmo typically dined out on Sundays. Emily wrote in June 1908, "May walked a few steps." In January 1909, May wrote, "Elmo draw me over home in cart." (Elmo took the place of the horse!)

When May and Elmo went out, he carried her to and from the buggy and, in later years, to and from the automobile. She didn't use a wheelchair, not even when she and Elmo were both in their sixties. May, like her mother, was a tiny lady. Occasionally she recorded her weight in her diaries. In 1898 she weighed 96¾ pounds. By 1909 she had lost three pounds and continued to shed rather than gain weight with age. Elmo, on the other hand, was over six feet tall and a trim 179 pounds in 1909. (He added a few pounds with age.) May and Elmo joined in activities like picnics and ball games, where he would have had to carry her to a seat. But often when Elmo went to town, he dropped her off at her folks ("over home") or with the Purdys, who lived on the way to Rockford. When they went to town on errands together, she often waited in the buggy or auto.

Although May lost the ability to walk, she used her hands effectively. May sewed, quilted, and helped prepare fruits and vegetables for canning. She wrote many letters, and her handwriting did not deteriorate markedly until the late 1930s. Occasionally she even drove the horse and buggy.

Those who still remember as I write describe in similar terms how she maneuvered around her kitchen with her short-legged chair to attend to her affairs. The legs of the chair were cut off, so that her feet could rest on the floor. It was a sturdy but lightweight wooden armchair, and with the strength in her arms, the force of her bodyweight, and some pressure with her feet, she would pitch the chair from side to side and forward, or in the direction she wanted to go, across the wooden floor. It may seem odd, but she got used to it, and she preferred it to a wheelchair.

Thus, May also managed meals with the help of others. Sometimes May would mention in her diary when Elmo had helped. ("He help me.") May's mother also came down regularly and helped. Usually when there was a hired man to feed, May had a hired girl to run for her and do the things she couldn't do. Cooking involved lots of peeling potatoes and washing and cutting up fruits and vegetables; these were things that May could do. May had grown up helping her mother in the kitchen, and as a woman in her thirties and beyond, she was comfortable directing the efforts of others, despite her handicap.

RHYTHMS OF FARM LIFE IN 1908

After a gap of five years, May began keeping her diary again in 1908, when she and Elmo were both thirty-four years old. She recorded not her thoughts and feelings but the activities and the rhythms of daily life on the farm. In her ledgers, she kept track of the business of farming, including purchases of new machinery and equipment.

The record of 1908 that follows draws on Emily's diary as well as May's and is fortified with notes from May's ledger. Emily was an energetic sixty-four years and ninety-eight pounds in 1908. Her husband, Joseph, was sixty-eight years old and was slowing down considerably; Starr and Elmo were working much of his land.

January

New Year's Day, 1908, was a "fine, clear day, 10° above in the morning." May and Elmo celebrated with dinner at Starr and Maggie's, along with Joseph and Emily and Starr's in-laws. They all enjoyed Starr's new phonograph and a cutter ride. (A cutter was like Santa's sleigh.)

Although snow covered the ground on January 1, the January weather was relatively mild with many sunny days. More snow came at the end of the month; Starr's wagon wheels were broken, so he used the bobsled for his milk route. (Bobsled runners could attach to the same wagons that used wheels on clear roads.)

Elmo spent most of the month hauling crops to town and cutting or hauling wood. He sold hay, corn, and hogs in Rockford, making one trip on any given day. Rockford was about seven miles away, and on these short January days, he often went in the middle of the day and had dinner in town (for a quarter). Elmo went twice with corn, once with hogs, and four times with hay. He used a gasoline engine to power the "buzz saw" to cut wood. He spent five days in January sawing wood, or hauling it up from the pasture or the woods, or taking it down to his mother in Cherry Valley.

Farmers' Institute in Rockford took one day for Elmo in January. (The Illinois legislature authorized such institutes in 1895. The University of Illinois provided speakers on agriculture and home economics topics.)[4]

Neither May nor Elmo had steady help during the month. Elmo's hired man from 1907 put in one day helping with wood. A Mrs. Pratt came just once a week to help May with the wash and other housework. When Elmo had dinner in town ten days during this month, it saved May the trouble of preparing a meal.

May devoted little attention to her own activities in her diary; she was more likely to mention who stopped by than what she did. Her mother came down the lane to visit about a dozen times (attesting to the mild weather), and several times when Elmo was going to be out, he dropped May over home. On one such occasion, May and Emily worked on a quilt that the local women's auxiliary was preparing for a charity project in Tennessee. Another time, when her folks were in Rockford, May watched Starr's children while Elmo sawed "wood for Papa." Miss Froom, the young schoolteacher at Bell School who had boarded with May and Elmo for part of 1906, spent the night a few times before boarding with them again starting in February. But much of the time, May was home alone with limited mobility. In the back of her diary, she listed twenty-four books read during the year. During January, May also made pillow shams and covered pincushions.

Elmo, on the other hand, was usually out and about. He went to an auction and stopped to see a neighbor's new engine. He went to see other farmers on business matters or to Cherry Valley or Rockford on errands. In the summertime, May might accompany him on such errands, but not in the cold. Elmo also went to Rockford one day late in January to retrieve the sister of a man who was suddenly taken ill; the man had worked for Elmo the previous year and now worked for Charles Kleckner. He died several days later, and Elmo attended the services.

Joseph and Emily were mainly occupied with some redecorating in January. They went into town to buy new carpets and have the others cleaned;

they chose new wallpaper for the bedroom and the vestibule. Emily prepared the rooms for the workmen to do the papering. She also read books, visited with May, and attended an auxiliary meeting at Mrs. George Picken's. Joseph and Emily had a lame horse; Elmo went over to "cut into foot & horse get better."

February

On February 1 the thermometer fell sixteen degrees during the day, the wind blew, and the snow drifted. It was 5° above zero before dark. Only the cream man and the mailman were out on the roads. The next morning it was 8° below zero but clear and still. The groundhog would have seen his shadow. The snow made for good sleighing on February 3; Papa and Mama

From May's 1908 diary.

went to Rockford in the cutter, and Elmo took the bobsled into town in the afternoon to buy coal and have a shave. The next day, Elmo cleaned out the icehouse; he intended to fill it, now that the Rock River had frozen and before the ice softened again. Mat Ralston and his hired man both helped Elmo, and the men brought six loads of ice to fill the icehouse on February 7.

A visit from May's aunt Alice brightened the month. Papa retrieved her from Rockford in time to help celebrate Starr's birthday on February 8, and she stayed for a week with Joseph and Emily. Emily hoped for a nice snow for good sleighing to take Alice back to Rockford, but the snow melted, so they went in the buggy.

Elmo took advantage of the good sleighing in early February to take a load each of hay and oats to Rockford on Saturday, February 8, and again on the following Monday. (Sunday was a day of rest in the Guilford community, but May and Elmo did not attend church these days.) Elmo took the bobsled to an auction on February 12, and Papa brought Mama and Aunt Alice down in the cutter to see May the same day.

Throughout the month of February, Elmo hauled goods to town and sawed wood. He took four loads of hay, a load each of oats and barley, and two loads of ear corn into Rockford to sell. Elmo and Mat Ralston spent a day hauling two loads of pigs to Cherry Valley for Papa. The day before, Papa was over to May's twice to use the telephone to sell the pigs. Elmo also sawed wood for Mrs. McFarland (Starr's mother-in-law) and another neighbor and took wood down to Cherry Valley for his mother. When Elmo was sick for two days, Walter McFarland (Starr's brother-in-law) took a load of corn to Rockford for him.

May had a quiet month after Aunt Alice's visit. She was over home several times to visit and also at the Purdys' when Elmo was in Rockford on errands. May and Elmo attended a surprise party at the Pickens' early in the month, and May attended an auxiliary meeting at her mother's. She also joined Starr and his family at Emily and Joseph's one Sunday. At the end of the month, May cut out two shirts to sew for Elmo.

The last week of February marked the arrival of the schoolteacher, Miss Froom, to board and the beginning of Annetta's long bout with illness. (Annetta, Starr's oldest, would be four in March.) Elmo went to Cherry Valley to pick up Miss Froom on February 23, and Emily noted the same day that Starr had been up for medicine, since Annetta was not well. The next day Maggie telephoned May that Annetta had pneumonia, and May went down with her folks to see the girl.

March

March came in like a lion: May wrote on March 1, "Thunder shower again last night, everything covered with ice. Cloudy, N. wind," while Emily noted, "Have not ventured outdoors today." But the weather soon cleared.

Annetta was sick again on March 3; Dr. Franklin and Mama were back and forth to see her all month long. First Annetta was sick and then Joey, but the doctor was not sure what was the matter. On March 6 he said they had Dutch measles. On March 8 Annetta had tonsillitis and Joey had a stiff neck; and then on March 12, "Annetta have typhoid fever." But on March 21, "Annetta has bronchitis," and the next day, Mama was called twice to help. Then "Dr. say pneumonia." Starr came to get Mama in the afternoon, and she sat up all night with Annetta, who was "very sick." Elmo and May went to see her the next day. A few days later Annetta began to improve, but Mama came down with a cold.

Mama had had a busy month. Her husband, Joseph, with the help of Mr. Grow, butchered a pig as the month began. (Elmo butchered a pig at the end of the month.) Emily made lard, and Joseph cut up the pig to salt; then they made twenty pounds of sausage. Emily was also working on a comforter and a baby quilt, since Maggie was expecting again and due the end of April. By midmonth, Emily started to set her hens with a nest of eggs to hatch, and Joseph cleaned the henhouse.

Annetta Lyford, ca. 1908.
Courtesy of John Pearse.

Spring was coming: Emily saw a meadowlark on March 11 and bluebirds several days later. The first little pigs were born on March 24, and before the end of the month, Emily and Joseph had twenty-six little pigs. May noted that Starr sowed clover seed on Papa's rye field on March 19. Elmo took Papa's cream separator out of the cellar on March 24. He brought home a new drag (to smooth the plowed ground) and a seeder at the end of the month, and he readied his machinery for the "spring's work." Starr and his hired man began hauling manure.

The hired help for both Elmo and May came on in March. Elmo went into Rockford on March 2 for his new man, Will Johnson. (Sometimes a neighborhood boy would work for Elmo; other times he found a fresh immigrant in Rockford—a "green Swede," as locals said.) Will worked in March at twenty dollars and board for the month; his wages increased to twenty-five dollars per month in April. Ruby Miller, whose family lived two miles to the east, began working for May on March 23, for two dollars per week. Both Will and Ruby boarded through the week and were off on Sundays. Ruby usually borrowed a horse to go home for the day on Sunday, but Elmo typically took Will back and forth to Rockford or to Cherry Valley, where he caught the interurban streetcar ("the car") to Rockford. When the weather improved later in the year, Will came out on his "wheel" (bicycle). Ruby was young, and judging from Will's wages, so was he. May referred to both Will and Elmo alternately as "the boys" or "the men." Ruby was old enough to help with the hay fork in the summer and young enough to attend play practice with the other young folks at Bell School.

Elmo sold more ear corn in March and also sold hay, oats, hogs, a bull, and seed oats; other times he sawed wood. Elmo hauled hay, oats, and corn to Rockford to sell at Upson & Burrows, a flour and feed dealer; he also sold hogs in Rockford. Mr. Molander bought close to fifty bushels of seed oats for his spring planting; other neighbors bought corn. A Cherry Valley livestock buyer bought the bull. Elmo sawed wood for Charles Kleckner, and Walter McFarland came to help saw wood for Elmo when Will was laid up.

Will's first month on the job was overshadowed by his encounter with Dinah, a horse. At the end of his first week, Dinah kicked him in the knee. Will spent the next week convalescing and doing a few chores in the evening; then he went home for another ten days, before returning to split wood and clean oats for sowing.

May noted everyone's comings and goings: Elmo and Will, Papa and

Mama, Ruby and Mrs. Pratt, the doctor for Annetta. Miss Froom boarded and went back and forth to Rockford on weekends. Farmers came for loads of corn and oats; a rag peddler came to trade rags.

April

Planting began in April, but not right away. The first few days were cold; Elmo and Will spent them cutting wood. The hen Mama set in March had five chicks on April 4. Later that week, Emily noted, "some farmers sowing oats." Elmo and Will burned weeds in the afternoon in the field by the schoolhouse; then they began to sow oats the next day. Starr was spreading manure up at Joseph and Emily's and got stuck in the mud. Mrs. Pratt was at May's to help with the wash. (Emily always noted whether the clothes actually dried; this time they did before it rained in the afternoon. Sometimes the clothes came in just as wet as they went out on the line and had to be hung in the attic.)

Elmo and Will worked in the oat fields most of the month, seeding, dragging, and pulverizing; they broke for wet weather. One wet day, Elmo went to Rockford to have the plows fixed, and Will cleaned the pig house. When they finished with the oats at home, Elmo and Will began sowing at Papa's. The men also hauled several more loads of last year's oats to Rockford. When the sowing was done, they let the cows out into the pasture and began fixing fence.

The April weather was extremely changeable. On April 14, the temperature soared to 80° by noon; Papa was planting early potatoes. Ruby sowed sunflowers, balsam, and pansy seed the day before. Cold weather followed. Then April 22 was another warm day; May sat on the porch to sew all afternoon, while Elmo planted potatoes and peas. Joseph and Emily also planted garden that day; they let the furnace fire go out. Arbor Day was celebrated at the schoolhouse with the planting of an apple tree, trumpet creeper, and honeysuckle vines. Joseph set out the strawberry plants before the end of the month.

April was much less dreary for May than the winter months. Ruby livened up the house substantially: she went back and forth to Mama's on errands, and her mother and siblings came to call. Ruby worked in the yard on pleasant days, and on April 25, when it rained all day, she and May baked. May was out only infrequently to Starr's, to her folks, and twice with Elmo to Cherry Valley. Most of the month, Elmo was busy in the fields, and when he was not, the weather was miserable.

May

The month of May began with a handmade "May basket," spring wild-flowers, and a large rainbow. Ruby took the May basket of flowers to Papa and Mama's. Elmo and Will worked on fence in the afternoon, and Will fixed the blackberry bushes, pruning and cutting out the old canes. The rainbow came in the evening after showers and hail. The next day was so cold the cream man wore a fur coat; flakes of snow appeared in the afternoon. Elmo and Will were still working on fence that morning, and Elmo hauled oats to Rockford in the afternoon.

Mama's cherry trees began to blossom on May 5, and her radishes, onions, and lettuce seedlings were up. She came twice to visit May that day, despite rainy weather. Emily declared on May 7, "the worst storm of the season." It rained hard all day, with high winds. The next day, Elmo and Will went fishing in the afternoon after fixing fence all morning. They fixed fence again when they returned. The men had also been using Papa's sheller to shell seed corn and had taken a load of wood down to Elmo's mother in Cherry Valley. Sunday, May 10, was clear and warm; neighbors and family came to call.

The corn planting began on May 12; Elmo and Will planted three acres. In addition to corn, they planted beans, pumpkins, and squash. The month was wet, and the muddy fields and roads slowed the work. On May 18, Emily and Joseph "set out tomato plants in the mud." Conditions improved, and the men planted corn for the next four days. When Elmo finished planting, Will was already cultivating the first corn planted. Starr had dinner at Emily and Joseph's that day, and they ate the first radishes from the garden. Starr finished planting corn the next day, while Elmo planted late potatoes.

Especially toward the end of the month, more people stopped over, and May was out more often. Sunday, May 17, was another lovely day: May and Elmo went down to Aham's in the afternoon, after Mama, Starr, Annetta, and Joey had paid a visit in the morning. The next day May was over to the Purdys' while Elmo was in Rockford buying corn planter wire and having the horses shod. A few days later, May Purdy stopped by with her mother. Mrs. Pratt was still helping with the wash once a week, and Ruby was practicing at the schoolhouse for a play some evenings. Mama was over frequently to see May, and she and Joseph were also out and about more often in the warmer weather. May was over home in the afternoon of May 30, making Papa a cart cushion. Starr was up with his hired man, hoping to drag, but it was too wet.

The month ended with a cool Sunday. May wore a thick dress and a coat when she and Elmo went to Cherry Valley for dinner. But by now the cherry blossoms were fading, Mama's garden was producing lettuce for the table, and the last flower seeds she planted were coming up.

June

On June 1 Emily proclaimed the hens finished setting; she had 105 chicks. Emily finished making Joey's shirt, washed the flannels, and scrubbed the floor. The next day she put on her short cotton drawers instead of her warmer underclothes. June had arrived!

Elmo and especially Will spent much of June cultivating corn. Many days, both men cultivated all day long, but Elmo also spent several days replanting corn south of the barn in the wet spot, where it hadn't come up. Elmo and Will went fishing June 6 in the evening after a hard rain, but Will was cultivating when Elmo went into town on June 9 for a new suit, shoes, and a belt, in addition to groceries.

Graduation exercises took place that evening at the town hall. May, Elmo, and Ruby attended. Howard Fitch, Linna Pratt, and Elsie Marsh were the only graduates from Bell School this year. On June 15, the school year ended with a picnic at Stevenson's quarry.

Will was cultivating again on June 15, when Elmo plowed up the last planting of potatoes that had rotted in the wet field. And Will was cultivating the next two days, when Elmo went to Rockford to buy over four hundred cabbage plants to set out in the former potato field. (He also sowed turnip and banana squash seeds.) Will was cultivating on June 19, when Elmo went to Rockford with Ruby. (He bought "camera printing paper" and groceries, and they had ice cream sodas.) It was circus day in Rockford, so they also watched the parade. A few days later, Elmo and Will dug ditches in the wet fields and transplanted corn, and then both cultivated for the next two days, and Will cultivated again on June 27.

May was out regularly this month—every Sunday and during the week as well; visitors came, and Mama was over almost daily, sometimes twice. Early in the month, Lyford relatives came down from Roscoe, and Florence Fitch called with her children. Elmo and May had Sunday dinners with her parents, with his mother and aunts, and with Aham and Carrie in Cherry Valley. They went for drives in the buggy and stopped to see various cousins. Starr came over with his children.

By mid-June, the strawberries and cherries were ripening, there were berries for the table, and the canning began. Emily noted the first meal of strawberries on June 15. Two days later, her cherries "taste fairly good." On June 20, "Ruby help Mama pick strawberries," and Mama was canning and making strawberry jam. (These strawberries were much sweeter and juicier than those of the next millennium. Their smaller size made them harder to find in the patch, however, and they had to be eaten or canned right away, because they spoiled quickly.) Joseph picked early cherries on June 22; May came to pit them, and Mama canned cherries while Ruby picked strawberries. Two days later the cherries were ready at Elmo and May's. Elmo and Will picked, while Ruby and May pitted and canned seven quarts. On June 27, Elmo picked cherries again for May and Ruby to can (in addition to hunting up stray young cattle, patching the barn roof, and going to a ball game). By the end of the month, the nasturtiums had bloomed, and the hollyhocks were just beginning. Joseph and Emily had eaten their first peas from the garden.

Mama turned sixty-five on June 30, and May threw her a small party with Mrs. Pratt and Ruby. Mama was impressed with how prettily the cake was decorated and with the "*pink* lemonade." The women sang, recited poems, and gave presents; they all had a "fine time."

July

The crescendo of nature's bounty continued into July. On July 1, May and Ruby canned four quarts of strawberries and mixed strawberries with currants to put on shortcake for dinner. The cherries were still coming on strong through the first third of the month; cousins and friends came to pick and have dinner. Then Emily's raspberries started producing on July 10; she mixed them with the cherries and canned two or three quarts every other day for the next week. Already on July 15, she had found ripe blackberries. The blackberries kept coming throughout the month of July—plenty for both families. Ruby went over to pick regularly, and she and May canned. Before the end of July, the summer apples began.

Emily reported a few highlights in her garden: the first new potatoes appeared in mid-July, and her green tomatoes were as big as the end of the thumb by July 23. On July 30, May noted, "peas for dinner, string beans for supper, & pickled 2 quarts of beans."

The men worked on hay in July and also cut rye, barley, and oats. Starr cut rye in early July, and Elmo cut barley later in the month. The grain was cut with a binder, and the bundles stacked to wait for threshing. Most of the rest of the month went to making hay: cutting, tedding (turning it to dry), and storing it in the barns. Ruby helped drive the horse for the hay fork, and an extra boy came to help for a week during haying. It could be tricky to get the hay cut, dried, and into the barns between rains, but this year July was fairly dry.

Most of the cultivating of the corn had been completed in June. The corn was usually cultivated four times before it was tall and leafy enough to outcompete the weeds. Emily noted that Starr finished cultivating corn for the fourth time on July 1. Still, there were the four hundred cabbages, potatoes, squash, and other garden vegetables to cultivate. In spare moments, Will cleaned up the barnyard or cut weeds around the farm buildings, and Elmo went to Rockford to have things fixed or to buy groceries. Elmo applied the "Paris Green" (an early insecticide) to the potatoes early in the month. One day, Elmo drove Fritz (a colt that needed training) to Cherry Valley. When he left to come home, the horse "drag him about 4 rods before he can get into cart." (Four rods is over sixty feet.)

July was another socially active month for May. When Starr worked at Mama's, he often brought Joey and Annetta, and Mama came down with the children to visit May. May was also out frequently. She and Elmo went to a picnic on the Fourth of July and went down to Cherry Valley more than once a week, usually in the evenings. On at least two of these evenings they had ice cream cones (introduced at the St. Louis World's Fair in 1904). May joined Elmo on various errands, and she visited regularly over home and spent time at Starr's on several occasions.

August

In August, telltale signs of summer's nearing end began to accumulate. Early in the month, Will hauled manure, preparing for next year's crops. May and Ruby pickled and canned and counted the jars of produce for the winter months. Before the month ended, Mr. Purdy reported light frost at the creek.

Threshing was the main activity for the men this month. Starr and Elmo both finished cutting and stacking oats during the first few days of the month. Joseph cleaned up his barn and barnyard and fixed the granary to get ready for the threshers. May and Ruby began preparing food. The threshing machine and engine arrived at Papa's in the evening of August 7; the men slept in Elmo's barn. The next morning, after the dew dried, they began threshing the oats Elmo had planted at Papa's. (The men would feed the bundles of grain into the thresher to separate the grain from the chaff and straw.) Mrs. Pratt had come early to help with the meal, and Papa and Mama brought over extra chairs. The men finished the Lyford oats and moved to Elmo's before they quit in the evening. Monday the threshing began again; and Mrs. Pratt helped May and Ruby with the noon meal. The threshers finished at 4:30 PM and then moved their machinery to George Brown's, where Elmo and Will helped thresh the next day. The threshing continued all month around the neighborhood, interrupted by rain. Usually either Elmo or Will went to work with the crew. On August 28 and 29, Starr threshed oats at home and then rye at Papa's; both Elmo and Will helped Starr thresh.

In between threshing, Elmo and Will did many other things. The windmill needed fixing early in the month. Midmonth the tilers came to lay tile to drain the field; Elmo and Will hauled stone and dirt and filled ditches for them. Will hauled manure when Elmo was sprinkling cornmeal on the

Threshing with a steam engine, Boone County, Illinois, ca. 1903. Courtesy of the Boone County Historical Museum, Belvidere, Illinois.

cabbages to counteract the cabbage worms, threshing around the neighborhood, and beginning the fall plowing. They both made apple cider and dug the first field of potatoes toward the end of the month.

As in July, May had many opportunities to visit with family and friends. When Maggie, her sister, Nettie, and the children were up to Mama's for apples midmonth, they spent part of the day at May's. (The children were growing: the youngest was Franklin, now four months old. Walter was eighteen months; and Joey and Annetta were three and four and a half years, respectively.) Florence Fitch came out to visit one day with her mother and baby Lee. Belle Whittle was also out again this month, with little Marion, to see May. Ruby's family came out to get cider and went to Papa's to pick crabapples. May was also out and about often this month with Elmo to visit family and neighbors.

Emily was mostly tending her garden and her chickens. She picked her last blackberries on August 13, but by then there were more apples. She picked her "first good ripe tomato" on August 24 and noted, "many touched with dry rot." One day when May wrote, "Tramp for dinner," about thirty of Mama's young chickens were found missing. Emily spent one day in Rockford visiting friends, when Joseph took the interurban to Freeport (west of Rockford) for the celebration of the Lincoln–Douglas debates.

September

September began with a cool, windy day; Elmo had taken wood to his mother the day before. School was starting. Miss Froom stopped by the next day to visit with May, but she boarded elsewhere this fall. Papa went to Cherry Valley for his first loads of coal for the winter months and heard reports of frost.

Ruby and May spent the month making all kinds of pickles, sauces, and preserves. First there were two quarts of crabapple pickles from the native "crabs" and "3 quarts sweet ripe cucumbers. This makes 9 in all." When Papa and Mama went to town on September 4, they brought back a bushel of peaches. May and Ruby canned nineteen quarts of peaches the next day. A week later Papa and Mama brought back a bushel of tomatoes from Rockford for Ruby and May to can. (That bushel made twenty-one quarts of tomatoes.) In between, they pickled four quarts of beets from the garden.

On September 16, they began the piccalilli (a cucumber relish), which sat for a while in the brine before canning the next day. Then came some chili sauce. A half bushel of pears, from town, turned into eight quarts of canned pears. Then still more tomato pickles, catsup, three quarts of beet and cabbage pickles, and four more quarts of chili sauce, not to mention the first two pumpkin pies. Another bushel of tomatoes and some onions arrived with Ruby's neighbor, and they were turned into three quarts of tomato preserves and nine quarts of "salt tomatoes." Relative to canning records in other years, this September was inspired, particularly in its variety. Ruby and May were surely having a good time of it; they even went up to Mama's to make catsup. Ruby finished working for May on September 29, after they celebrated their birthdays together.

Emily's canning records were not so extensive this month, but in addition to canning, she was also dressing chickens, watching Starr's children occasionally, and out frequently. She canned tomatoes throughout the month, a quart or so at a time, from her garden. She also made grapes into juice, made beet pickles, and canned a few quarts of peaches bought in town. As she did throughout the year, Emily made bread, "fried cakes" (cake doughnuts), and yeast regularly. She counted the roosters as they landed on the dinner table, for example, "Dressed 7th rooster." (In all, eight roosters were dressed this month.) She and Joseph went to Rockford several times, and friends and relatives called. Joseph's brother, Dudley, was down with "some nice melons." Emily also attended her monthly auxiliary meeting, as she had every month all summer. And, of course, she came frequently to see May.

Dry warm days in early September meant the corn was ready to cut and shock by midmonth. Elmo shared the corn binder with Starr, so they needed to juggle their activities. The first week of September, Elmo and Will plowed and spread manure after Elmo fixed the spreader. The next week was spent helping neighbors who were threshing again. Midmonth, when Starr was using the binder to cut corn, Elmo and Will took more oats and hay to town. They cleaned the cellar to get it ready to store produce for the winter. They ground feed for the pigs and cut some corn by hand for the livestock (the cows or the pigs). Elmo also checked on the balers, who were moving around the neighborhood with a stationary baler, baling hay stored in the barns back in July. Elmo helped two neighbors bale hay before the end of the month. When Starr finished with the binder on September 22, Elmo and Will cut corn and set up the bound shocks in the field.

Before corn cutting began, Elmo attended two popular area fairs—the Boone County Fair in Belvidere, and the fair in Elkhorn, Wisconsin. Belvidere was just six miles to the east, but he took the train to get to Elkhorn, about forty miles away. Elmo also squeezed in a ball game one Saturday afternoon at the Prices'.

May didn't attend the fairs or the ball game, but she and Elmo were out together on several occasions. Besides dinner in Cherry Valley and over home some Sundays, they had dinner with a friend in Rockford and went to a social at the Ralstons'.

October

October began with a heavy frost; the growing season was just about over. October 2, May wrote, "Frost last night killed tomato vines. Picked green ones." Elmo and Will were finishing up with cutting corn and setting up the shocks to further ripen and dry. Tying the shocks together was the final step, until shredding began in November. Much of the corn was still standing, however; husking would begin later in October.

After the heavy frost, the potatoes were ready to be dug. Elmo and Will dug sixteen and a half bushels of them on October 8. (Some years Elmo put fifty bushels or more in the cellar, but this year one field of potatoes rotted before they sprouted. Most of the cabbages they planted to substitute were still in the field, awaiting harvest.)

Besides the corn husking and hay baling to be done this month, plowing had to be done before the ground froze hard. Starr spent two days in early October sowing rye for next summer's crop. One day the men flailed out the dry beans they had pulled the previous month. (The beans amounted to one and a half bushels, more than enough for next year's seed.) Elmo also cleaned up the barn on October 13 for the hay balers, who came the next day. The men worked all day and baled over eighteen tons of hay. (May served two extra men for breakfast and six extra men for both dinner and supper that day with the help of Mrs. Pratt.) After the hay baling, Will left for Rockford and didn't return, apparently unexpectedly. Elmo looked him up, learned of his new job, and then started looking for another man to help husk corn. Walter McFarland and his brother, Verne, began husking for Elmo on October 20; they also husked some days for Starr. Elmo spent most of the rest of the month plowing, at home and at Papa's. He also fixed the corncrib, hauled hogs and oats to Rockford, ground barley for feed, and had the plow sharpened in Rockford. On the last day of October, Elmo fixed the hayrack and took a load of baled hay to Rockford.

With Ruby gone, May had minimal help in preparing meals. Mrs. Pratt worked a full day once a week, and she put in two extra days when the balers came, including the day before to get ready, and two other extra afternoons. Mama was over almost every day, however, and occasionally May noted that she helped start dinner preparations. Otherwise, May managed the meals with assistance from Elmo; only three expense records of dinner in town appear for October. May mentioned meals in her diaries infrequently, but when she did, she treated them as her responsibility and something that others helped her with.

Although it was a busy month for fieldwork, October held many warm and pleasant days, so May was out regularly, every Sunday at least, to Cherry Valley or over home for dinner, to the Fitches' in the evening, or to another neighbor's. Neighbors called, and May spent several afternoons with her folks. (Emily noted on one of these days that they sewed for the children.) May also went along to the Kleckners' when they hosted the "shredder meeting" midmonth.

Emily did her auxiliary work, still had an eye on her garden and her chickens, and often watched her grandchildren. Early in the month, she attended her auxiliary meeting and a week later attended the annual dinner and sewing bee up at the Argyle church; she and Maggie Jane Ralston packed a box of aprons to send to a charity in Tennessee. Joseph picked snow apples several days this month. Emily's cosmos were just budding on October 4; she picked them all on October 20, "thinking it would be cold." The nasturtiums had been blooming since June; she picked one last bouquet the next day. Emily noted the first coal fire in the furnace on October 25. All month long, Emily and Joseph dressed roosters for the table; by October 30, they were up to number seventeen.

November

Shredding and husking the rest of the corn occupied November. The cornstalks that were cut, bound, and set up in the fields in September and early October were now fed into a shredder, powered by a steam engine. The result was a mix of corn and roughage, appetizing to the cattle. (Cornstalks could also be used as feed without shredding, but the cattle would leave most of the rough stalks and then need hay to fill up.) Last year's expenses recorded a fifty-dollar "share in shredder." Besides Elmo, shredding together this year were John G. and Mat Ralston, Jim and Hugh Reid, George Brown, and Charles Kleckner. (Most of these men and their sons would work together for the next thirty years.) The men spent two to three days working at each farm, running the shocks of corn through the shredder. A new boy, Alvin, was working for Elmo. From November 4 to November 21, all day every day, except on Sundays and once when the machine broke, the two of them shredded cornstalks with the other men. The McFarland boys had husked twenty acres of Elmo's corn, but more remained for Elmo and Alvin to husk when the shredding was done. Elmo also hauled two loads of oats and a load of hay to Rockford this month and more wood to his mother.

Neither May nor Emily had much to say about their own activities but rather focused on the men's work. Getting the corn in and other work done before winter arrived in full force always created some tension. This year the "first real snow storm of the season" was on November 14, but it didn't stop the shredding. For the first time on November 17, Emily found no eggs. The hens also knew that winter had come.

Elmo's aunt Phrone spent a week with May in early November, but otherwise May had only a few visitors this month besides her mother and Starr's children. Starr spent many days working at his parent's farm, either husking

Farmers with a McCormick–Deering husker and shredder, Frankfort, Indiana, ca. 1919. Machines in use in 1908 were similar. Courtesy of Wisconsin Historical Society (image 23682).

or plowing or loading hay. One day when he brought Annetta and Joey to spend the day, May noted that the children found a dandelion blooming when they walked down to visit her. Emily fixed dinner for Starr much of the month; May also attended to meals, although while shredding throughout the neighborhood, Elmo and Alvin ate at other farms. Mrs. Pratt helped May with meals when shredders came to the Davis farm, and she also put in a full day once a week with some extra half days. While Emily visited almost daily as usual, May was rarely out this month, except to spend time with her parents. On Thanksgiving, however, May and Elmo celebrated with a family gathering at May Purdy's.

December

With the husking finished and the hired boy gone, Elmo spent December on odds and ends. He mended his fur coat one morning, and he spent several days checking at neighborhood farms to find a pig suitable for breeding. Many days he hauled loads into town: ear corn, barley, oats, shelled corn, and baled hay. He ground feed, fixed the corn sheller, shelled corn, and helped Papa and Mr. Grow butcher a beef. He went to Hugh Reid's to help fix the shredder and met with his shredder group twice to discuss business. Elmo's cousin Archie also came from Wisconsin to pay a three-day visit.

Elmo's thirty-fifth birthday was December 14. May and Elmo celebrated on Sunday with a birthday cake and popcorn that Mrs. Pratt had made when she came to wash the day before.

Both Joseph and Emily were feeling poorly for parts of December. May was over home more often, and Mama came down to May's less frequently than in November. Mama had a bad cold early in the month, and May stayed with her twice while she was sick. Emily was also too sick to attend her auxiliary meeting, but she and May spent the day sewing.

Christmas preparations and celebrations highlighted the month. Early in December, May helped Mama pack the "Kansas boxes" with gifts for May's cousins, Puss and Kate, and their growing families in Wichita. As Christmas approached, Emily noted the gifts she was sewing: a "waist" for Joey, "aprons" for Walter, Annetta, and May. At midmonth, May helped Mama "work on stars for tree." When Mrs. Pratt came to work on December 22, they strung popcorn for the tree. Elmo went up to Papa's to put up the Christmas tree the next morning and then went into Rockford to pick up May's new bookcase—an early Christmas present. When Elmo went to town on the 24th to retrieve a box of gifts from May's Kansas cousins, May was over home all day, working on decorations to trim the tree and for the Christmas table. Starr came with his family and the phonograph to celebrate Christmas Eve; May wrote, "Elmo is Santa Claus." Christmas dinner the next day was also at May's parents, and many presents were exchanged.

On the last day of 1908, the temperature dropped into the single digits. Elmo was grinding feed. Papa had loaded the remaining roosters up in a crate to take to Rockford to sell, and Mama was tending the tallow from the beef butchered earlier in the month.

SIGNS OF THE NEW CENTURY

Midwestern farmers ran their own businesses, but more than one-quarter of all workers in the country worked for the largest 1 percent of companies by the early 1900s. Corporate America had come of age. Although the contrast between urban and rural America already seemed great, changes in the urban industrial environment and those on the farm were still closely linked.

Many of the largest corporations in America were midwestern companies based in agriculture. They included Chicago meatpackers such as Armour and Swift. International Harvester, the descendant of the company that produced the McCormick reaper, was the target of much antitrust action. The result of many mergers around the turn of the century, it had plants from New York to Minneapolis. Many other American industries also sold products to farm families.

In the early 1900s, few urban residents had telephones, but the telephone was key to shrinking distances in rural areas. Independent private telephone cooperatives sprang up rapidly in the rural Midwest in the early 1900s. By 1907 May and Elmo, Joseph and Emily, and Starr and Maggie all had telephones, and so did many other midwestern farmers. By 1920, more than 70 percent of farms in Illinois, Iowa, Kansas, and Nebraska had telephones, while most urban residents still lacked this modern convenience.[5]

The Kodak camera and the phonograph were also arriving in rural homes early in the century. Elmo received a Kodak camera for Christmas in 1906. Throughout 1907 and 1908, the Davis ledgers are full of home developing expenses. Starr's children, the circus parade, and Mama's chestnut tree in full bloom were captured on film. The phonograph that Starr brought up to Joseph and Emily's for family gatherings was purchased in 1907. May received a phonograph and twenty-eight records for Christmas in 1909.

The most dynamic aspect of American industry at the turn of the century was its machine tool industry. Factories in cities that grew up supporting the manufacture of farm machinery were now making drills, lathes, saws, milling machines, and standardized parts (e.g., pumps, pulleys, belts, and regulators) and selling them around the world. Rockford's Emerson–Brantingham Company (which had produced the Manny reaper in the 1850s) was among the midwestern farm machinery companies that served an international market.

Many such midwestern companies were already producing automobiles powered by gasoline engines. But the internal combustion engine was first developed for stationary use, and in 1910, farmers were using many more gasoline engines than there were automobiles registered in the United States.

Powers and Engines

Elmo bought a gasoline engine in November 1906 for $215 (the equivalent of about five months of factory wages). In addition to using the engine for cutting wood with his buzz saw, he also used it with a new corn sheller purchased in 1907. Previously, Elmo either had to load up his corn and take it somewhere to have it shelled, for a low fee, or pay a much higher fee for someone to come to the farm to shell it with a sheller and a steam engine. Small amounts (like the seed corn) he would do with a hand-cranked sheller.

Cutting wood with a buzz saw powered by a portable gasoline engine, ca. 1905. Courtesy of Wisconsin Historical Society (image 9572).

For cutting wood he had used the buzz saw with a horsepower. Horsepowers (known in short as "powers") used gears to harness the power of one to ten or more horses. Some of these machines were of the treadmill type; others were a sweep style, in which the horse or horses walked around in a circle. Small treadmills were even available for dogs or goats.

Powers and steam engines had both been in use since well before Elmo was born and had served more or less interchangeably for decades. Either could run a machine with a belt and pulley system. Most of the earliest threshing machines in the 1850s were powered by large horse sweeps, but in the 1870s, steam engines began threshing midwestern grain. At the turn of the century, horsepower was more common for things like grinding feed, shelling corn, sawing wood, and running cider presses, elevators (to load crops up into barns), and fanning mills (to clean grain).[6]

Stationary (or portable) gasoline engines began to appear on farms about 1900. A contemporary expert estimated the number of gas engines on farms at over one million (or perhaps 16 percent of U.S. farms) by 1914.[7] Prosperous northern Illinois farmers invested early in the new technology of gas engines, which soon came in all sizes and were competitively priced. In 1908, Sears, Roebuck and Company sold a Kenwood engine of two and a half horsepower for $95.25. Seven years later, Montgomery Ward sold a two-horsepower model for $48.[8]

Cities and towns all over the Midwest had local manufacturers of gas engines in the early 1900s. One historian catalogs over two thousand such companies, although many of these firms were in business for only a short time. Fairbanks–Morse in Beloit, Wisconsin, just across the state line from Rockford, soon became a world leader in engine production; its clients included railroads and the mining industry in addition to farmers. International Harvester also sold many gas engines to farmers. At least two firms produced engines in Rockford, including Rockford Engine Works. As early as 1904, this company produced gas engines in sizes from four to thirty horsepower, with the four-horsepower size weighing in at 1,250 pounds. Many of these engines were mounted on wagons to be drawn by horses. Smaller sizes of one and a half to two and a half horsepower were introduced within a few years.[9]

May mentioned no tractors in her diaries or ledgers until 1919, but she made numerous references to engines before then. Elmo's engine was not suitable for large jobs. (Judging from the price and how he used it, it was probably about five horsepower.) He used it with the saw, the corn sheller, a grinder, and with a new fanning mill purchased in 1913. By 1913, several other neighbors had gas engines large enough to run a hay baler or silo filler. The Guilford farmers (including Elmo) who bought the corn shredder together in 1907 had initially used a steam engine for shredding. In 1914, many of the same men pooled their resources to buy a large gasoline engine for their new thresher.

Gas engines held many advantages over steam engines. Although May recorded "engine bother" with both types of engines, gas engines started and stopped with less time and trouble, and no water team was required. Safety was also an important consideration: steam engines were dangerous. After not working well at Elmo's for the corn shredding in 1910, the shredders' steam engine exploded when the men hauled it a mile or so to the next farm. No one was hurt, and they fixed it up to use again the next season, but the same was not true of a steam engine that blew up during the 1919

Horses pulling an International Harvester water-cooled Titan gasoline engine, ca. 1905. Courtesy of Wisconsin Historical Society (image 41501).

threshing season in the Guilford neighborhood. One man was killed and another badly scalded. The steam engines also required engineers to run them; May often noted the engineer in her diary. Almost every midwestern farmer, however, in the first decade of the century began to learn about gasoline engines, and many were already tinkering with them.

The Icehouse, the Potato Patch, and the Grocery Store

Big business was heavily involved with food by the turn of the century. Chicago's meat industry dominated much of the U.S. market and increasingly moved into other foods requiring refrigeration, such as fruits and vegetables. Major players were also rising in retail cereal products, and grocery store chains such as A&P, Kroger, and the National Tea Company were just beginning to expand their reach.[10]

More and more brand names appear in May's records of grocery expenses with each passing year of the new decade; so do purchases of fruits, vegetables, fish, and meat. For instance, bananas, pineapple, oranges, and cranberries appear regularly. So do oysters, salmon, herring, and codfish, in addition to mutton and beef. February grocery records occasionally include lettuce and radishes from farther south. Commercial canning techniques had improved by this time, and canned corn appears among grocery purchases. Breakfast cereals such as Grapenuts, Post Toasties, Cream of Wheat, and Quaker Oats begin to appear regularly. The Nabisco and Ralston brand names also pop up. Ivory soap, Bon Ami cleanser, and Lenox soap are regulars, but Coca-Cola appears only once.

Many food products were produced on the farm: milk, eggs, poultry, beef, pork, and a cellar full of potatoes, in addition to garden fruits and vegetables. Beef and pork were still butchered on the farm, even while Sinclair's novel *The Jungle* made consumers think twice about store-bought meat products. Although Starr butchered beef, Elmo rarely did. He helped Papa butcher, and May and Elmo often bought beef from Papa, Starr, or other neighbors. Elmo usually butchered a pig in the early spring until 1917; after that he stuck to dressing chickens. Although a local butcher existed in Cherry Valley and a meat packer in Rockford, much of the beef and hogs produced on the farm were shipped by trains into Chicago.

Curiously, the same innovations that facilitated the provision of fresh meat, fruits, and vegetables to urban residents led to the demise of icebox refrigeration and the icehouse on the farm. Elmo filled the icehouse for the last time in 1908. Icebox refrigerators of the time depended on a block of ice from the icehouse to stay cool. According to May's diaries of 1901 to 1908, Elmo filled the icehouse for a two-dollar charge or less for the ice and the help of a couple of other men. He waited until the temperature plunged far below zero and went to the Rock River to get the ice. The ice from the river was cut into blocks with specialized equipment. The mild winters, however, in both 1907 and 1908 made it tricky to harvest the ice before it thawed. Moreover, rural areas were outside the delivery route of the manufactured-ice plants that provided regular deliveries to urban consumers in northern Illinois by this time. So when the supply of natural ice became impractical, farmers relied on cellars and wells to keep foods fresh. In urban areas as well, ice was considered overpriced, and iceboxes troublesome. Even by 1930, only about half of U.S. homes had some kind of refrigeration.[11]

The Modern Dairy Industry

Urban markets and new innovations were modernizing the dairy industry. Creameries, such as the Argyle creamery, had sprung up all over northern Illinois and Wisconsin in the 1880s, with the advent of centrifugal cream separators. Then at the turn of the century, hand-cranked separators became common on farms. The Lyfords bought a separator in 1898, and mentions of churning fell from several times a week in 1896 to about once a month in 1898. Elmo and his mother stopped selling butter in 1899; by the time May had begun keeping records, she and Elmo bought their butter from the dairy. In 1902 they also bought a separator (for eighty dollars) and began selling cream rather than milk.

Change in the dairy industry continued to induce changes in Elmo and May's milk marketing over the decade. By 1890, Wisconsin was the second largest cheese-producing state in the nation, second to New York. Northern Illinois, however, was a corn and hogs mixed-farming area in the early 1900s; it had more creameries than Wisconsin, to satisfy the tastes of urban consumers. Hand-cranked cream separators made good sense for mixed-farming operations. Farmers could feed the skim milk to the pigs and sell small amounts of cream to dairies for regular cash income. Other advances at about the same time made it possible to test the butterfat content of milk accurately, and creameries multiplied in both Illinois and Wisconsin. Before long, refrigeration allowed for the storage of milk, and urban demand for milk and ice cream grew. Milking machines became practical around 1910, and mechanical refrigeration also became an option for farmers who chose to invest and specialize.[12]

Like most Corn Belt farmers who raised corn, hogs, and "fat cattle," May and Elmo did not invest in specialized dairy equipment but rather milked a few cows for home consumption and sold the excess cream and milk. The largest sale of milk or cream from 1901 to 1910 was $257 in 1902, a little more than one-eighth of the farm income for that year. In 1910, the sale of cream was only $102. Elmo's cousin Frank Davis, on the other hand, specialized in dairy. Before 1916, Frank had "thirty-eight high grade Jersey cattle" and "a modern cow barn with cement floor, patent stalls, compressed air milking plant, and other very desirable, improved appliances."[13]

Expanding Operations

Although May and Elmo did not invest in dairy during the century's first decade, they invested heavily in the farm. In particular, they made payments on the farm and expanded it to 150 acres. When the farm belonged to Elmo's father, it was 120 acres: 40 acres surrounding the schoolhouse and crossed by the creek, and 80 acres with farm buildings south of that. Sometime before 1902, Elmo's mother bought twenty acres of woods a quarter mile still farther south along Bell School Road. In 1902, adjacent to the twenty-acre woods, Elmo and May bought ten acres of improved land, which Elmo used as an extra field for corn or oats or hay. The woods provided fuel for the winter months.

During the ten-year period of 1901 through 1910, Elmo made payments to his mother that totaled approximately $3,400 for rent, note, interest, and unspecified ends. He also kept her well supplied with wood for fuel. Another $350 payment in 1904 was marked "balance on the 10 acres." Elmo had likely made other payments to his mother before he married. Farms were expensive in Illinois, even in 1900; 150 acres in Winnebago County, not including buildings, would have cost $7,200—the equivalent of about fifteen years of factory wages.

In addition to the investment in the land, May and Elmo invested in buildings, machinery, and horses. Elmo put in a well, fixed the haymow, and added several small buildings, including an icehouse, a hog shed, a henhouse, a tool house, and a corncrib. In 1910, he expanded his barn (for $373). He spent more than $160 tiling the fields for better drainage between 1907 and 1910. These capital expenses amounted to $1,220 over the ten years, not including his time and that of the hired man.[14] Purchases of equipment came to $886 over the ten years. The equipment included the gas engine, two manure spreaders, a cream separator, a wagon and two wagon boxes, a hay rake and hay loader, two cultivators, seeders, a drag, a sulky plow from Starr, a pulverizer, a feed chopper, a bobsleigh, a horse cart, and shares in a potato digger and the corn shredder. During the decade, May and Elmo bought ten horses, including three young foals. The prices paid for horses and colts varied considerably: one colt cost $200; a foal cost $7.50. (Three horses were also sold and at least one lost to illness.) The investment in horses came to about $570.

All told, these investments in buildings, machinery, horses, land, and total payments to Elmo's mother came to more than $6,000 over the ten years. Gross farm income (that is, produce sold and paid farmwork) for the period was $19,252. Thus, May and Elmo were able to reinvest roughly one-third of their gross income into the farm after paying for all other farm expenses, property taxes, livestock costs, and living expenses.[15] Furthermore, over this period the accounts registered savings of $950, after all investment and expenses were subtracted from income.[16] Clearly these were good times. In part, the comfortable budgets may have owed to the generosity of May's parents. Starr and Elmo farmed much of their land (one hundred acres) from 1907 to 1910, apparently sharing the value of this production with the elder Lyfords, since no direct expenses for rent were recorded. The young men did, however, alternately fill Joseph's barn with hay.

May and Elmo's situation was rather typical. The size of their farm in 1910 was 150 acres, with 130 of that improved. The average farm in Winnebago County was 135 acres, with 117 of that improved. Farmers in the county increased the value of their buildings by 58 percent and the value of their equipment by 79 percent between 1900 and 1910. Average farm values in Illinois doubled over the same period, while the average size of a farm increased slightly. Farm values across the Midwest and much of the United States were also increasing at about the same rate. But Illinois farms were fertile, close to good markets, and among the most valuable in the country—more than twice the nation's average. At the end of the decade, the average Illinois farm of 129 acres with buildings was valued at close to fourteen thousand dollars.

Farm values were up because prices for farm produce and profits were increasing. Although consumer prices rose by only 12 percent from 1900 to 1910, wholesale prices for farm products increased by 47 percent. Elmo sold hogs at ten dollars per hundredweight in 1910; average U.S. hog prices were half that in the early part of the decade.[17] May recorded hay selling at thirteen dollars a ton in 1908 and at seventeen dollars a ton in 1910.

Hay was becoming a good business for Rockford area farmers. While stationary balers had been in use in some areas since the 1870s and earlier (powered first by horses and later by steam), Elmo sold only a few loads of loose hay in the winter until 1907. For the first five years of the decade, hay represented less than 3 percent of gross income. As urban areas demanded more hay for horses, gas engines facilitated hay-baling operations. Bales of hay were easier to haul into town and could also be shipped on to Chicago. From 1908 to 1910, hay increased to more than 10 percent of gross income. In 1910, Elmo expanded his barn to hold more hay, and Starr built a new barn the next year.

The overall prosperity of the decade was marred little by the Panic of 1907. The financial panic in November served as another reminder that money was not necessarily safe in banks, but J. P. Morgan's efforts to co-ordinate the actions of New York bankers were successful, and disaster was averted. Neither diaries nor farm ledgers revealed anything amiss. Business in Rockford proved resilient as well. Even greater prosperity was just around the corner.

Chapter 2

The Glow of
The Golden Age
1910–1914

Following a decade of rising farm prices, the years from 1910 to 1914 were the heart of the Golden Age of Agriculture. The war years that followed were as frenetic as golden, but farmers have held fond memories of the years before the war. Some of these memories involved automobiles, which were taking the country by storm at the time. Farm prices were high relative to other prices farmers faced, so farm income went further. And the prices of automobiles were falling, so many farmers, including Elmo and May, bought their first automobile.

The auto industry boomed. The Midwest was still an agricultural heartland, but it quickly became the industrial heartland as well. The midwestern industrial economy that took root in the 1850s, manufacturing reapers, plows, and other farm implements, matured into an industrial economy driven by the automobile. Scores of companies that produced bicycles, buggies, wagons, farm machinery, and gasoline engines tried producing automobiles too, including about a dozen Rockford companies. But by 1910, Detroit was the center of automobile production.

Rockford profited handsomely from the automobile trade. Although its early automobiles failed to amount to much, Rockford's machine tool industries supplied the tools and machines that automobile manufacturers needed, not only in the United States, but around the world as well. Moreover, soon Rockford was producing "clutches, joints, spark plugs, door bumpers, piston rings, gaskets, locks, heaters, upholstery and other parts and accessories."[1] Rockford's population numbered about forty-five thousand in 1910 and would increase by 45 percent within the next decade.

While immigration, industrialization, and urban growth continued strong, the farm population slowly fell in relative terms. In 1910, 35 percent of the people in the United States lived on farms; by 1914, this percentage fell to 33. Although the farm population in the country as a whole was still increasing slowly, the farm population in Illinois had peaked at 1.3 million in 1900 and then began to decline. A gradual trend toward fewer and larger farms was already underway. The size of an average Illinois farm, having risen from 124 to 129 acres between 1900 and 1910, rose to 135 acres by 1920. Improvements in machinery in general and the power from gas engines in particular made it possible for farmers to manage more land.

The most dramatic change on Guilford farms during these years was the advent of the automobile, yet reliance on horses, buggies, and bobsleds continued. Tractors excited the imagination of farmers at state and local fairs, but few were in use in Illinois fields. Farmers invested in buildings and equipment but maintained the same mixed-farming crop and livestock rotations that had served them well for decades of Corn Belt agriculture. These were tranquil and happy years.

The Automobile Arrives in Guilford Township

May first mentioned an automobile in Guilford in early May 1909. She wrote, "Heard H. Reid has automobile." Undoubtedly this was the first auto in the Bell School neighborhood, and the news spread quickly. In June 1908, May had noted that she and Elmo began a subscription to *Outlook,* a magazine for motorists; Elmo had had a "long auto ride" in Rockford a few weeks before that. In October 1909, both May and Elmo had an auto ride, probably a test drive.

The Farmers' Market for Automobiles

Until about 1906, automobiles were primarily amusements for the wealthy, and Rockford had its share of wealthy industrialists and businessmen. Rockford's colony of automobiles grew from about 100 in 1904 to 216 in 1908. Already in 1904 Rockford had its first garage.[2]

But by 1906, automobile manufacturers began targeting farmers as their next major market. Country doctors were among the first owners of automobiles with business rather than purely pleasure on their minds. The automobile allowed them to make their rounds more rapidly (when roads were good) and to arrive more promptly when their services were urgently needed. Farmers, however, made up a larger market; they had long distances to travel on a regular basis, gasoline was inexpensive, and many farmers were already familiar with the workings of gas engines. Even those farmers who didn't already own a gas engine had spent their lives monitoring innovations in farm machinery and dealing with mechanical failures. County and state fairs, since the turn of the century, had exhibited automobiles alongside the commercial exhibits of farm engines and machinery. Moreover, the farming prosperity thus far in the new century made automobiles affordable to many farmers.

To satisfy farmers, however, the automobile had to be reliable, durable, and reasonably priced. In 1906, the time was ripe to begin mass marketing, and Henry Ford began producing the kind of car that many farmers had been waiting for. His first major success was the fifteen-horsepower Model N, introduced in 1906 for $600. The famed Model T followed in 1908 for $850.[3] (This was substantially more than a year's factory wages; May and Elmo took in about $2,500 in annual gross income during 1910–14.) With four cylinders and twenty horsepower, the car was mounted high to negotiate poor country roads. Demand for the vehicle swelled. It was so successful that Henry Ford decided to focus production exclusively on the Model T, continually striving to lower the price. The Model T, which became known as the Tin Lizzie, was a bare bones vehicle that came only in black, but it was rugged, reliable, and easy to drive and maintain—ideal for many farmers.

Not all farmers, however, had their heart set on a Tin Lizzie. Other cars had more style. The Buick Motor Company was the industry leader in 1908, and many other manufacturers offered alternatives to the Model T. By 1914, annual production of passenger cars skyrocketed to over a half million vehicles.[4]

Between 1910 and 1914, farmers were the most rapidly growing market for automobiles, and they often bought their autos at the local farm implement dealer. In 1910 an estimated 11 percent of all registered autos were on farms. By 1914, farmers owned over 20 percent of all registered automobiles. The farmers' share of automobiles continued to rise until the end of World War I, when farmers represented 30 percent of the population and owned almost 27 percent of registered automobiles. Many farmers in Guilford Township were among those owners.[5]

Automobiles around the Neighborhood

After only a single mention of Hugh Reid's auto in 1909, suddenly in 1910 automobiles were all over the Guilford neighborhood and very much on May's mind. In February, Elmo went into Chicago to attend an auto show. One Sunday in April, when May and Elmo were out for a ride with their young horse Fritz, they passed Hugh Reid in his auto. May noted that Fritz was "not scared a bit." (The motorist magazines commented on the quarrels some farmers had with motorists touring the countryside. They drove too fast, scared the horses, and raised great clouds of dust.)

The summer of 1910 brought numerous auto rides with neighbors who had new cars. May and Elmo's classmate from Bell School, George Picken, offered the first. George was over in mid-June to take May and Elmo and their hired help to Cherry Valley for ice cream. Ten days later, Mat Ralston was over with his new auto; May, Elmo, and their help all rode around the neighborhood with Mat before going into Rockford for ice cream. The following Sunday, Mr. King stopped by to offer a short spin. In early August, Frank Reid and his parents were out with their new auto, and Elmo and May went off riding in the evening with them to Belvidere and Cherry Valley. Before the summer was over Elmo had several other rides with the farmers he worked with, and when the men were shredding on Election Day in early November, May noted that they all "go to election in autos."

Not all of May's references to automobiles in 1910 were happy ones. An automobile killed the "little Barnes boy" in June. (The Barneses were prominent Rockford industrialists.) But horses and buggies were not entirely safe either. Less than two weeks after the Barnes incident, Carrie Davis was thrown from a buggy and broke her hip.

Aham Davis and family in auto, ca. 1912.

May and Elmo's First Automobile

May and Elmo's first automobile seems to have been on order through much of 1910, because producers had trouble keeping up with demand. Elmo built an "auto shed" in September 1910, and before Christmas an auto agent stopped by in a vehicle. On February 11, 1911, when May and Elmo's automobile arrived in Rockford, Elmo took grist into town to grind and made the down payment of $750. But he didn't bring the auto home. The roads were bad because the snow was melting and everything was quite muddy. On March 4, he paid the balance of the bill; the total payment was $860. But still he had not brought the car out to the farm. Finally on March 9, he and the auto agent came out from the garage and gave May and the hired girl a ride; then the men took the car back to Rockford again. The next day, Elmo went to Cherry Valley, had dinner at his mother's, and took the interurban to Rockford to retrieve the automobile and bring it home in the evening.

Then the fun began. Starr and his two older boys, Joe (who was five and a half) and Walter (who had just turned four), were up the next day, right after breakfast, for "a ride around the school square" with Elmo and May. They got stuck six times before returning. Later in the day Elmo used the horses to take a load of hay into Rockford. The next day was Sunday, and Elmo "try his auto in PM." But he had little success: "rained last night, so roads quite sticky." Monday, already, the automobile went back to Rockford for some adjustment. The following Saturday evening, Elmo brought it home again, and by then the roads were better. Sunday morning, Elmo was over to the Pickens' and the Browns' in the auto. Then in the afternoon, May and Elmo were over "to Papa's, Starr's, Purdy's and back to Starr's," where May stayed "while Elmo take Starr & boys over ½ way to Belvidere & back." Emily wrote, "Elmo & May have been riding in their new auto, but it does not go very well yet." Two days later Elmo took the auto into Rockford for some auto grease. May noted that the auto "go good."

May never mentioned the make (or the color) of the automobile, but an invoice found among Elmo's papers confirms that the car was a Maxwell touring car. The Maxwell didn't sell like the Ford or the Buick, but it was a popular model. (The Maxwell–Briscoe Company later evolved into the Chrysler Corporation.) The Maxwell garnered significant attention in 1909, right when May and Elmo would have been considering various models. A young woman by the name of Alice Ramsey, along with three other women, drove across the country in a Maxwell touring car, from New York to San Francisco, in fifty-nine days.[6] Not until the late 1920s did May and Elmo make long cross-country road trips. But this Maxwell and the cars that followed it were clearly purchased with May in mind. May couldn't walk, but she loved to ride in the automobile.

May recorded various expenses for the Maxwell in the months following its arrival. The automobile came equipped with a removable top and acetylene lights for night driving but no speedometer. Elmo paid $18.50 for a speedometer in May. He had already purchased two inner tubes, auto batteries (twice), an auto license, and a pressure gauge for the tires, in addition to oil and gasoline. (The gas had totaled about twenty-three dollars.) After the cost of some chains to help with muddy roads, there were no further significant expenses, save gasoline, oil, and grease, until later in the fall, when the car suffered "a breakdown about 4 miles from Starr's" and had to be pulled home by horses. Elmo took the "broken pieces" into Rockford the next day, and later the auto was hauled in as well and stayed there a month, while the carburetor was replaced for twenty dollars. After that, the machine ran better than ever.

Throughout the spring, summer, and fall, May and Elmo's social life, in particular, revolved around the auto. Sundays they went for drives, unless it was too muddy. The shiny new automobile increased the incentive and reduced the time it took to visit Lyford relatives fifteen miles to the north, in Roscoe, and Campbell relatives twenty-five miles to the northwest, in Durand. Frequently May and Elmo took May's aunt Alice and aunt Augusta, who lived in Rockford, for rides, and they were often down to Cherry Valley with the auto. May and Elmo went to the Beloit Fair in the automobile, with different passengers in tow each way. Elmo often took the auto to Rockford on an errand, and May was frequently with him; sometimes Emily was too.

The Automobile Age

More and more neighbors were mentioned with automobiles in the next few years. When the Bell School children had a picnic in June 1913 at a new park in Rockford, five automobiles congregated at the schoolhouse to take them. When Rockford had an auto parade in June 1912, May's hired girl went with Mat Ralston and his family; unfortunately the Maxwell was "out of fix" just then. In late 1913, Rockford hosted an auto show, and Elmo drove the Maxwell in to see the new models.

Starr was one of the later farmers in the neighborhood to get an automobile, but he was building a new barn in 1911 and a grand new house for his growing family in 1913. When Starr brought home his first auto in June

1914, he came by with his boys and the auto agent, learning to run the machine. Starr's auto had plenty of use and much mention that summer, especially in Emily's diary; for example, "Starr & 5 children up in auto," "Starr & all the children up in auto." (The total number of children was now six; the youngest, Emily, was not yet two years old.) Starr and his family took the auto to Chautauqua, in Cherry Valley, and to the Ringling Brothers Circus in Rockford. In less than a year, Starr had bought a second auto; one of the two was an Oakland. By that time, May and Elmo had traded their Maxwell for a new Buick.

By 1914, automobiles had become commonplace in Guilford, and some of the shine, but certainly not all, had worn off. By the end of that year, Elmo had spent many days and half days working on the automobile, by himself, with the hired man, or with the Picken boys, and he had taken the car into Rockford and worked on it all day with the guys at the garage. He had had several "blow-outs," had run out of gas, had been pulled from the mud by the horses of various neighbors, and had done his share of pulling others out too. In the summer, May complained of the autos raising dust on the roads: "Very warm & dusty. Six autos & 2 motorcycles on this road."

But the automobile added enormous pleasure to their lives. On occasional nice days, May enjoyed sitting in the auto near where Elmo was working. Or in the evening they went together in the auto to gather the cows in the pasture or to take some of Starr's children along for a ride to Cherry Valley or Rockford. In early September 1914, May and Elmo attended the Rockford auto races. In early October they took an all-day Sunday automobile trip with Aham and Carrie in the latters' auto, over thirty miles west through Rockford and Pecatonica to Freeport. Then they circled back to the northeast and visited Campbell relatives in Durand, finally arriving home about 8:30 PM.

May often noted what she was wearing when she went out in the auto, and there's no doubt that she was dressed stylishly. (Both May and her mother noted the progress of their new clothes at the seamstress, and Mama sometimes stopped in on the way home from Rockford to show off her new suit, coat, or hat.) In part, May noted her clothes on these occasions to indicate the weather; for example, "I wear blue serge dress & winter coat" and "So warm I not put on coat till I start home & so still I wear hat with no pins or veil." Emily, too, enjoyed rides to her auxiliary meetings in the autos of various neighbors.

By August 1914, even the mailman drove an auto; automobiles were more than fun; they were also efficient. In some eastern cities, automobiles delivered mail on an experimental basis as early as 1899. Rural carriers received permission to use automobiles in 1906. As carrier wages increased—to eleven hundred dollars a year in 1912—and automobile prices fell, more rural carriers used autos. Soon rural routes had to be reorganized, because automobile routes could be twice as long as horse routes.[7]

Not everyone had an automobile, of course. Joseph and Emily did not, although Joseph regularly borrowed and read *Outlook* and enjoyed rides with Elmo or Starr. At the other end of the age spectrum, John Pratt, Elmo's hired hand, couldn't afford an automobile. In 1910 and 1911 he came to work on a bicycle, but by mid-1912 John had a motorcycle and traded up for a new one the next year.

HORSES, BUGGIES, WAGONS, AND SLEIGHS

Despite the seeming pervasiveness of automobiles in Guilford Township by 1914, horses could still look forward to a long future there. Tractors and trucks appeared on few farms before the 1920s. Until then, for hauling loads and braving mud, snow, and slush, the horse was still king of the road. For good reason early motorists were told to "get a horse!"—it was the only way to get the automobiles out of the mud.[8]

Riding the Roads

May and Emily constantly reported the state of the roads. There was considerable variation to behold. For example, the roads could be "rough," "muddy," "icy," "drifted," "sticky," "dry," "smooth," "slippery," "dusty," "sloppy," "frightful," "passable," and "pretty well broken." The road report was often part of the weather report, especially in the winter; for example: "Fine day overhead, but roads bad." "Thaw till roads are sloppy." "Roads very muddy, but freeze by night." "Snow thaw fast, spoil sleighing." "Blizzard, it snowed most of the day; watched the sleighs go back and forth from school house." "Look some showery in AM, roads dry except for mud holes." "20° below. Men & teams are breaking through the drifts."

In general, road conditions were poor all over the United States. In the country as a whole in 1909, fewer than 9 percent of roads were surfaced at all.[9] Rural roads were largely unimproved, except by the efforts of the farmers themselves. In the wintertime, the neighborhood farmers plowed out the snow, and especially after they started driving cars, they went out to drag and grade the roads.

Pressure to improve roads was building in Guilford and across the country in the 1910–14 period. Bicycle enthusiasts began agitating for improved roads before the turn of the century, and the introduction of rural free delivery beginning in 1896 also encouraged better roads. The post office could refuse delivery when roads were not maintained, so farmers made efforts to maintain them. But the arrival of the automobile on the farm made better roads a higher priority for farmers and for local governments too. In February 1914, Elmo went around the neighborhood with a road petition. A road meeting followed in March and another on April 1, when May noted, "Commissioners not grant petition." More road meetings followed in early May and late October. In early November, men were "surveying our road."

In the meantime, however, automobiles were simply not up to the road and weather combinations during much of the year. Unquestionably, the horse and buggy were a better match for mud. Sometimes May and Elmo started out with the auto and went back for the horse or went with horses in the first place because it was too muddy. For example, "Sun shone in morn, but soon cloud over. Wind turn to NW & rain, snow & sleet much of PM. Elmo get Aunts from Valley in auto, but have to take them home in top buggy." Although the auto age had dawned, the horse-and-buggy days were far from over; May and Elmo bought a new buggy in 1914.

Whenever there was hauling to do, horses did the honors. Large loads of hogs, hay, or corn went to town on the wagon or the sled hitched to a team of horses. When the load was smaller, the "democrat wagon" would suffice. (The democrat was a smaller and sportier flatbed wagon that Elmo took to town when he had a load of grist for the mill, some potatoes to sell, or errands to run on a day when the roads were bad.)

Throughout much of the winter, the sled or the cutter was the vehicle of choice. Emily and Joseph had a cutter, for traveling in style in snow. Emily loved a good sleigh ride; she regularly noted her first sleigh ride of the winter. Both Emily and May commented through the winter months on the quality of the sleighing. For example, Emily noted, "Turned to snow & has been blizzardy all day. Must be fair sleighing." May wrote, "Men draw pigs on sleds, pretty good sleighing to Cherry Valley." Comments like these also appear regularly: "Much snow in places on center road, but we get through with one-horse buggy." "We go Cherry Valley in buggy, but find snow deep a good deal of way, better for bobsled."

A common refrain for the winter slush and mud was "neither good sleighing nor wheeling." Fortunately, however, they had both of these options and more. The wagons, usually drawn by a team of two horses, could be fitted with either bobsled runners or wheels. And when conditions merited, an additional horse or an extra team could be added to haul heavy loads. In February 1913, Elmo hauled gravel with a three-horse team; a month later it took four horses to haul the hay baler.

At times the conditions were too much even for the horses. On a late December day in 1909, it was 4° below zero in the morning, and Mat Ralston's horse was stuck in the snow with a load of corn. Elmo helped Mat get the horse out of the snow bank. Another time Elmo went into Rockford with a load and got caught by a blizzard; he had to walk the horses all the way home with the "snow [up] to their bodies in places." Sometimes the only alternative was to wait till the roads improved. One day in late January 1911, May wrote, "Elmo drive up to Argyle in PM to see how roads are." The report came back: "Mud 6 inches deep in spots." Elmo intended to haul hogs to Argyle, but heavy loads and deep mud didn't mix well. He waited several days until the ground froze to haul the hogs. Still the roads were "very rough."

Road conditions in the winter months were often bad enough to tip the loads the men were hauling. The winter of 1910 was full of snow, and the men used sleighs to haul. In mid-January, May noted, "Elmo take load of hay to Rockford, tip over before he get to corner. Leave part of load & go on & tip over twice more going through Kleckner's." Days later, "Elmo take last of his hay to Rockford, not tip over till he get to Rockford. Then in crossing tracks, get caught in streetcar tracks & break king bolt & tip over." Such incidents were handled in stride, certainly in the diaries; for example, "Elmo tip over with pigs on streetcar track, none hurt. Average 315#."

Counting on Horses

Clearly horses were yet to be displaced by machines. Gas engines powered many jobs on the farm that had been run by horsepower, but Elmo used his engine in the off-season primarily. At this time, it was more often the steam engines that were displaced by gas engines. The total number of work animals on farms did not peak in the United States until 1921 (although the number of farms also increased until about the same time).[10] Nowhere in the diaries or ledgers did May mention how many horses she and Elmo owned, but she did mention the horses by name regularly. She mentioned when they were shod or sharp shod for ice and snow, and when they were sick, and when they died. She mentioned when a horse was bought or sold. While it's impossible to know with certainty how many horses they had at any one time, in 1910, May and Elmo had at least eight adult horses and three young colts. In 1914, they had at least seven adult horses, three young horses still in the rambunctious stage, and at least two young colts.

Not all of those horses worked at any one time. But often two teams were working—one team with Elmo and the other with the hired man, when both men were cultivating, for example. Three or even four horses might be used for plowing or pulverizing, and one team of horses might work in the morning and a fresh team in the afternoon. Sometimes a mare might be taking care of colts, and an older horse would be out to pasture. Old horses generally lived out their lives on the farm; their care and feeding beyond working years were the reward for years of service. On the other hand, Elmo sometimes called an old horse into draft service again. He went out to the pasture to get "Old Ned" in 1915 for a third horse to plow with but found him with a sore foot and was forced to plow with two horses.

Dogs received brief mention in May's diaries, but horses were part of the family, some for twenty to thirty years. The older horses were the ones they took to town or loaned to the hired help to take home on Sunday. Molly and Sam were working in the field as a team in 1902. In 1909, Molly was the horse that went home with the hired girl; in 1912, Molly was out with the colts in the pasture. Sam received the most frequent mention in the

June Breckenridge, Elmo's great niece, driving horses and grain binder, ca. 1914.

1910–14 period. He was the horse of choice to take into town, the hired girls drove Sam, and even May drove Sam across to Papa's in 1914.

Elmo was busy, however, with a variety of horses in the 1910–14 period. Since 1908, he'd been training Fritz, apparently a colt born on the farm. Fritz was the horse that dragged Elmo behind the cart for several rods on the way home from Cherry Valley in 1908 and the horse that wasn't a bit scared of Hugh Reid's auto in 1910. Fritz was sold in early 1912 for $150. By that time, Elmo had other colts to tend to, including June and Colonel. During 1912 and 1913, Elmo was breaking June; he then traded her in early 1913 to Mr. Seele for an older horse, Dan. (He netted thirty dollars in the trade.)

When a horse was sick, Elmo stayed up late into the night with it. When Dandy was sick with indigestion in May 1909, Elmo sat up till 2:15 AM, but to no avail. Although the horse got over the indigestion, heart trouble set in. Dandy died during supper the next day. Bonnie was hauling pigs to Cherry Valley with Elmo when she became ill. Elmo "get her into Aham's barn," and Aham took the pigs into the Valley while Elmo tended his horse. Elmo came home that evening at about 9 PM to take May to her folks to spend the night; then he returned to Aham's in the auto to spend the night with Bonnie. For the next three days, the horse stayed in Aham's barn, and Elmo went down to check on her. Bonnie went on to live a long life with Elmo and May. But the "big horse" Shamrock that belonged to the Fitch family died suddenly from the same ailment. May and Elmo visited the Fitches when the horse was ill, and May noted the time of its death in her diary, just as she did when relatives and neighbors died.

Horses could be sensitive to illness, a drawback relative to machines. Horses were mentioned with colic, flu, colds, indigestion, stomachaches, and other ailments peculiar to them. They could also overheat and drop dead. May often noted the caution Elmo used to avoid overworking the horses. One hot July day in 1916, the temperature was 100° in the shade; Elmo went to Belvidere for lumber; he had to "water & rest horses much on way home for the heat was extreme, 32 horses taken to Belvidere rendering works on account of heat." Motor vehicles didn't drop dead in the heat, but in 1914, horses were still more reliable than the machines that later replaced them.

TRAINS, FAIRS, AND FLYING MACHINES

Although horsepower reigned on the farm and on the country road, and automobiles were the wave of the future, railways were still the backbone of distance travel for produce and people within the United States. From the

1850s through at least the 1920s, steam-powered locomotives dominated long-distance transport for grain, livestock, merchandise, and passengers. Electric streetcars had a shorter heyday. They boomed around the turn of the century, connecting suburbs to urban centers and moving people around cities; then they fizzled when the price of the basic Model T fell to under three hundred dollars by the mid-1920s.[11]

The use of steam-powered locomotives for freight and passenger trains, across the United States, peaked around 1914. Through that time, miles of track continued to increase, connecting more and more rural communities by rail. Thousands of freight trains came through Rockford each year, and other trains moved passengers every day between Chicago and Rockford.

Passengers could also travel from Rockford to Chicago by electric rail. By 1910, interurban lines extended thirty miles north of Rockford to Janesville, Wisconsin, thirty miles west to Freeport, and forty miles east to Elgin, which was already connected by electric rail to Chicago. The Rockford and Interurban Railway Company conveniently and rapidly carried more than six hundred thousand passengers a year, in addition to tons of freight.[12]

Although May and Emily took train travel for granted, the interurban line, known locally as "the car," received frequent mention. From the time the line between Rockford and Cherry Valley was completed in 1902, May noted whenever Elmo took it from Cherry Valley to Rockford. The hired help, the schoolteacher, and visitors also caught the car back and forth from Cherry Valley to Rockford. (May, on the other hand, was never mentioned taking it.) Joseph and Emily made regular trips to Roscoe on the car to visit relatives. Emily even had roosters delivered by "interurban express" in 1914.

Relatives from farther distances arrived by train; so did parcels and boxes; and most produce went into Chicago by train. Every year at Christmastime, May and the other Lyfords shipped and received boxes of gifts by train, exchanging with their Kansas relatives. Elmo's relatives, Bertha and Ely Breckenridge and daughter, June, came to visit from Tacoma, Washington, on the train in 1910 and 1914.

Many of the major amusements of the day for rural America, such as the circus and the circuit Chautauqua, arrived by train. In America, the circus grew up with the train in the nineteenth century. Train travel was a financial boon for circuses; they could choose which towns to play in, fill their tents with patrons, and reinvest their proceeds. Performances improved, because performers could sleep overnight on the train on the way to the next big town. The golden age of the circus began in the mid-1880s and lasted until the Depression of the 1930s dampened its glow. When the Ringling Brothers bought out the Barnum and Bailey Circus in 1907, each of these circuses filled about eighty railroad cars with their shows. Although these two were the greatest, they were not the only circuses around. In 1909, about thirty circuses traveled by rail, each with some thirty or forty railroad cars. Many other circuses still traveled with horses and wagons.[13]

On circus day, Rockford was filled with excitement that affected the entire community. Emily mentioned the "great crowd" in Rockford on circus day in 1908. Elmo was there to see the circus parade through the center of town. May didn't go to the circus, but Elmo often caught the parade at least, up through 1914. That year, the Ringling Brothers Circus came to town; Elmo and the hired man saw both the parade and the show.

Chautauqua also came to town on the train during the Golden Age of Agriculture. The original New York Chautauqua Institute was established in 1874 to offer lectures and performances for adult education. At the turn of the century, many midwestern communities sponsored their own Chautauqua programs; May recorded Chautauqua expenses in 1902. By 1913, however, circuit Chautauqua, which first sprang up in Iowa in 1904, was displacing community Chautauqua. The traveling Chautauqua could provide more arts, education, and entertainment more cheaply than the hometown variety could. The circus trains came to big towns like Rockford, but Chautauqua came to small towns like Cherry Valley and stayed for several days. The smaller spur line railways that were built up through 1914 and beyond facilitated the movement of Chautauqua from town to town. Starr and his family went to Chautauqua in Cherry Valley in 1914, and May and Elmo attended the Chautauqua there in 1922. By the mid-1920s, however, many small rural towns could no longer afford Chautauqua, and it began to decline.[14]

Besides bringing such entertainment to town, trains also took farmers and others to state and local fairs. The fairs offered both amusements and important information for farmers. Fairs presented opportunities to learn about new breeds of livestock and methods of farming. Farmers could see for themselves the innovations they read about in magazines like the *Prairie Farmer, Better Farming,* and the *Wisconsin Agriculturalist.*[15] Fairs demonstrated all kinds of exciting developments in new technology. Golden Age fairs pitted new tractors against horses and featured automobile races (along with the classic horse races) and, most amazing of all, flying machines. The Iowa State Fair featured a flying machine in 1906, just three years after the Wright brothers took flight. The first air flight in Minnesota was in 1910 at the state fair. The same year, an air flight from Chicago to Springfield attracted crowds (Elmo among them) to the state fair in Springfield. After that, barnstormers were a regular attraction at the state fairs.[16]

Between 1910 and 1914, Elmo took the train twice to the Illinois State Fair and once to the Minnesota State Fair with other farmers. When May and Elmo drove the Maxwell to the Beloit Fair in 1911, Emily noted that they "saw a flying machine." They returned to the Beloit Fair in 1913, and a few days later, Elmo was off to the fair in Minneapolis. (A postcard preceded his return four days later; expenses were $25.50.) May didn't mention what Elmo saw at the fairs, but among other things, he surely examined the gas engines, farming equipment, and improvements in silos. In 1913, Elmo built a silo, and in 1914, he and his machine group bought a new gas engine to run their new thresher, shredder, and silo filler.

FARMING IN THE GOLDEN AGE

Farming in northern Illinois during the Golden Age of Agriculture was both prosperous and stable. Farmers invested in buildings, new equipment, gas engines, and automobiles. But few tractors turned up on Corn Belt farms. Yields per acre for most crops held essentially constant within normal, highly variable ranges. Farm prices, having risen from 1901 to 1910, remained high during the 1910–14 period. Technological advances continued in dairy and poultry, and farmers also experimented with new breeds of livestock and some new crops.

For Elmo and May, good help increased the tranquility of these years. John Pratt began working for Elmo in early March 1910 and continued through December 1914. (John's mother had been helping May with the wash for several years already.) John began work in 1910 at twenty dollars a month and worked till husking was done in early December. The next year his monthly wages increased by five dollars, and he worked through the end of the year and on into January and February at ten dollars per month during the off-season. His wages continued to increase through 1914, when he worked for thirty-two dollars a month. Two of John's sisters (Linna and Mattie) also worked for May during these years.

Silos Sprout in Guilford Township

One eye-catching change on many farms in the 1910–14 period was the addition of a silo beside the barn. Dairymen were the first to feed silage—

chopped green cornstalks and ears that fermented in the silo. The Babcock butterfat test, first marketed in 1891, soon proved that feeding silage enhanced butterfat. With intensive dairy in neighboring Wisconsin and in the Chicago area, Guilford farmers were exposed early on to the feeding technique. A turning point came in 1910, when fat cattle producers became convinced of the need for a silo, producing "insatiable" demand for silos and silo fillers during the next decade.[17] (The silo filler both chopped the green cornstalks and moved the silage up into the silo.) Techniques for working with concrete had also improved, making poured concrete silos practical.

By all indications, silos sprouted quickly in the area. May first mentioned them in June 1910, when lightning rod and silo agents stopped by. Then, the day after Christmas in 1912, Elmo and John began hauling gravel to build a silo. The silo didn't actually go up until the following June, but the winter months, when the ground was frozen, were best for hauling. Elmo bought dynamite to down the bank at the gravel pit; by early January, the men had hauled twenty-two loads of gravel. May recorded a six-dollar payment for forty loads of gravel when Elmo and John finished hauling at the end of the month.

The cement for the silo arrived in Rockford by train on June 3, and in less than a month the silo was up. Charles Kleckner, Mat Ralston, and Frank Reid all helped Elmo and John haul cement the day after its arrival. Then, for two days beginning June 9, Elmo and Harry Molander dug the "silo hole" while John cultivated. (Half a wagonload of dirt caved back into the hole overnight.) Before the "silo men" came on June 16, there were more preparations to do and supplies to get. Ed Pepper brought a cement mixer and engine that morning. At least two silo men in addition to Mr. Mohns, who directed the job, worked through July 3, pouring the concrete into forms, which moved upward as the silo was raised. Then the cement mixer went back to Ed Pepper, and the last of the forms came off by July 7. A bit more work was done on the silo in mid-August, and finally, after it had been filled with corn, Mr. Mohns put on some final touches, including whitewashing the roof.

By September 1913 most of the men in "Elmo's crowd" (as Emily referred to them) had silos and filled them together. (By this time Mitchel Breckenridge had taken the place of his brother-in-law, John G. Ralston, in the group, and Frank Reid had taken the place of his father, Jim.) The night before Elmo went to Minneapolis for the fair that month, several of the men came over to talk about silo fillers. After Elmo returned, the men began to fill silos. That year and the next, they used an "old machine" that acted up;

then in 1915, they bought a new machine that worked so smoothly two corn binders couldn't keep up with it.

Mama's Incubator

The poultry business was also changing during the Golden Age. While most farmers still set a few hens in the spring and let nature take its course, others began to use incubators to hatch the eggs and brooders to keep the little chicks warm.

Traditionally, raising chickens fell to the farmer's wife; Emily Lyford took the job seriously. In 1908, she noted her usual activity of setting hens and counting chicks in the spring and selling eggs around the neighborhood and in Rockford. But in 1909, she and Joseph visited a neighbor to see his incubator and brooder, and the following spring she had her own new setup. The best part was when the chicks hatched. The first incubator began to hatch on Easter Sunday 1910, when May and Elmo were at Mama's for dinner to see the chicks begin to come out.

Once hatched, the chicks stayed in the drawers of the incubator for a day or so, before going into the brooders. A brooder was a box with glass panes on top and a lamp to keep the chicks warm. Normally, the brooders stayed outside in a special "brooder house," but Emily's incubator was inside her house. The incubator held over 200 eggs. Of the first batch that hatched

May and Elmo's barn with silo.

in 1910, 138 chicks made it to the brooders. (Unfortunately the Maltese cat killed 24 of them a few days later.) In mid-May, Emily and Joseph set the incubator once more with 212 eggs. Three weeks later the chicks began to "pipe their eggs" and hatch. This time 139 chickens came out.

Tending the incubator and brooders turned out to be a rather fussy affair. The hatches that first spring were the best of the six years that Emily used the incubator. After 1910, she set the incubator only once per year, and in most years about half of the eggs hatched. In 1914, however, May noted that only 65 hatched; Emily explained, "The thermometer would not stay in place & I expect I roasted or smothered very many of them, for eggs were piped and 12 or more that had got out all right, dead." Frequently, Emily had difficulty regulating the temperature of either the incubator or the two brooders. Once, one of the brooders stopped working altogether, and she and Joseph had to put all the chicks in one brooder. Another time when the brooders acted up, the chicks stayed in the house for several days, in boxes in the bathroom near the heat ducts.

Once on their way, however, the chickens grew rapidly. Many years, the first rooster was ready for the table by the Fourth of July, and the young pullets laid their first eggs in late September. By Thanksgiving, Emily and Joseph had normally dressed a couple dozen roosters for the table, and perhaps the same number had been sold in town. Then, each year at the end of the year, when the pullets were shut up in the henhouse for the winter, Joseph and Emily brought a few roosters from other farms to keep the hens company. In the spring, a week or so before the incubator was set, they started saving eggs to fill it up. Throughout most of the year, Emily had eggs to sell. In 1913 she gathered up to forty-two eggs a day to sell to neighbors and in town.

Emily was up-to-date on advances in poultry farming. One year in January, she began feeding the hens a special "egg food." In the early spring of another year, Joseph went to Cherry Valley to pick up some special chick feed. Thanks to Joseph, the brooder house and the henhouse were kept nice and clean. The henhouse was also sprayed once a year to control disease.

While Mama fussed with the incubator and brooders, May also paid more attention to chickens in her diaries. May rarely mentioned chickens in 1908, but throughout the 1910–14 period, she counted the chicks born in the spring. Perhaps her attention increased because her and Elmo's flock had dwindled during this time; no egg sales were recorded for 1911–14, but most other years they sold some eggs. Or it may reflect May's increasingly precise farming records as she moved into her prime years. In either case, May noted when Elmo set the hens; sometimes they took eggs from Mama to set. One year the efforts to set hens yielded little; from the two hens that Elmo set, only one chick was born and it died, whereas from the hens that hid their nests, twenty-one chicks were born.

Market Crops in the Golden Age

Farm income for May and Elmo in the 1910–14 period continued to come primarily from cattle, hogs, corn, oats, and hay. Once again, as in the first decade of the century, hay surged as an income crop. Hay prices were high in 1911 and 1912, and after Starr finished his new barn 1911, Elmo filled Joseph's barn with hay. (Apparently Starr had previously used the space in Joseph's barn.) The percentage of income from hay rose from about 10 percent during 1908–10 to almost 20 percent during 1911–14. Hogs produced the most income, at almost 30 percent, and cattle fell to 15 percent of their income, down from more than 40 percent during the first five years of the century, when hogs produced less income. Sales of corn accounted for about 10 percent of their income and sales of oats for about 15 percent (up slightly from the previous five years).

During the 1910–14 period, hay was still handled as it was in 1907, when the balers first came. Elmo bought a hay loader in 1907 for use with a side-delivery rake. The loader picked up the rows of hay and used a belt to deposit the hay on the wagon. May didn't describe the process by which the men "get the hay up in barn," but local residents still remember the big forks that lifted the hay into the barns with the help of ropes, pulleys, and horses. From that point, balers came with a stationary baler and a gas engine to bale the hay that was stored in the barn. Sometimes the balers came in August, September, or October, but just as often they came in November, December, or January. Then during the winter months, Elmo hauled hay to town.

Livestock was still the major income source, although Elmo shifted among cattle, hogs, and corn with changing market conditions. During the 1910–14 period, the market was relatively strong for hogs, whereas in 1901–5 it was stronger for cattle. Year-to-year variation was also significant. In 1911, Elmo sold no corn, and in 1912 he sold no cattle (except for an old cow). In 1913, his sales of corn (both ear corn and shelled) were roughly equal to his sale of hogs, but cattle brought in the most income then.

From 1910 to 1914, Elmo marketed from twenty-five to fifty hogs each year and usually from seven to ten steers and heifers. He added to his livestock from local sources. In November or December, Elmo typically looked around the neighborhood for a pig to buy. Then in the spring, May kept a count of the piglets as they were born. Piglet mortality could be high; their numbers went up and down throughout the spring. Additions to the cattle herd were also only occasional: four steers from Retzlaff, two calves from Molander, a cow from Seele—all from neighbors, except for one purchase of two steers from a Cherry Valley livestock buyer. The livestock were sold either in Cherry Valley, or Rockford, or Perryville (a railroad depot between Rockford and Cherry Valley). The men rose early in the morning to drive cattle to market. In 1912, Elmo and John were up at 1:15 AM to drive cattle to Rockford. The hogs, on the other hand, were hauled to market in wagons.

Oats, which served primarily as feed for horses, were an important market crop during the 1910–14 period. Although electric streetcars had displaced many horses in urban areas by 1910, the horse population remained high, with most horses serving farmers and rural residents. Prices for oats were fairly stable during this period, and excellent yields increased sales somewhat relative to the 1905–10 period.

Elmo also planted minor amounts of two other crops for the first time in 1912—millet and soybeans. Neither was sold. The millet and the soybeans were planted and harvested at the same time. When harvested, the millet was cut, stacked, and put into the barns. No word on what was done with the beans. In 1914, however, Elmo helped Frank Reid thresh soybeans. Not until the mid-1920s did Elmo plant soybeans again, nor, indeed, did many farmers in the United States. (Millet was not mentioned again in May's records.)

The Mixed-Farming Rotation

In the absence of chemical fertilizers and pesticides, Elmo depended on animal manure and crop rotation to care for crops. Different crops make different demands on the soil and provide different contributions. Corn, which loves nitrogen, was often planted on clover sod, since clover is a legume that fixes nitrogen in the soil. Then oats, barley, or rye followed the corn. The next year, hay (based on timothy grass or perhaps clover again) would follow the small grain crop. Volunteer grain from last year's crop enriched the hay. Similarly, May noted the regular movements of the pig pasture. The old hog pasture became a potato patch and then the following year went into beans, peas, and oats. The animal manure left behind enhanced the subsequent crops. Manure left in the barn by livestock was also spread out on the fields.

Such mixed-farming systems helped control pests and diseases. Root diseases, fungus, nematodes, and insects were kept at bay by following a susceptible crop with another that would not serve as a host. Corn planted in successive years on the same ground could generate problems with root aphids, root worms, and corn borers. Some pest cycles could be broken with an alternate crop in a single year; others required longer rotations of four or five years.

The mixed-farming methods also spread the work evenly throughout the year. The men sowed oats and hay in the early spring, well before the corn, which was planted in May. The corn required considerable labor; it needed cultivating at least four times, taking most of June. Oats, barley, and rye, on the other hand, were left alone until harvest; sometime in July the grains were cut with a binder and stacked, waiting for threshing. Making hay was wedged in between several times over the summer, as rains permitted. Corn husking was another labor-intensive job, but it waited till November, when the other crops were in and the corn was dry. Caring for livestock required more labor in the winter months, when the only other jobs were hauling crops to town and chopping wood.

Volatile market prices for grain and livestock and unpredictable weather conditions also favored a mixed portfolio of produce to sell or feed. Diversification helped to guarantee a minimum income. In 1910, Elmo sold hogs at ten dollars per hundredweight, up from less than seven dollars the year before, but by the following April, prices had fallen to just over six dollars. Prices for oats moved from twenty-nine cents a bushel in April 1911 to fifty-six cents a bushel a year later. The oats on the creek piece yielded seventy-six bushels an acre in 1912, but in 1914 Elmo's oat yield was just over thirty-eight bushels per acre. Oats thrive on plentiful rains, but barley does well in cool and dry weather. Barley and corn both made good feed for pigs and cattle; the one yielding the higher price could be sold, while the other was fed to the livestock.

Threshing, Baling, Filling, and Shredding

Large crews of men worked together with farm machines throughout the Golden Age. Most of the machines of the day required many hands to get the work done efficiently and were also too expensive for ownership by a single farmer. So, various ownership patterns and labor arrangements were employed. A custom operator might both own the machinery and provide a crew of men. Or an organized "ring" of farmers might hire the owner of the equipment, and the ring of farmers would work around the neighborhood, providing most of the labor, until the work was finished on all farms. Finally, a group of men might jointly purchase machinery for their own use and perhaps to hire out as well.[18]

Elmo's machine company got its start in 1907, when the men purchased a corn shredder together. (Initially they used the shredder with a steam engine that was not jointly owned.) Then in 1913, a somewhat reconstituted group bought a used silo filler together. Some of members had gas engines to run the silo filler, but these engines were not quite up to the job. In 1914, the men bought their own thresher, a large gas engine to run it, and a new corn shredder, and they built a shed on the Breckenridge farm to house their machinery. From then on, that gas engine was used for threshing, shredding, and filling silo. Some additional machinery was also purchased jointly later. Especially early on, the men used their machines on other neighborhood farms as well to help pay bills. In 1914, they threshed together at five other farms in addition to their own.

The responsibility of keeping accounts rotated among the six or seven members of the machine company. At the end of the year, accounts were

Filling silo with a gas engine, ca. 1905. Courtesy of Wisconsin Historical Society (image 41499).

squared and dividends distributed. There was also a point person who made sure the machinery was ready to use, but when repairs were required, everyone helped.

Until 1914, Elmo was part of a large threshing ring whose membership varied from year to year but always included the members of his machine group after 1907. The ring hired the thresher and steam engine to go from farm to farm. Similarly, until 1918, an outside hay baler came to bale hay. Between 1910 and 1914, several different names were associated with baling operations. Late in 1918, Elmo and his machine company bought a used baler (apparently), after shopping around among farmers who had previously baled hay for others.

But whether the machinery was owned by others or by his own machine company, Elmo and his hired man spent many days threshing, baling, shredding, and filling silo on other farms. Elmo and John threshed at ten other farms in 1910 and at nine other farms in each of the next two years. Their threshing ring made no payments to the men for this work, but the number of days each worked was specified. If one of the men couldn't make it, he sent a substitute. Fewer men were needed for the baling operation, so Elmo spent only a few days a year helping others bale hay. The silo filling and shredding were done on the farms of those in the machine company and sometimes at one or two other farms.

Whether the men were threshing, baling, shredding, or filling silo and irrespective of how the payments were handled, they needed to be fed at dinnertime. May described the feeding of these large groups of men only briefly but usually noted their number. The threshing crews were the largest, with nineteen or twenty men to feed. The balers tended to number only eight to ten hungry men, but they often stayed for both dinner and supper. The silo fillers came with ten to twelve men, and the shredders were noted to be seventeen men in 1910. May also usually noted who was there to help her, generally her hired girl and one other woman. Elmo often went to Rockford to get the meat the night before, Papa would come down with extra chairs in the wagon, and the hired girl would go up to Mama's several times to borrow something as the three women prepared the meal.

The number of men coming to dinner was always a moving target, and the date was not fixed either. Depending on breakdowns and weather conditions, which farm wife was serving dinner might be adjusted at short notice. In 1911, Elmo went into Rockford early one Saturday morning in mid-August "for thresher food." (He bought coffee, pickles, cheese, corn, and meat. Potatoes, bread, garden vegetables, and home-baked desserts would also be on the menu.) Mrs. Ostberg came over early to begin dinner plans and preparations. But at 9:30 AM, Mrs. Brown telephoned that she would have the threshers for dinner, because work wasn't proceeding as rapidly as anticipated. May's dinner waited for the following Monday. Then again in mid-August 1915, May expected to have threshers for dinner, but the men finished early and moved to the next farm at 10:30 AM. May wrote, "Annie Rutz come soon after 6:30 AM & we cook meat & make pies & cakes, go to mama's for chairs, etc, and then they go to Faulkner's to dinner. Elmo take Annie & meat, bread & potatoes in auto over there."

Pass the Potatoes

Potatoes were not an important market crop for May and Elmo (they never amounted to more than 3 percent of the gross income), but they were important for the table. Elmo planted early potatoes, late potatoes, garden potatoes, and field potatoes. A good crop of potatoes brought a sigh of relief and the peace of a well-stocked cellar to last till the new potatoes came on in early summer. If one ran short before that time, relatives or neighbors were happy to barter a few old potatoes in the spring. When too many were left over come spring, relatives and neighbors who ran low came calling, and the potatoes could also still be sold in town for a fair price. In the spring of 1910, however, Elmo had a hard time getting rid of the excess potatoes. Apparently the 1909 crop was good for everyone; the forty bushels he sold in the spring went cheap.

Average yields per acre barely budged on most Corn Belt crops from 1897 to 1935, but potatoes were an exception. As a result of improved varieties, potato yields across the United States increased from eighty-one bushels per acre on average at the turn of the century to ninety-five bushels per acre a decade later.[19] In 1909 and 1910, Emily and May both remarked on impressive potato yields. Starr harvested 230 bushels from 1.5 acres in 1909, according to Emily—155 bushels per acre. In 1910, Elmo harvested "149 bushels from about an acre."

Because limited acreage was devoted to potatoes, the potato planter and potato digger machines were shared around the neighborhood. Each year from 1910 to 1914, Elmo went around the neighborhood to find a potato planter; he found the Retzlaff planter at George Brown's in 1910. Likewise, the potato diggers floated around the neighborhood. Although Elmo, Starr, and Joseph bought a potato digger together in 1905, seven years later it had moved into the public domain. These implements floated on an "if-it-breaks-you-fix-it" basis. No expenses were recorded for the use of the potato planter, but May noted, in 1912, that the planter found at Jim Reid's had to be fixed to get it to work right.

Extras for the Table

A medley of minor crops broke the monotony of the yearly routine and added variety to the table. Hickory nuts fell from the trees every year, but some years the yield was extraordinary, and everyone was out "nutting." A freight charge of ninety-one cents on forty pounds of nuts even appeared in the ledger in 1911. May first mentioned a harvest of honey in 1910. "Elmo cut bee tree at eve, from which we get 1½ quarts strained honey." He returned to that tree for honey several times in the next few years.

Emily and Joseph took special pains with their fruit crops and usually had plenty; May and Elmo were less consistent, but they tended apples, cherries, grapes, and blackberries. The 1910 apple crop was lost to a late frost; but in 1911, even though they seldom sold apples, May and Elmo sold thirteen bushels for about ten dollars. That was after making thirteen quarts of cider applesauce, twelve quarts of canned apples, ten quarts of apple pickles, two jugs of boiled cider, and plenty of fresh cider to drink. In addition, they typically stored several bushels of apples in the cellar to use over the winter and into the spring. May and Elmo also harvested cherries regularly, although they were less dependable than apples and had to be canned to keep. For cherries, 1913 was a good year; May canned eighteen and a half quarts. In the spring of 1915, Elmo planted ten apple trees, two cherries, and six pie-plant (rhubarb) roots.

Emily and Joseph had an exceptional berry year in 1913. Emily picked the first small bowl of strawberries on June 13, and two days later on Sunday morning, Elmo picked a big kettle full. Less than a week into the season, Emily noted that the strawberries were "very, very abundant"; three of Starr's boys, Elmo, and Mattie Pratt all picked that day. Elmo and Mattie both picked regularly that season; so did Starr's children and his sister-in-law Nettie. When the strawberries finally gave out, Emily's black raspberries and currants were producing, and then came the red raspberries. These last three produced only modest quantities, but the blackberries were "very thick and ripe"; they produced heavily for a month. Elmo and May had blackberries of their own, but before long Mattie was up picking at Mama's too. Emily also shared them with many neighbors who came to pick.

New Investments

May and Elmo continued to invest in the farm while the Golden Age moved into its heyday. They made some final payments to Elmo's mother and payments to settle the estate after she died in 1912. The silo, built in 1913, cost $378.71 for contracted labor and materials, just a bit more than the addition to the barn in 1910. Lightning rods for the barn addition ($50) and shingling for the corncrib and hog house ($58.75) were other significant farm building expenses from 1911 to 1914.

Investments in machinery and horses surpassed the building costs. Elmo replaced both his corn binder and his grain binder with new machines in 1911 and 1912 for $115 and $148, respectively. The old binders may have been in use since before he and May were married; similar binders had been introduced in the 1870s. (Elmo took both old binders apart in 1912 and sold a load of iron for $5.75.) Other farm equipment for Elmo included a new wagon, a fanning mill, and a hay tedder. He bought three horses for a total of $270. Together with the other farmers in his threshing and shredding group, he went in on the thresher, the engine, the silo filler, and the shed that housed all this machinery on the Breckenridge place; Elmo's share of these group expenses was $375.32.

Household expenses were also significant in this period, with a new automobile, a new buggy, and work on the house. May and Elmo had the exterior of the house painted and the steps fixed, and they put a cement floor in the cellar and bought a new furnace.

May and Elmo's house.

Relative to the first decade of the century, in the second one May and Elmo invested less income in the farm and put more into the new automobile and cash savings. If buildings, machinery, horses, final payments to Mother Davis, and settlement of the estate are all lumped together for a rough estimate of new farm investment, the total was about $1,985 for 1911–14. Gross farm income (or total produce sold) for the four years was $10,781, so investment was about a fifth of the gross income. Over the 1901–10 period, almost a third of the gross income went back into the farm as new investment. Most of the difference relates to the shrinkage of payments to Elmo's mother and the growth of cash savings. With the farm paid off, net farm savings for these four years (net of all farm and household expenses) was about $1,190—more than the $950 for the ten years from 1901 to 1910. May and Elmo also made some loans to friends and relatives with the savings; the interest payments were recorded in May's ledgers.[20]

Elmo also expanded the available acreage for pasture and future cropland by grubbing parts of the twenty-acre woods that had belonged to his mother. Elmo first fenced the woods and used it for pasture in 1910. Then in the next few years, he removed considerable wood from the area. John Pratt spent several winters cutting wood and otherwise "working in the woods." Often Elmo worked with him. Late in 1913, Elmo and John grubbed out tree stumps with dynamite. Elmo first planted crops on part of the "20" in 1915.

Accidents and Nature's Wrath

Despite the general farming prosperity of these years, the possibility of calamity on the farm was ever present. Capricious acts of nature could destroy a harvest or burn a barn full of crops and animals. In 1910, a heavy snowstorm and a cold spell in late April froze the apple and cherry blossoms that came out with an early spring and eliminated these crops. Even the blackberries were few and far between. January had so much severe cold that a "coal famine threatens Rockford." Hail in July the same year, with "stones large as big hickory nuts," stripped the corn leaves and broke off branches of the potatoes and tomato vines. The storm also broke off the heads of the oats in the field right at harvest time. Fortunately, Elmo had already cut most of his oats. On November 11, 1911, the weather was very warm (76°) and windy, but black clouds brought the "worst storm of the year" with heavy rain, thunder, lightning, and hail. By the next morning, the temperature had plunged to 16°, and the wind blew hard from the west and northwest all day. Emily later wrote, "Reports of Saturday's storm from surrounding towns showed we escaped almost miraculously." In June 1912, a storm again produced "hail stones as big as hickory nuts down at Starr's & Mr. Purdy's large as egg." Fortunately that storm came well before grain harvest.

Heavy electrical storms, with high winds, lightning, and sometimes hail, were a constant threat in the summertime. In July 1913, lightning struck and fire burned Hugh Reid's granary, the crops inside it, and the milk house as well. Just a month later, a rye stack (shocked bundles of rye, standing in the field waiting to be threshed) at Mitchel Breckenridge's was struck by lightning and burned. Lightning in June 1914 shattered a large oak in May and Elmo's creek pasture, and in August, lightning struck and burned the barns on two area farms. A fire (of unknown cause) at Robert Brown's in July of the same year burned the barn in addition to "most of the out buildings and four horses." Elmo went to help, as did all available men, whenever fire threatened neighbors.

Farmers took measures to protect themselves by buying insurance and installing lightning rods on their barns and granaries. When Elmo made a sizable addition to his barn in 1910 and Starr built a barn in 1911, both men had new lightning rods installed. Elmo paid fifty dollars for the installation of the rod. Entries for insurance appear in May's ledgers every year from 1901 on.

Other kinds of accidents were also common; the physical nature of farmwork involved hazards. Fortunately, when the steam engine exploded after the men had just used it to run the corn shredder in 1910, no one was hurt. But when Elmo helped Mat Ralston haul tile from Belvidere in 1912, a man fell from a load of Mat's tile and died the same day with a broken back. In 1913, Charles Kleckner ran a pitchfork into his leg; a week later, he had improved. But tragedy was never far away. In 1914, Emily noted that Minnie Behling's husband was killed in the gravel pit.

Organizations of Rural Life

Rural life was reorganized a bit in 1914 with the creation of the Cooperative Extension Service under the Smith–Lever Act. The Extension Service was a joint venture between the U.S. Department of Agriculture (USDA) and states to extend advances in farming technology to farmers. The land-grant universities, initiated with a law signed by Abraham Lincoln in 1862, when the USDA was also established, played the key role. During the Golden Age of Agriculture, the land-grant university system came of age.

The University of Illinois was among many land-grant institutions that had already been working with Farmers' Institute. Elmo attended Farmers' Institute meetings each winter during the 1910–14 period, as he had done since the turn of the century. States such as Illinois were already moving toward a cooperative extension program before 1914. The Winnebago County Farm Improvement Association was formed for that purpose in 1913, and Elmo joined that year. Similarly, boys and girls clubs began to form in the early years of the century; in 1911, they competed at the Illinois State Fair. Later, during World War I, these clubs became known as 4-H clubs, but working with such clubs was already part of the role of extension agents, outlined in the 1914 act.[21]

The Grange had returned to the social and educational purposes that had inspired its founding in 1867. It remained an important rural institution, particularly at the local level. Many new granges were established in Illinois during the Golden Age—1,774 by 1914.[22] While it failed to take hold in some regions of the country because of its nature as a secret society (Catholics and Lutherans frowned on it, and others found its rituals tedious), part of the Grange's appeal as a social organization lay in its inclusion of both men and women on relatively equal footing.[23] In 1899, a woman even served as "worthy master" of Guilford Hope Grange; more typically women held special female offices or served as secretary.

Guilford Hope Grange was alive and well in the Golden Age. During 1913 and 1914, it met every two weeks, usually in the homes of members. Attendance ran at only ten to fifteen members in 1913 but increased in 1914. The group discussed road improvements, made joint purchases of sugar, and listened to educational talks on topics such as alfalfa. Music, singing, and humorous readings were ever present, and the group also gained a reputation for their banquets, picnics, and other feasts.[24] May rarely mentioned Grange, however. She and Elmo were not yet members, although they attended Fourth of July Grange picnics in 1911 and 1914.

CHILDREN, MORE CHILDREN, AND OTHER FAMILY CHANGES

Scenes full of children, especially Starr's, round out the picture that May and her mother present of the Golden Age of Agriculture. The children would come over to play and find kittens in the barns, or come by to show the new puppy (named Guess) or to see Elmo's colts. When they had birthdays, Emily made cakes and sent presents. Starr's family was completed in 1915 with the birth of yet another boy, for a total of seven children, five boys and two girls.

Schoolchildren and Toddlers

The school routines of the children brightened the days of both May and Emily. Since both women lived between Starr's house and the schoolhouse, the children often stopped by at one place or the other on the way to or from school. Both May and Emily noted when snow, subzero temperatures, or illness closed the school. School picnics, spelling contests, and entertainment at Christmastime all received mention. When Joe fell in the creek over the noon hour at school, he came up to May's "for repairs." Sometimes the schoolchildren stopped in at May's with the teacher, bringing flowers or cake, candy, and nuts from the school social or to give May a special showing of a performance the children were practicing. Other times the younger children waited at May's while Starr was at the schoolhouse with the older ones.

As each child started school, another toddler was ready to accompany Starr to work at Joseph and Emily's. Sometimes four or five children would have breakfast with their grandparents and Starr in the morning before the older ones went off to school. The older boys seemed to prefer being out with their father to attending school. Once not long after Joe started school, he was up to May's with Walter and Franklin, apparently skipping school. Emily wrote, "Joey said he was too tired to go to school." Another time Emily noted, "Walter here too, as he hurt his knee, so he cannot go to school." By the fall of 1914, Joe and Walter, despite their young age, were

Lyford boys with pony, ca. 1914. Courtesy of John Pearse.

integral to their father's part-time workforce; for instance, they stayed home from school one day to help dig potatoes. If Emily disapproved, she also noted that they "got out a lot of potatoes."

The children of Florence and Ed Fitch also attended Bell School and were regular visitors at May and Elmo's. In the fall of 1914, the Fitch children had a new pony to take them to school; the pony stayed at Elmo and May's during the school day. Because the Fitch children and Starr's children often stopped by, so did many of the other schoolchildren that walked or rode ponies from the south up to Bell School.

Children Working

The line between play and work was rather fuzzy in the Starr Lyford household. Certainly when the two older boys (nine and seven and a half years) stayed home from school in 1914 to help harvest potatoes, they were clearly working. But the following Saturday, according to Emily, Starr and three boys were "up in the afternoon to pick seed corn." Franklin was the youngest of these three, at six and a half years. To what extent was Franklin working? Two weeks later Emily noted, "Starr brought up 4 boys when he came to husk before 7 AM. Russell [almost five years] stayed all day, the rest to school." The older boys were surely working, or at least learning to work, when they came up with their father, and the younger ones were surely right behind. The fact that all five of Starr's boys farmed as adults suggests they enjoyed the work and play of their childhood.

By 1914, Starr's older boys were also adept at handling the horses and could run errands for their folks. They came up to borrow Joseph and Emily's "horses and carriage to use. Drove themselves." A week later the boys were up "for horses to go to Belvidere with." They may well have been learning to drive the car at about the same time. Annetta later recalled that she and her brothers began driving cars at nine or ten years of age, initially out to the pasture to get the cows and, before long, on the country roads as well.[25]

Middle Age in the Golden Age

May and Elmo entered middle age in the Golden Age. By all indications, it was a time of peace and tranquility in their family life. Significantly, they both had come to terms with May's immobility. Years later (in regard to a Democratic landslide victory), May noted, "What can't be cured must be endured." It was surely a concept she had taken to heart regarding her rheumatism. Although she stayed home frequently when others were out, never a word of complaint hit the pages of her diary. May didn't let her disability and the resulting desire to stay home keep Elmo from seeing the circus parade, going to fairs, or driving around and visiting his relatives. Most of the time, she was with him when he had dinner at the Whittles', the Purdys', or at Aham and Carrie's, but other times she spent a Sunday with her folks while he was out. On the other hand, May also noted when Elmo helped with the housework, when he surprised her with a new "blanket coat" in subzero weather, and when he took the place of the horse to pull her up the lane in the cart. She took pleasure in being near where he was working. And on winter Sundays, May read aloud to Elmo. During these Golden Age years, although the notes in her diary are mostly dry reports of the day's weather and activities, the tone is cheerful with regular mentions of warm, pleasant days and fine, sunny mornings, as well as a beautiful rainbow.

Elmo and May both turned forty in 1913. On her fortieth birthday, September 25, May had two cakes; Mama made one, covered with marshmallows and a pennant with verse, and Mattie Pratt made another, trimmed with fern. Mattie also decorated the sitting room with ferns, flowers, apples, and corn. Papa and the schoolchildren came to help celebrate. Elmo's fortieth birthday fell on a Sunday in December; his sister May Purdy hosted a birthday dinner that May and Elmo both attended.

Some of the children of the next generation were already approaching adulthood. Florence Fitch, who was the same age as Elmo and May, had her first child when she was twenty. Her son Howard, by the fall of 1913, was a student of agriculture at the University of Illinois. So was his cousin, Fred Davis. Since Fred's parents, Aham and Carrie, now had no children at home, May and Elmo spent even more time with them.

Some members of the older generation were passing away, including Elmo's mother, who died in the summer of 1912 at the age of seventy-four, after several years of failing health. May's uncle Dudley Lyford died in 1914 after an operation for appendicitis; he was seventy-eight. Another of May's uncles died suddenly only four days before Uncle Dudley. Although Elmo attended funerals quite regularly, May did so only infrequently, but she did attend her uncle Dudley's funeral and Elmo's mother's funeral.

May still had the luxury of both parents alive and just up the lane. In 1914, Emily and Joseph completed seventy-one and seventy-five years, respectively. Joseph's health was increasingly frail after a bad fall down the hay shute in mid-1911. Although he recovered from the fall, he was ailing with the "old trouble" the next year and used an inhaler in 1914. Elmo often did Joseph's chores for a week or so when Joseph was ailing, but Joseph still made farming decisions, helped Emily with her chickens, and tended the berry bushes. He stopped raising pigs after 1912, but even then, when Starr butchered in 1913 and 1914, Papa cut up and salted the half pig Starr brought up. Emily was healthy and energetic throughout these years. She had more help with housework than in previous years. But she was still gardening and canning, making bread and fried cakes, fussing with her incubator and brooders, caring for grandchildren, cooking for her son and his hired man, and making birthday cakes and clothing for her grandchildren. She made buckwheat cakes for breakfast in the winter months and sometimes sent a few down to May; she canned maple syrup in the spring. She also provided help and companionship to May: when Florence Fitch had an oyster dinner, Mama came to help May dress for it. They made rag rugs and sewed together; they visited and played a card game called Flinch.

Throughout the 1910–14 period, Joseph and Emily still hosted holiday dinners—both Christmas and Thanksgiving until 1913 and 1914, when May and Elmo hosted Thanksgiving dinner, and her parents did Christmas. (In these years May still had hired girls working in late November to help her with the holiday meal. Emily surely helped, too, and Elmo.) In 1910, Joseph and Emily had a big Fourth of July picnic at their farm, with all the Lyfords down from Roscoe. Elmo dropped May off there before 8 AM to help her folks with preparations, and then he went to Rockford for ice cream. In 1914, May and Elmo took Joseph and Emily to the Grange picnic in Robinson's woods on the Fourth of July, and in the evening May and Elmo went into Rockford to see the fireworks.

Women's Voice

The extension of limited voting rights to women in the state of Illinois in 1913 began to change family dynamics. Women were granted the right to vote in municipal and national elections, but the state constitution was not amended to allow them to cast ballots on state issues. Emily voted at Guilford's Town Hall on April 7, 1914, although May didn't join her. In preparation for her new voting privileges, Emily and Joseph read eight volumes of MacMasters' *History of the People of America*, followed by another four volumes of Wilson's *History of the American People* between September 1913 and the end of February the next year.

Women around the world were waging battles during these years to gain a voice in public policy. In the United States, five thousand women marched down Pennsylvania Avenue on the eve of Wilson's inauguration in March 1913. Some weeks later, ten thousand women marched in New York. In both cases the primary issue was women's suffrage. The National American Woman Suffrage Association had already been working with limited success for over twenty years, going state to state to extend voting rights to women. A national amendment to the Constitution became the next target. Although Emily voted in 1914, May didn't choose to vote until 1920, when all women across the country were granted voting rights with the ratification of the Nineteenth Amendment.

Prohibition was another hot issue among Rockford women and women across the country. The local organization that became the Woman's Christian Temperance Union was established in Rockford in 1874, several months before the national organization was established. Rockford women cast ballots for prohibition in an advisory referendum on the issue in 1881, only to have the all-male Rockford City Council ignore the results. But with only men voting in 1908 and 1912, Rockford voted dry and then wet again. In 1914 with women voting, prohibition prevailed by a wide margin.[26]

Guilford women tried to make a difference with their auxiliary work. The group known as the Guilford Gleaners had been an outgrowth of the Sunday school at Bell School and had reorganized under that name in 1898. The women met in one another's homes once a month with their Bibles and hymnals and typically worked on a sewing project for deserving recipients. They collected dues and raised money for scholarships; they saved magazines and newspapers and packed up missionary boxes to send off. Emily attended regularly and hosted a meeting most every year. In 1913, she hosted an all-day quilting session. Tables were set up on the lawn through both dinner and supper on a "lovely warm day" in mid-July. May usually attended only the meetings that took place at her mother's, but she hosted a meeting herself in 1912.[27]

In June 1913, near the height of the suffrage battles, Emily attended a special alumni banquet of Rockford College graduates. Although this event was more subdued than the marches in Washington and New York that same year, the Rockford College women discussed relevant issues of the day. Since its founding in 1850, the Rockford Female Seminary had energized women's politics in Rockford. Many of its graduates, such as Jane Addams and Catharine Waugh McCulloch, established national reputations as social reformers and suffragists.[28] Emily noted in her diary, "Joseph took me to Rockford after an early lunch. And with Mrs. Brazee as escort, I went to Rockford College and attended Alumnal business meeting and banquet." May and Elmo retrieved Emily in the evening when the event was over.

CHAPTER 3

THE GREAT WAR AND ITS AFTERMATH 1914–1920

The Great War, which began in Europe in 1914, would leave the world, including May and Elmo's portion of it, vastly changed. Automobiles and airplanes were transformed from luxuries and curiosities into accessories of war, and industries developed a multitude of other mechanisms of modern warfare. The war sped up social changes already in the pipeline. Women's skirts were moving up toward midcalf as war broke out in Europe. When men went off to fight, women filled factory jobs, and after the war women were allowed to vote for the first time. During the war, labor unions organized to demand wage increases; and the U.S. government successfully experimented with a command economy. The U.S. economy boomed while industrial and agricultural exports poured into Europe. Farm prices skyrocketed, and farmers turned their profits into Liberty Bonds to help win the war. U.S. citizens united in voluntary weekly sacrifice of meat, sugar, wheat, and other comforts and pleasures to support the war effort. Death and destruction reached almost every corner of the globe, but far less from the shots that were fired than from the devastating Spanish flu, which hit hard in towns all across America and the rest of the world.

For May and Elmo, family events during the war years were as tumultuous as world events. After the war, life on the farm would never again return to anything resembling the peaceful, prosperous days of the Golden Age of Agriculture.

1914–1915, WAR IN EUROPE, ROCKFORD GEARS UP

War broke out in Europe in August 1914, and the United States declared neutrality almost immediately. But the effect on the U.S. export economy was far from neutral. Foreign demand for U.S. goods, especially from the

Allied forces, began to rise. When the Germans sank the *Lusitania* in May 1915, the British liner was carrying over sixty tons of ammunition bound for Great Britain from the United States. Nearly 2,000 people were also on board, and more than half of them drowned, including 128 Americans. President Wilson declared the United States "too proud to fight," but he increased army reserves.[1] Meanwhile, U.S. exports to Britain and France continued, increasing 70 percent from 1914 to 1915.[2]

Rockford industries soon benefited from the war in Europe. Already humming with the rising demand for automobiles and the machines and parts to make them, Rockford's foundries and machine tool factories responded to the demand for new hardware for modern warfare. A local historian noted that "companies proved their adaptability by manufacturing parts for engines, tanks, airplanes, machine guns, artillery projectiles, fuses, uniforms, and military instruments."[3] Business boomed in Rockford in 1915, and as the orders came in for war products, many local factories instituted night shifts. The total number of industrial employees in Rockford rose from about ten thousand in 1914 to almost fifteen thousand five years later.

By the end of 1916, demand for food exports also started to soar, along with farm prices, but in 1915, U.S. farmers were concerned with another kind of battle on the home front.

The Foot-and-Mouth Outbreak

Not long after war broke out in Europe, U.S. farmers faced the worst outbreak of foot-and-mouth disease in history. In October 1914, the disease gained entry into the Chicago stockyards and other major markets. From there it spread rapidly to infect over thirty-five hundred livestock herds in twenty-two different states before it was defeated a year later. To control the disease, more than 168,000 animals were slaughtered at a cost to the government of $4.5 million.[4]

Despite relative proximity to the Chicago stockyards, Winnebago County avoided the foot-and-mouth infection until fairly late in the game. Finally the disease broke out in Burritt Township, just west of Rockford, in March 1915. From there it spread to infect about a dozen farms in Burritt, Rockford, and Cherry Valley townships.

May recorded the initial outbreak in Burritt and during the next several months made various references to it. The county was under quarantine within a week. Before the cream could be sold, Elmo and May had "to procure affidavit that cream is all right, animals free from foot & mouth disease, from notary public." Soon, a veterinarian was "out to inspect stock" before Elmo took pigs to market the next day. A few months later when Elmo sold cattle and hogs, the vet also came to inspect the stock. According to a local historian, the disease ultimately infected nine herds of cattle in Winnebago County. All cattle and hogs on these sites had to be slaughtered and buried in quicklime.[5]

Out in the Buick

Notwithstanding both the war in Europe and the foot-and-mouth scourge at home, 1915 was much like another Golden Age year for Elmo and May, at least through the end of the summer. They traded their Maxwell for a new Buick in the spring, and after its arrival, adventures in the new auto eclipsed most other activities of the year. Neighbors hosted barn dances over the summer, and the autumn brought an abundance of apples and grapes.

January and February were quiet months. Elmo and May worried about their horse Gypsy. She had been kicked in the ankle, and the wound became infected; May gave almost daily updates on her progress. Gypsy finally improved but nevertheless died midyear. May also noted books that she and Elmo were reading on snowy Sundays and noted when the Molander children stopped or brought the mail on the way to or from school. John Pratt had moved on to other employment; neither May nor Elmo had steady help until March 1, when Lizzie Rutz, a neighborhood girl, started working for May, and Charley Johnson came out from Rockford to work for Elmo. (Wages were already on the rise. Lizzie started at four dollars per week; last year's girl had worked for three dollars. Charley started at thirty-five dollars per month; John Pratt had last worked for thirty-two dollars.)

Valentine's Day was the occasion for a big family dinner and good-bye party, the first in a series of family changes. Elmo's half sister, May Purdy, and her husband moved off their farm that year and out to Tacoma, Washington, to join their daughter and her family.

The Buick arrived on April 1 amid considerable excitement. (Elmo traded in the Maxwell for a $285 credit and paid another $700 for the new car.) Right away Elmo took May for a ride around the neighborhood. The new car was a good excuse to visit all kinds of relatives and take them for day trips on Sundays. In early July, they drove forty miles or so along the Rock River down to Oregon, Illinois, to see Black Hawk Statue, a fifty-foot-high concrete monument, named for the Indian chief whose defeat in 1832 had opened up northern Illinois to white settlers. In early September, they took an overnight trip to Starved Rock State Park, about seventy miles straight south of Rockford, to see the canyons and sandstone bluffs along the Illinois River. A few days before May's birthday, on September 25, May and Elmo drove Aham and Carrie to the fair in Elkhorn, Wisconsin. When the schoolchildren threw May a surprise party for her birthday, they all got rides in the new auto too.

In between Sundays, however, plenty of farm work occupied Elmo and Charley. Charley spent much of March clearing and cutting wood in the twenty-acre wooded piece down the road, and Elmo often worked with him. In mid-May, after most of the corn had been planted, Elmo bought fifty pounds of dynamite to grub out stumps there. An extra hand helped Charley and Elmo with the grubbing, and then the men built a fence. Elmo borrowed a special breaking plow from the Pickens to plow the newly grubbed land, and the men planted potatoes and corn. Elmo was still tending part of Joseph Lyford's hundred-acre farm (perhaps half of it); Starr also worked in his father's fields. Elmo had fields of corn, oats, and hay this year at Papa's. In July and August, an extra hand helped with the haying.

In late September, Aunt Phrone, the elder of the three Campbell sisters who had lived together in Cherry Valley, took sick with pneumonia at the age of eighty. Elmo visited his aunt almost daily for the next month, often accompanied by May or Florence Fitch. As executor of her estate, Elmo made several trips to Durand before the end of the year, often with May.

Not two weeks before Aunt Phrone died, a tragedy hit just down the road. Mrs. Grow, who lived on a farm to the south, suffered an "awful accident." She was "horribly burned when starting a fire with kerosene" and died in the hospital the day after the accident. Her husband was the neighborhood handyman, the one who had always helped Joseph butcher a beef or a hog; his skills were numerous. Just this past spring, he had helped Elmo with some carpentry work and later fixed a stock pump.

Emily and Joseph had a quiet but pleasant year until October. They enjoyed sleigh rides in the winter months early in the year and went to town regularly in the spring and summer in a new carriage purchased in early May. They went for rides with Elmo and May in the new automobile, and Joseph's sisters, Alice and Augusta, came to visit. Emily was still busy with her chickens, housework, berries, garden, and the Guilford Gleaners auxiliary. Starr and the children were also up frequently. But beginning in early October, Joseph's "pleurisy" kept him in bed, and Elmo took over his chores for much of the rest of the year.

1916, FAMILY TRANSITIONS

Life was altered substantially for May and Elmo in 1916. Multiple changes in the family made this a pivotal year in their lives. The war in Europe was also changing the world (and raising farm prices), but it had yet to hit home for Elmo and May.

Detailed notes in May's farm ledgers nevertheless confirm that the war-time farm economy was heating up. Anna Rutz began to work for May that year at $4.50 per week, up from the $4 per week her sister had received the year before. (Anna was given a 25-cent raise to $4.75 after her eighteenth birthday, in October.) Emil Carlson came out from Rockford in early March to work for $36 per month for the rest of the year, a dollar more than Charley had received the previous year. By the end of 1916, grain prices were up about 50 percent from the year before. Cattle, hogs, and hay were also up but not quite so much.

Scarce mention was made of the war or farm prices, however, as family transitions took center stage. May did note when the "C regiments of Illinois State Militia were called out to guard Mexican border" in mid-June. Several days later, Elmo, May, and Anna went to Rockford to see the troops leave town. The only mention of farm prices in the diaries was at the end of May, when Elmo went into Chicago to sell a carload of cattle. It rained all day, and a big run of cattle came in; the market was off forty cents per hundredweight. Both Emily and May noted what an unpleasant day Elmo had in the rain at the Chicago stockyards. Still, he received $8.90 per hundredweight, up about 25 percent from prices received the year before.

Much of the year was overshadowed by Joseph Lyford's poor health. May's parents missed the traditional New Year's Day dinner at Starr's and got out very little this winter. Only occasionally did Emily leave her husband and come down the lane to visit May.

Emily took advantage of her confinement, however, by getting out the sewing machine. In early January she wrote, "Have been stitching on machine. It seems odd—so long since I have sewed any." She was working on a shirt for Joseph that she cut out the day before. A week later the shirt was done and she started a second shirt, and then a third before that week was out. The next project was a kitchen apron, and then Emily began some patchwork too, before February was scarcely begun.

Suddenly in early February, Aham Davis went into Chicago for a cancer operation. May had telephoned Carrie and learned the news. Elmo hurried down to see Aham and Carrie just as they boarded the train. The operation took place several days later. May wrote, "We hear from Aham at eve. They operated in AM. No hope." Elmo went into Chicago to see him the next day.

Aham's sister, Florence Fitch, and her family were in the midst of their own transition. Just ten days before, they had a sale on their farm that both May and Elmo attended. (Elmo bought a mechanical corn husker for thirty-six dollars at the sale.) On February 24, Florence and Ed Fitch moved their family into Rockford. This would make it easier for their three younger children to attend high school. On the day of the move, Elmo was in Chicago again to see Aham, and then Aham returned home a few days later.

During the next few weeks, May and Elmo went back and forth to visit Aham, who had little time left to live. But there were crops to haul, a pig to butcher, young colts to be trained, and spring planting to prepare for. Elmo took his turn sitting up with Aham through the night on March 30.

A week later, on April 6, Aham died of cancer at the age of fifty. The ground was frozen that day, and Elmo, May, Mama, and Anna Rutz had all gone into Rockford in the auto. They heard of Aham's death while there. The next day, Elmo helped Fred Davis make arrangements for his father's funeral while May stayed with Carrie.

Meanwhile, Emily Lyford had been looking after her ailing husband and sewing up a storm. (She didn't bother with the incubator this year.) Her further sewing projects included pillowcases, "lounge covering blocks,"

Emily Lyford, 1916.

"crazy slumber robe blocks," three potholders, and an apron for May, two skirts for her granddaughters, and a petticoat too. In addition, Anna helped her put two comforters together.

During the early summer months, Joseph and Emily took some short Sunday rides with Elmo and May. Two auto loads of Lyford relatives from Roscoe came down one Sunday afternoon. But Emily rarely noted any activity on the part of Joseph. Once in mid-June she wrote, "A nice warm day. Joseph has sat out a good deal & went for mail."

Emily, on the other hand, was quite active this summer—cooking, cleaning, picking berries, and canning. And Starr and the children were often up. Joey, who would be eleven in September, was doing lots of fieldwork, especially after school dismissed for the summer. He drove the team to town with hay and put in long hours dragging and cultivating. Walter and Franklin (nine and eight) came up to mow their grandmother's lawn. Walter also hitched up the team these days, and all three boys helped load up straw in February. One day in late June, Annetta (twelve) came up to help Emily get dinner for Starr and the boys. May hosted a birthday party for her mother as usual, on June 30, Emily's seventy-third birthday. Russell (six) arrived on the pony with flowers for his grandmother.

Toward the end of July, Elmo started building a new granary, and it was just about this time that May's father took a turn for the worse. It began

Joseph Lyford, 1916.
Courtesy of JoAnne Reid.

with a recurrence of some hip trouble, and then the weather turned oppressively hot—103° in Rockford on July 27. Two days later the heat continued unabated. Elmo was drawing lumber from Belvidere for the granary and had to stop several times to water and rest the horses. Starr's children took water to the men cutting oats in their grandfather's fields. When Sunday came, Emily wrote, "Another very, very hot day with no breeze. It is a mercy to man and beast it is a day of rest. Don't think many could endure work today. Joseph feels very weak & poorly." The next morning a cool northeast breeze began to blow, it continued to "blow harder & grow cooler through the day." Emily wrote, "A cool breeze today is helping men and horses." But late that night Joseph was in severe pain, and after August 2, Emily's diary ended for the year. Her husband died on August 11.

After her husband's death and funeral, Emily went back and forth between her house and May's, struggling to find her bearings. Sometimes Elmo and May spent the night with her, and other times she stayed with them. Joseph had died right in the midst of threshing season. Just two days after her father's funeral, May prepared dinner for eighteen men and two boys. Another round of threshing followed a week later, and sixteen men came to dinner again. Then Elmo left for a three-week trip to Tacoma, Washington, to visit his sister in her new home. Emily stayed with May while he was gone; by the time he returned, Emily was ready to move in permanently.

Meanwhile, Carrie and Fred Davis were adjusting to life without Aham, and they also depended on May and Elmo for support. Fred was still working on a bachelor's degree at the University of Illinois, and now he had a farm to manage as well. Fortunately, the train provided good transportation to Champaign-Urbana, but Carrie was planning to move into Rockford so that the farm could be rented.

As fate would have it, the year held yet another family crisis. Nettie McFarland, Starr's sister-in-law, who still lived with the family and helped with the younger children and the housework, was suddenly "real sick" in early December. By the time the doctor sent her to the hospital, it was already too late. Nettie's life was cut short early in 1917, and the role of caretaker for the Lyford family passed to Starr's eldest, Annetta.

1917, War Bound from Camp Grant

As 1917 dawned, it was becoming more difficult for the United States to remain neutral in regard to the war in Europe. Within another few months, American soldiers would be headed for France, and before Thanksgiving,

Rockford's new Camp Grant would be ready to house over forty thousand troops to train for deployment in Europe.[6]

By February 1, Germany had renewed unrestricted submarine warfare on the U.S. ships bound for Great Britain and western Europe, prompting President Wilson to sever relations and to call for armed merchant ships. Not long thereafter, England intercepted a telegram between Germany and Mexico, proposing an alliance to help Mexico win back lost territory in Texas. Finally, when yet another U.S. ship was sunk on April 2, armed and bound from New York with 3,727 tons of foodstuffs and supplies (worth more than five hundred thousand dollars), Wilson asked Congress to declare war on Germany and urged American men to sign up for military service.[7]

On Friday, April 6, the same day that Congress officially declared war on Germany, Elmo sold pigs at $15.10 per hundredweight. May and Emily had been noting the prices of hogs in their diaries. Starr had sold at $13 per hundredweight on March 3, and Elmo had sold at $14.50 per hundredweight on March 20. While hog prices were normally quite variable, these prices were already double those of 1914. Wages were also rising; Emil Carlson had worked for Elmo the year before at $36 per month, but this year, after some negotiation, he started at $44 per month in mid-March.

In mid-April, May stopped keeping her diary for several months. Her eyes were bothering her; she had developed a small ulcer on one eye. Except for a few entries here and there, she didn't resume until mid-July. Emily did keep a diary, however, beginning again in January after her husband's death, and made brief notes. May and Elmo were back and forth to the eye doctor all through the month of May; then May stayed two weeks with the Fitches in Rockford to be closer to medical care. Emily also noted that Emil Carlson quit work after only a month and that the new man went into Rockford to register for the draft on June 5. He was among almost ten million men to do so that day across the United States.

After Emil quit in mid-April, Elmo had no steady help until almost June; it was a difficult year for hired help. With the labor market already tight in Rockford, the movement of men into military service further depleted the unskilled labor market. Those with dependents or jobs essential to the war effort didn't have to serve, but 2.8 million men were inducted into service almost immediately, thus diverting about 16 percent of the male labor force.[8] One of them was Fred Davis, who was called into federal service by the National Guard on July 10. He had been a member of the Reserve Officer Training Corps at the university. Fred spent his service stateside as a drill sergeant in military camps in both California and Texas.

When construction began at Camp Grant, on Rockford's south side, additional demands were made on the local labor market. Moreover, during the war, immigration from abroad slowed to a trickle. Nevertheless, Elmo managed to hire a man at only thirty dollars a month during the summer months, but he worked less than twelve weeks and then unexpectedly failed to return to work in mid-August. For the first time ever at year's end, Elmo's day-help wage bill for outdoor help exceeded the wages he paid to steady help. Mrs. Frigast, early in the year, did the wash once a week for May, as she had done for the last few years. Several of the Molander girls, from down the road, also helped May this year; Edith worked at $4.50 a week.

The biggest news of the year by far, in the Rockford area, was of Camp Grant. The announcement that the War Department had chosen Rockford as the site of the Illinois Army cantonment came in mid-June. About the time construction began at Camp Grant, at the end of June, May and Elmo bought a flag and later took a Sunday drive with Emily out to see the site for the cantonment. In total, the War Department built sixteen cantonments around the country to train army divisions and an additional sixteen camp sites for the National Guard.[9]

The effect of the camp on Rockford was dramatic. The U.S. government leased four thousand acres of farmland just south of Rockford, along the Rock River. The camp included twelve miles of trenches and parade grounds in addition to barracks for tens of thousands. Another three thousand acres

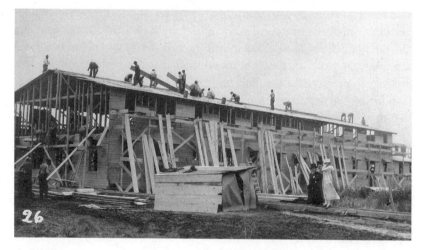

Building Camp Grant, ca. 1916. Courtesy of Midway Village and Museum Center, Rockford, Illinois.

became a rifle range. Construction began at the end of June, and before the end of the summer, almost eight thousand civilians were employed, erecting and equipping more than fifteen hundred buildings. The city virtually exploded overnight as job seekers and their families streamed in. Rockford's population swelled from 45,000 in 1910 to 65,650 by 1920. Restaurants, hotels, barbershops, and movie theaters were overrun with customers. By some estimates, Camp Grant added up to one million dollars a month in sales to Rockford businesses.[10]

Over the course of the war and on through 1919, more than one million men came through Camp Grant, to be either trained or discharged there. When completed, the barracks held fifty thousand men, the hospital had space for fifteen hundred patients, and almost a thousand people worked in the commissary. The commissary "daily served 225 quarters of beef, 800 pounds of chicken, 30,000 eggs and countless pies, cakes, cookies, biscuits, ears of corn and loaves of bread." With seven thousand mules and forty-five hundred artillery horses at Camp Grant, the new demand for oats and hay was also impressive.[11]

To finance the war effort, the Treasury Department began to borrow money from the public by issuing war bonds. Elmo bought four hundred dollars of Liberty Bonds, on June 12 and 14, on the strength of his spring hog sales. With the second issue of Liberty Bonds in October, he bought an additional one hundred dollars of bonds.

The ambitious building agenda, the cost of munitions, and the expense of feeding, clothing, and equipping the soldiers and paying their salaries increased government expenditures enormously and injected cash into the already booming U.S. economy. Federal expenditures during the war rose to at least twelve times prewar levels. The Liberty Loans were one way to deal with the costs. The newly established Federal Reserve System kept interest rates low by easing credit. The easy credit, combined with gold pouring in from abroad to pay for U.S. exports, ultimately resulted in a massive increase both in the supply of money moving through the economy and in price levels. (Elmo received fifteen dollars a ton for hay all through January, February, and into April. In mid-June he received twenty-four dollars a ton.)

Emily returned to her typically active self again after her husband's death. She visited Starr's family, attended the Guilford Gleaners auxiliary meetings, and spent time with other relatives. Since Emily drove neither automobile nor buggy, she needed a lift to get where she was going. Annetta (thirteen) sometimes served as chauffeur of the buggy, often with her two youngest siblings in tow—back and forth to Starr's or back and forth to Cherry

Valley, where Emily could catch the interurban. Emily also joined Centennial Methodist Church.

At the end of October, Emily rented out the farm that had been her home since her children were small, and at this point she stopped keeping her diary and apparently did not pick it up again. On October 27, Emily wrote, "Got pretty well cleared out," referring to the house. The next day she noted only, "Cloudy, sprinkled." And that was her final entry. Midmonth, she had noted the settlement of the estate and the lease of the farm to Mr. Ed McLarty.

In November 1917, Elmo still had several acres of "Mama's corn" standing waiting to be husked. It had been a heavy year for work without much help. Big crops of oats and hay in 1916 meant lots of hauling in January and February. With no extra help for chopping wood until mid-March, May and Elmo used more coal in the furnace this year. Emil worked only one month in the early spring, quitting even before the oats had been planted. By that time, May's eyes needed care, and Elmo was taking her to the doctor while scrambling to find help and trying to get the crops in. Joe Connelly worked through June, July, and part of August but left before the threshing was done. Elmo rounded up day help from the neighborhood for threshing, and then in mid-September the fiancé of the hired girl worked for about two months (at forty dollars a month). Mr. McLarty put in some time on the husking, working for two dollars a day. Meanwhile, Starr's boys had stayed home from school several times that fall to help with fieldwork, especially the digging of the potatoes.

The year came to a quiet close amid signs of a difficult winter ahead. When the Lyfords celebrated Thanksgiving at May and Elmo's, Elmo had not finished husking corn. It turned cold in early December; temperatures plunged below zero for several mornings while Elmo was shredding with his shredder group. It warmed up briefly midmonth, when there was hay and straw to bale. Elmo and Mama took the buggy in the mud to go to Rockford then for errands and Christmas shopping. By Christmas it was cold again; on December 28 it was "6° below zero at 7:30 AM," when Elmo went to finish the husking at Mama's. Later that afternoon, a fine snow fell and "blow through the air like a young blizzard, but not amount to much."

1918, On the Home Front

The year 1918 would hold many surprises, not the least of which was a record-breaking winter. At winter's end, American men began to swarm the battlefields of Europe and quickly turned the tide of the war; the war effort on the home front also intensified. But as the war wound down in October, a completely unexpected devastation swept the globe.

The Winter of 1918

The new year of 1918 roared into northern Illinois with an unforgettable winter blast. Blizzards came in from all directions with blowing winds and falling temperatures. Elmo spent most Sundays in January plowing out roads. Mail came infrequently, and the milkman had a terrible time getting through to haul the farmers' milk into town.

It began snowing the morning of January 1; by midafternoon, it was snowing fast and kept it up until dark. A northeast wind brought in more snow the next morning. Elmo got cornstalks from the field for the cattle, dressed a chicken, and went out to husk some of the eight acres of corn he still had standing. In the late afternoon, he got down the sled and spent most of the next few days hauling oats and baled straw to Rockford and coal from Cherry Valley.

The first blizzard came on Sunday, January 6. It lasted all day, snowing and blowing from the east. The next day the north wind blew and filled up the east–west roads with drifts. Elmo helped the milkman more than halfway to Rockford. The roads were so badly drifted, the two men took the sled through the fields in many places. There was "no mail, no school." But school resumed the next day, and so did the hauling of the oats and hay.

The next blizzard hit on January 11 and 12, just after May and Elmo heard from Florence that Aunt Harriet was "very low." Morning temperatures were well below zero both days, the snow was fine, and the wind was coming from the northwest and west. Now the north–south roads filled up with snow, and the neighbors all helped the milkman. "He leave his team here and Elmo take his load to A. Marsh's, then others take it. . . . No mail." The 13th was a Sunday, another below-zero morning; it was spent digging out, plowing roads, and helping the milkman. Aunt Harriet died the next morning.

The cold winter was taking a toll on coal supplies around the country— coal urgently needed for the war effort. A spectacular cold wave had pushed through the Northeast at the end of December, with readings of 13° and 15° below zero in New York and Boston. By mid-January, the Fuel Administration (part of the governmental apparatus set up to guide the country through the war) called a coal holiday. May wrote, "All the factories and the high school close for 4 days on account of coal shortage." The temperature that morning was 14° below, and the next few mornings were almost as cold. On January 21, May noted the "general holiday throughout cities in 28 states on account of coal shortage." All industries east of the Mississippi were affected by the order, except for the most critical war plants; "heatless Mondays" followed for the next nine weeks.[12]

January 23 dawned with a temperature of 11° below, but the temperature rose through the morning, and by the afternoon, winds from the south had brought in yet another blizzard. January held even more snow and days spent plowing roads and hauling crops. But February 2 was sunny and still, "groundhog surely see his shadow today." The day before had dawned with a temperature of 17° below, and a few days later it was that cold again when Elmo and Charley Kleckner took loads of hay and straw to Rockford. (Charley tipped his load on the streetcar track and froze his nose.)

Despite the forbidding winter, farm prices in early 1918 made hauling crops through the snow and subzero temperatures worthwhile. Elmo was getting thirty dollars a ton for baled hay, double the price of just a year earlier. Oats went for eighty-one cents a bushel in early February; the previous year at the same time, oats had brought fifty-four cents a bushel. Elmo had not sold baled oat straw since 1907, when he first began baling. In 1907 it had sold for seven dollars a ton; in 1918 it brought twelve dollars a ton, making it profitable again to bale and haul into town. With thawing and rain in early to mid-February, however, the sleds were cutting into the packed snow on the roads, making hauling more difficult.

May made little mention, all through these wintry days, of her own or Mama's activities. She focused, rather, on Elmo, the milkman, and whether and how the mail arrived. Sometimes the mailman left it at the schoolhouse for Elmo or Mr. McLarty to pick up there. Few people were out to stop by. Mrs. Frigast came only once every two weeks; she helped can beef and make mincemeat, among other things. On February 11, May noted that Mama had finished her fifth sweater.

By the middle of February, Mr. Prindle, the milkman, had apparently had it with the formidable road conditions. The big thaw wasn't helping matters at all. May noted "2 feet of water at our corner" on February 12, with Mr. Molander stuck in it. Elmo and the neighbors got their milk to town among themselves that day. The following day Mr. Prindle was "stuck at our corner" and "says he draw no more milk." So Elmo and the neighbors traded off taking milk into Rockford through the end of March. The temperatures plunged below zero once again after the first February thaw, but the end of February and all of March were fairly mild and muddy.

February also marked the first time that Elmo and May paid federal income tax—$17.94 on February 20. The Sixteenth Amendment had passed in 1913, creating a federal income tax, but until the war demanded increased revenue, married persons with incomes less than four thousand dollars did not have to pay. War needs reduced that exemption by half. May and Elmo paid federal income taxes in 1918, 1919, and 1920, and then not again until the next war was at hand.

In mid-March, Elmo had still not finished husking last year's corn. He'd been husking by hand on and off since it warmed up in mid-February. He finally finished up with the help of Mr. McLarty on March 22.

The War Effort at Home

American units were not deployed on European battlefields on a large scale until the spring of 1918; that was also when efforts on the home front heated up. People pitched in across the country with Liberty Loans, Red Cross circles, victory gardens, and the voluntary conservation of critical commodities. May's diaries and ledgers reflect a flurry of wartime activity on the home front. On March 30, 1918, for example, she wrote, "We turn clock ahead 1 hour." It was the first instance of daylight savings time in the United States, part of an effort to conserve energy.

The Third Liberty Loan was launched in the spring of 1918; people were also buying smaller denomination war bonds. Farm prices had risen so much that in the first three months of the year, May and Elmo's sales of farm produce had totaled almost twenty-four hundred dollars, about the equivalent of their sales for the whole year in 1914. They bought six hundred dollars of Liberty Bonds on April 5, when the campaign began, and spent an additional twenty dollars on a War Chest Loan. At the end of February, the schoolchildren had been in selling War Stamps, and May also recorded purchases of War Thrift Stamps in mid-March. In late April, Elmo and May were out "about the neighborhood on Liberty Loan business." Before the campaign wrapped up in early May, Elmo bought an additional two hundred dollars of Liberty Bonds.

Emily Lyford helped organize two Red Cross circles in the summer of 1918: one for the ladies and another for the schoolgirls. Founded in 1881, the American Red Cross virtually exploded from a small base during the war, although it later shrank again. May mentioned the Red Cross for the first time in December 1917 and recorded a small purchase of Red Cross Stamps. The Guilford circle, however, was first organized on June 5, 1918, at a meeting that took place at May's. The Red Cross circle met there at least three more times in June and July, with Emily apparently providing the leadership. Emily and Mrs. McLarty made calls around the neighborhood to recruit members. Subsequently, when the circle met at other neighborhood homes, Emily attended regularly and May occasionally. In early August, Emily was at Starr's all day with a Junior Red Cross meeting. The Junior Red Cross later met at May's and then moved to the schoolhouse when fall classes began. Emily got projects ready for the Junior Red Cross meetings and sent work packages up with the children on their way to school.

May didn't describe the activities of the circles, but Red Cross circles around the country were making bandages and other articles for servicemen and clothing for refugees. Later that fall when the Spanish flu hit Camp Grant, area Red Cross circles provided fifty thousand gauze masks and enlisted 150 women to help the overburdened army nurses. They handled the records of the influenza victims and sent letters and telegrams to the families.[13] The Guilford circle met for the last time in May 1919.

Patriotism ruled in 1918, across the country and not least in Rockford. On the Fourth of July, May and Elmo were among the hundred thousand spectators who bid farewell to a division of twenty-eight thousand soldiers that paraded through Rockford before going off to fight. After a picnic dinner with "relations," they watched the Camp Grant fireworks through the distance from the farm.

Farmers and urban folks alike were called on to conserve key commodities and produce needed foods. The Food Administration was established in 1917 to guide the wartime production and distribution of foods. In addition to the heatless Mondays of the winter of 1918, "meatless days," "wheatless days," and "sugarless days" were also regularly observed during the summer of 1918. "War gardens" sprouted in towns and urban areas. May and her hired girls shelled beans (encouraged as a substitute for meat) in 1917 and 1918; May also recorded two poems about beans that she and her hired girl had composed.

Wheat and pork were both critical commodities for the war effort, and the government sought to ensure adequate supplies. The Food Administration encouraged production by guaranteeing a minimum price for wheat and by stabilizing hog prices.[14] Elmo had not raised wheat since he and May were married but did so during the war and for several years thereafter. Although 1918 was not a particularly big hog year for Elmo, his sales of hogs as a share of farm income peaked (at 32 percent) during the 1915–20 period. May also recorded increasing sales of eggs during the war.

Fourth of July parade in Rockford, 1918. Courtesy of Midway Village and Museum Center, Rockford, Illinois.

Much of the patriotic propaganda encouraging both conservation and food production was channeled through the Cooperative Extension Service, formalized in the Smith–Lever Act of 1914. From January 1917 to July 1918, the number of county extension agents increased by 75 percent. Boys and girls 4-H farm production clubs mushroomed when the nation's youth were enlisted in the war effort.[15]

During 1918, the war effort continued to dislocate much of the farm labor force. That year, Rena began working for May in early March, but Elmo had no steady help until late May, when Hamar Osterberg began to work. Rena worked for five dollars per week, which was fifty cents more than last year's girl. (Rena was a big lady—174 pounds, according to May's diary. She even helped Elmo drag oat fields in April.) Curiously, Hamar worked for only $4.50 per week throughout June and July. He must have been very young, very inexperienced, working for patriotic reasons, or perhaps all of the above. He came out to work from Rockford on a bicycle, stayed through the week, and went home on Sundays. During hay season, Elmo hired another hand, who was paid almost fifty dollars for less than a month—more than twice Hamar's wage rate. Once again Elmo's bill for day help that year exceeded the bill for steady help. Clarence Martenson, a young neighbor enrolled at Bell School, had been helping after school since early May, when the potatoes needed planting. Roy Grow, from down the road, also helped out with the threshing; he worked for three dollars a day.

All told, Elmo's outdoor wage bill fell from about $250 in 1917 to approximately $200 in 1918; during 1914–16 he had spent about $350 per year on outdoor help. For a time when wages were rising rapidly, these facts are curious. Less acreage to farm was part of the explanation. Elmo was no longer farming on the Lyford farm, which reduced his acreage by perhaps as much as 50 acres, to 130 acres plus whatever had been cleared in the 20-acre wooded piece. Labor-saving technology was also a factor. Late in 1918, Elmo fixed up the mechanical husker, bought at the Fitch sale in 1916, to do his husking. (The husker was not so satisfactory, however.) Elmo also husked little corn this year; he bought corn for feed from McLarty the next spring. The unavailability of good help and its prohibitive expense also played a role in the ironically low wage bill; Elmo simply cut back on labor, put in more hours himself, replaced woodcutting with coal purchases, and postponed some jobs. Finally, government propaganda encouraged boys to take the jobs of men, helping to keep the wage bill down.

The summer of 1918 also held pleasures and pain unrelated to the war. During the early summer, May counted the mice that she and Mama caught in their cellar, noting twenty-four over the course of a month. One day in June, Dr. Shambaugh from Cherry Valley committed suicide, and a pig ate the little ducklings, all recorded in the same entry. A barn dance followed a few weeks later. As usual, the new potatoes, the blackberry pudding, and the sweet corn all tasted good. In August, May and Mama began collecting eggs in a "water glass" to preserve them through the year by immersing them in water to which lime and salt had been added, per a tip in Emily's 1917 diary. By the end of September they had nine dozen eggs in the water glass.

Of all the home-front efforts to support the war, by far the most difficult for May were the "chugless Sundays" that began in September. On most Sundays throughout the summer, May and Elmo had dropped Mama off at church in Rockford and had then gone for a drive. But on Sunday, September 1, May wrote, "Home all day as no one is supposed to go pleasure riding." The following two Sundays were lovely warm days with no drives, because "the Fuel Administration asks people not to use their autos." September 22 was the "4th Chugless Sunday. One buggy all that has passed here so far." The next day May, Elmo, and the hired girl all went to Rockford in the auto.

Spanish Flu, Forest Fires, and Autumn Leaves

In early October, the Spanish influenza, which raced around the world killing millions in the autumn of 1918, hit hard in Camp Grant and in Rockford. Carried far and wide by soldiers mobilizing for war, the disease spared only rare corners of the globe, and it killed primarily young adults. May's diary in October reflected an ironic blend of exceptionally lovely fall weather, occasional smoke from deadly forest fires in Minnesota, and reports of the epidemic in Rockford and Camp Grant.

October 4 was "warm, windy, summer-like . . . Spanish Influenza so bad they close school in Rockford." The *Rockford Daily Register-Gazette* for that day reported the closure of not only schools but also theaters, movie houses, churches, dance halls, and other gathering places. Church suppers and services were banned. At least 850 cases of flu had been reported in Rockford, and the city health commissioner estimated that an additional four thousand may have been affected by the epidemic.[16]

The closures did not stop the Fourth Liberty Loan drive, however. Newspaper ads ran on October 4 urging loyal citizens to show up at their polling places the next day to "register for as many Liberty Bonds as he or she can possibly pay for. . . . Uncle Sam needs your money NOW."[17] In an article on one newspaper's front page, the mayor of Rockford entreated everyone to turn his or her face to the east on October 5 in silent prayer, "imploring that the Fourth Liberty Loan may be doubly redouble subscribed, so that the blasphemous hopes of our enemies may perish."[18] Elmo, Mama, and May all went into Rockford that morning on errands, stopping at the Guilford Town Hall to buy Liberty Bonds. Elmo bought an additional thousand dollars worth of bonds that day and spent the afternoon and part of the evening assisting in some capacity at the town hall.

The flu epidemic raged for about a month in the Rockford area, while the leaves turned beautiful colors and fell. Bell School was closed from October 7 until November 5. On October 10, May wrote, "Mostly sunny, warm beautiful days. Foliage never prettier. . . . Epidemic waning in Camp, bad in Rockford." More than two hundred soldiers and civilians in the area died on that day alone.[19]

While the flu epidemic ran its course, forest fires raged in Minnesota. On October 12, the fires, made worse by dry conditions and high winds, swept across northeastern Minnesota killing 450 people.[20] May wrote that day, "Just lovely outdoors. 58° above at 8 AM. . . . Very dry to plow. Very hazy from Minnesota & Wisconsin forest fires which are very serious. Even smell smoke." Several more warm, fair days followed. October 15 was a "fine warm day, very windy. . . . Epidemic bad yet in Rockford." Two days later, the wind changed and came down strong from the north: "Air full of haze and strong odor of fires. Minnesota fires reported started again." After that, both the epidemic and the fires began to subside and received no further mention.

Fatalities from the flu were staggering: more than 1,400 at Camp Grant, 323 in Rockford, and nearly 100 in other parts of Winnebago County. A Rockford historian described the scene: "People on the street wore face masks. Emergency hospitals were established in the Rockford Boys Club, Lincoln School, and the Knights of Columbus club. A downtown garage was turned into a morgue. Flag-draped coffins stood in huge stacks at train stations. Grieving families of dead soldiers poured into town to claim their loved ones."[21] All told, the Spanish flu killed 548,000 Americans both at home and in the trenches. Worldwide, an estimated thirty million died— far more than perished as a result of the war itself.[22]

Armistice

Finally, on November 11, 1918, "whistles in Rockford about 3 AM announce Germany signed armistice." Elmo and Charley Kleckner went into Rockford at about 4:00 AM to hear the news and celebrate. Similar celebrations went on in the wee hours of the morning in cities all over the country. Elmo and Charley returned to spend the morning baling hay with the used baler that Elmo's group had just bought. Later, after dinner, May, Mama, and Elmo went into Rockford to see the parade.

The children were off school again on that first Armistice Day. Classes had started up at Bell School on November 5, after the epidemic, and although some children went to school on November 11, the teacher didn't come. Then in mid-November, diphtheria closed the school for another week.

Fred Davis got "home from camp in Texas" the day after Thanksgiving, and he spent much of the rest of the year working with, or in place of, Elmo. When Elmo went into Chicago with Fred Whittle for the "Fat Stock Show" on December 3, Fred Davis came out to shred in Elmo's place and stayed on shredding for several more days. Then, Elmo came down with a cold, and Mama was also tired out, so both Fred and Carrie came out again to help. Carrie stayed about five days, and Fred stayed on until just before Christmas. Most of the time he plowed, but he also split wood, did some other odd jobs, and went with Elmo to look for a pig to buy.

May and Elmo invited all the Fitches to Christmas dinner that year. A blizzard on December 24 filled up the east–west roads, so Elmo went to town the next day with the team to get Florence and Ed and their children, because "no auto can get through." Starr and his family had all been up to celebrate Christmas on the 23rd.

1919–1920, THE POSTWAR BOOM

Although many feared that the end of the war would bring falling prices and recession, that didn't happen right away. U.S. loans to Europe continued, mostly for that continent to finance its import of U.S. agricultural products. And although some soldiers were released soon after the armistice was signed, the full process of demobilization took at least a year. During that time, Camp Grant served as a demobilization center for thirteen midwestern states; more than 250,000 men came through to be discharged, benefiting business in the Rockford area.[23] Farm prosperity continued, and industries, too, were able to reorient their production quickly from military to domestic ends. Liberty Loans were followed by Victory Loans, and the easy credit that accompanied the loans pushed prices even higher.

But it was also a time of great uncertainty for farmers and a time when everyone was struggling to absorb the enormity of the war, the bitter irony of the flu epidemic, and the changed world they found themselves in. Soldiers still marched through the streets of Rockford in June 1919. Sugar was hard to come by through October of that year. Things had not returned to normal yet, and it was clear that some things would never be the same again.

The Ubiquitous Model T

The immense popularity of Henry Ford's Tin Lizzie was one of the more agreeable changes in the early postwar years. The energies of the automobile industry had shifted to war production during the war. Production of trucks in the United States had tripled from 1914 to 1915, primarily as a response to European war demands. By 1918, U.S. manufacturers produced almost ten times as many trucks as they had in 1914. The production of passenger vehicles had reached an all-time high of 1.75 million cars in 1917, almost double the production of 1915. But during 1918, producers were forced to cut back to conserve steel. They built fewer than one million cars in 1918, instead producing trucks, ambulances, and aircraft engines to fulfill government war contracts.[24]

After the war, the automobile industry lost no time switching back to domestic production. In 1919, production jumped to 1.65 million passenger vehicles, more than half of which were Model Ts. Both Elmo and Fred Davis bought Fords in February 1919. By 1920, half of all the cars in the world were Model Ts; the share was even higher in the United States.[25]

During the war, Ford, and other manufacturers too, had earned respect for the performance of their vehicles. Young men wrote home of their experiences riding in and maintaining trucks. The European roads were far more suited to motor transport than roads in America. But particularly in the difficult terrain of the combat zones, the Model T outperformed heavier European cars and trucks. By the end of the war, Henry Ford had become a figure of legend. Not only had he invented the assembly line and mass-produced cars for half of the U.S. market; he had also developed a car that was rugged, reliable, and economical. He had stunned workers and industrialists alike in 1914 by offering the working man five dollars for an eight-hour day—roughly double the going rate at the time. Although his wages did not increase to keep up with inflation, Ford shocked the world again—and pleased at least the female half of it—when he offered the same wage to women in 1916.[26] By 1919, Ford was also poised to capture the market for farm tractors with his new Fordson lightweight tractor.

Ford finally attained status worthy of mention in May's diaries in 1916. By that time, he had produced over one million cars. Until that time, May had not mentioned the make of any car except for a single mention of Starr's stylish Oakland. But in mid-1916, an auto agent dropped by and tried to sell Elmo a Ford, and a few weeks later, May's cousin Tom Lyford drove up in a new Ford. Starr and the children stopped by in their Ford in mid-1918. May's mention of Starr's Ford may not have referred to a new one; it could have been one of the two cars he bought in 1914 and 1915. What *was* new was May's respect for the Ford.

May was ready with praise for the Ford when Elmo brought the new car home in mid-February 1919. The roads were "rough & snowy," she wrote, "but car go good." This Ford was clearly a utility vehicle. Elmo used the Ford to haul grist to have it ground, in addition to hauling other small loads in it. It didn't replace the team and the wagon or sled for hauling, however, and although May frequently mentioned how well it performed in poor road conditions, the Ford didn't replace the buggy either. When the roads were "just *deep* with mud & ruts" in mid-March, Elmo took Mama to Rockford in the buggy. The Buick, on the other hand, didn't come out of the garage until early May that year.

Model T on muddy Argyle road. Courtesy of Wallace Ralston.

Facing Death Again, Back on the Farm

Indeed, the first time the Buick was used in 1919 was for the funeral of Carrie Davis, in early May. Less than two months earlier, Fred and his mother had moved back to their farm, just north of Cherry Valley. Fred bought a team of horses in early February, not long before he showed up at May and Elmo's with his new Ford.

Carrie was just fifty-three years of age at her death. Her health had not been good. Both she and her husband had health problems already in 1913, as was reflected in letters to Fred at the university. Neighbors came to bring May and Elmo the news, since their phone was out of order from an overnight storm. They went down to Fred's to do what they could. During the rest of the month of May, Elmo and May saw quite a bit of Fred. On Sunday, May 25, they attended the memorial exercises at Cherry Valley Cemetery, adjacent to Fred's farm and where both of his parents were now buried, and they stopped at Fred's after the exercises.

As he often did around Decoration Day, on May 29 Elmo went over to the Davis Cemetery, alongside the old Thaddeus Davis homestead, to do some maintenance work. Elmo's own parents were both buried in that cemetery, along with his grandparents, his brother and half brother, and many of his Davis aunts and uncles.

A Changed World, Still Writhing

The personal lives of May and Elmo, and certainly Fred, were entirely altered by all the family changes in these last few years, and the greater world they lived in was also transformed during the war.

Labor strikes and race riots rocked urban areas during the summer of 1919. When the flow of immigrants from Europe was halted by war, northern industrialists turned to the South for unskilled workers. A wave of black migrants responded, and the black population doubled in a few short years in cities such as St. Louis, Chicago, and Detroit. At the same time, the stresses of the war increased tensions between management and labor unions, and the rising cost of living and poor working conditions made strikes common. A strike in Chicago in mid-July meant Elmo had trouble getting parts for his broken grain binder. A week later, deadly race riots exploded in Chicago. To compound the hysteria, the Russian Revolution of 1917 had frightened the world with visions of communist uprisings. Bombings occurred in many cities, including Rockford, in the summer of 1919.

On June 14, May noted the bomb that exploded in the W. F. and John Barnes factory. Such bombings were typically blamed on communists.

The nervousness about communism provoked a crackdown in thirty-four cities across the country on New Year's Day, 1920—the "Big Red Scare." In Rockford, 180 people were arrested on suspicion of subversive acts; across the country, arrests totaled more than 1,500. (Little evidence was found anywhere to support the suspicions.) According to a local historian, "The Rockford crackdown . . . was by far the biggest in the country relative to population, with more arrests than in Boston, Philadelphia and Chicago combined."[27]

Social upheaval was also apparent in the eternal war between the sexes. Women around the world emerged from the Great War with a new sense of themselves. In 1919 and 1920, American women achieved specific victories on the issues for which they had fought long and hard. The Eighteenth Amendment, establishing Prohibition, was ratified on January 29, 1919. In August 1920, the Nineteenth Amendment was ratified, granting women full voting rights. In November of that year, May noted simply, "Elmo, Mama & I vote." Women had also entered the formal workforce in large numbers during the war, performing well (albeit at lower wage rates) in jobs formerly dominated by men. Although most women were pressured to give back their new jobs to soldiers returning after the war, they had gained confidence and respect from some quarters during the process of work. Women's fashions were also changing dramatically as the decade ended. Hemlines rose first in Europe and then in the United States. In addition, corsets were going out of style; some of the latest fashions featured flatter chests and roomier waistlines.

Children Growing Up

This new world belonged to the next generation, and Starr's children were already embracing it. His three oldest children were all driving automobiles on the country roads in 1919. Annetta was fifteen, and the two oldest boys were fourteen and twelve.

Annetta graduated from Bell School in 1919 and started high school in Rockford in the fall. Annetta and the three other girls in her Bell School class passed exams at the courthouse in Rockford a month before the commencement exercises. Annetta was a good student. A few years earlier, May had noted her achievement in a townshipwide spelling contest. When attending high school classes, Annetta stayed in Rockford with her great aunts, Alice and Augusta.

Over the summer, the children worked on the neighboring farms. Labor was still scarce in 1919, and May and Elmo relied on the youth in the family and in the neighborhood for their workforce. The Molander girls helped May after school from January through March. Later, in mid-April, Starr's third oldest boy, Franklin, who was eleven, started doing chores on a regular basis, for fifty cents a week. Sometimes his younger brother Russell would join him or fill in for him. Even little Stanley, who was just four, got into the act and did chores for May. (She recorded five cents paid to Stanley in the farm ledger.) Walter Lyford (twelve) worked all summer for May and Elmo, especially with the haying. He also mowed the lawn and sprouted the potatoes. In late June, another neighborhood boy began cultivating; he worked regularly throughout the summer and came back in October to help husk, at about two dollars per day. Mabel Fitch, Florence's elder daughter, eighteen years old in 1919, stayed through the week during July and August, and then another neighborhood girl took over the work for May.

The young labor force continued in 1920. But this year, Elmo hired some adult help too; Carl Sell worked from June 21 to mid-August at the rate of $65 a month with board. May also kept track of the work Elmo exchanged with the other men he farmed with. In 1919 and 1920, Elmo's outdoor wage bill was only about $160 each year, even less than in 1918, when it was about $200.

Rising Prices, Victory Loans, Tractors, and Expanding Agriculture

May's records confirm the continuing postwar frenzy in 1919 and 1920. Labor was still hard to find, and wages and prices of many commodities were still rising through much of 1920. Yet, many farmers knew the high prices wouldn't last. Elmo's father had surely told tales of how wheat prices spiked during the Civil War and fell precipitously thereafter. Meanwhile, May's record keeping reflected a heightened interest, as she carefully recorded prices and quantities for almost all products sold during the 1915–20 period.

Farm prices rose throughout 1919 and into 1920, with U.S. lending to Europe financing exports from U.S. farmers. Prices in general rose with the Victory Loans and easy lending policies of the Federal Reserve, but farm prices rose most of all, and farm income continued to swell. In 1918 and 1919, May and Elmo's gross farm income was more than fifty-two hundred dollars each year—about double the average level in the prosperous years of 1910–14. When prices started to fall in 1920, gross farm income fell back that year to about forty-two hundred dollars.

Produce Sold continued.   1919.

		$			
Mar. 3.	28 B. hay to N. & B., 2385#, $25. a ton,		81		
" 11.	Oats to Chick, 85 bu. 15#, 55 a bu.,	47	00		
" 15.	Int. from Fisher & North,	66	68		
" "	" " Lib. Bonds,	20	20		
" 27.	28 B. straw to Mettimer,	7	00	156	81
" "	35" tim " " " , 3045#, $15. a ton,	22	83		
" 28.	12 hogs, weight 3030#, $19.50 @ 100. = $590.85;				
	Freight 4.52, y'dage. 1.20, inspec .06, corn 111, hay	581	56		
				768	20
Apr. 2.	Oats to Ed. Pepper, 38 bu. 56 a bu.	21	28		
" 5.	9 doz. eggs to Fritz, 35 @ doz.,	3	15		
" 8.	Int. from Mrs. Hutchins,	27	00		
" 12.	8 doz. 7 eggs, 35 a doz.,	3	00		
" 16.	Int. on Liberty B.,	20	20		
" 17.	Oats to mill, 2750#, .63 a bu.,	54	24		
" 18.	" " " " "	58	93		
" 19.	2 doz. eggs, 35 a doz.,		70		
" 18.	13 hogs, weight 3140, $20.65 @ 100, = $648.41,				
	Freight 4.70, y'dage. 1.30, corn 2.18, com. 2.60,				
	Mgs. .. 2.51, ins. .63,	$634	49		
" 21.	32 bu. 11# oats to Frigast, 63 a bu.,	22	37		
" 23.	22 B. hay to N., 1895#, $26. a ton,	23	76		
" 29.	9 doz. eggs, 38 a doz.,	3	42		
				866	44
May 5.	Oats to mill 97 bu. 21#, .65 a bu.,	63	47		
" "	From M. car co. for Pres.,	37	50		
" 10.	Eggs 9 doz. .40 a doz.,	3	60		
" 17.	" 6 ", 43 ",	2	58		
" 26.	Int. on bonds,	4	26		

May's records of produce sold in the spring of 1919.

Farmers such as Elmo bought the Victory Loans almost as aggressively as the Liberty Loans, and many also invested in expanding their farming operations. Between April and June 1919, May and Elmo invested $2,257.50 in Liberty Bonds and Victory Bonds. Elmo also began a major addition to the barn in 1919, spending about nine hundred dollars on it that year and the next. Still, despite the investment in the barn, the purchase of the Model T in 1919, and $120 for May's eye trouble in 1917, May and Elmo put aside more than 40 percent of their gross farm income as savings during the 1917–20 period. By 1920, their farm income was supplemented by about $450 of interest income, including the interest on the Liberty Bonds, bank interest, and interest on personal loans. Average U.S. factory workers had to work about four months to earn $450 of income in 1920.

Yet if 1919 and 1920 turned out to be prosperous farming years, they were also uncertain ones. Farm prices did not all move in tandem throughout the period, and certainly farmers across the country, even across the county, reaped different rewards. The wheat price was stable by government design from 1917 to 1919, at a level more than double 1910–14 wheat prices, but other grain prices were less predictable. Elmo sold about 120 bushels of barley for $2 a bushel in 1918—almost three times what he earned from barley in 1915. When its price fell to $1.10 a bushel the next year, he sold only about 60 bushels. Oat prices did not rise so dramatically during the war; they less than doubled prewar levels. Elmo received his best prices for oats in early 1918; a year later, the price had fallen by 25 percent. The market for hay, on the other hand, was high and stable during the war and postwar years. Most of the hay he sold from the end of 1917 through 1920 went for thirty dollars a ton, about double the 1910–14 prices, but in the late spring of 1920, he sold hay for forty dollars a ton. Hay sales generated over 20 percent of gross farm income from 1915 through 1920.

Hogs were also good business during the war and the postwar boom, whereas cattle prices paled in comparison. Hog prices rose sooner and higher than those for most other farm products. In 1919, Elmo sold hogs at about twenty dollars per hundredweight—three times the 1915 levels. By early 1920, hog prices were down 25 percent from the 1919 levels. Cattle prices peaked for Elmo at twelve dollars per hundredweight in 1918, just 70 percent higher than in 1915. From 1915 to 1920, Elmo fed rather than sold his corn in most years, but even so, he sold considerable corn in 1917 and 1920, when its prices rose relative to hog prices. He also bought corn in the spring of 1919. Over 30 percent of gross farm income came from hogs during the 1915–20 period.

Some local farmers bought tractors during this boom period, encouraged to do so by the shortage of labor. Although Elmo didn't buy a tractor himself, neighborhood tractors helped him get his farmwork done. Frank Reid came with his tractor (a Waterloo Boy, later bought out by John Deere) in 1919 to pull Elmo's husker. For the next two weeks, when it wasn't too muddy, Frank and Elmo worked together on the corn husking. Some days Frank brought his tractor and they husked at Elmo's, and on other days Elmo and his man went with the husker to husk Frank's corn. No payments were exchanged for services on either side until the spring, when Elmo squared accounts with his machinery company group.

More tractors appeared on neighboring farms in 1920. Howard Fitch did some plowing for Elmo with his Fordson tractor in mid-May, and in the last week of October, Fred Davis brought up his new tractor and worked with George Brown's boys to pull the husker and husk Elmo's corn.

Elmo and Fred Davis also worked together on the addition to Elmo's barn. Elmo had built a new granary in 1916, but during the war, restrictions were placed on the use of building materials. When the restrictions were removed in 1919, pent-up demand for private construction created the beginning of a building boom. Elmo's barn addition was completed in two stages in the late summers of 1919 and 1920. Both years Fred came with his cement mixer to work with Elmo and the carpenters.

While farmers such as Elmo added value to their farming operations in 1919 and 1920, the value of their farmland itself soared. The high prices that farmers had been receiving for their products generated a major land boom, especially in the Corn Belt. The boom began as early as 1916 and achieved more dramatic proportions in 1919 and early 1920. Farmland values in the country as a whole increased by 70 percent between 1913 and 1920, but for some counties in the Corn Belt, the price of land doubled between 1914 and 1920.[28] In Winnebago County, farmland that had cost $81 per acre in 1910 increased to $149 an acre in 1920. In 1920, the average farm of 134 acres in Winnebago County cost almost twenty-five thousand dollars. (The buildings accounted for about 20 percent of that.) These figures for Winnebago County were very close to the state average.

As 1920 Winds Down

Life was not completely consumed in the frenzy of the postwar boom. Elmo and May began to take long Sunday drives again once the war ended. Although the mentions of having ice cream in Cherry Valley were rare during these busy years, Elmo did find time to pull numerous automobiles out of the big mud hole that had developed down by the semiwooded acreage he used for pasture. And when General Pershing (who led the U.S. forces during the war) was in Rockford in January 1920, Elmo went to see him. May noted when she and Mama made valentines for the children, when the bluebirds returned in March, and when the children found spring beauties and bloodroot in April. May was pleased with all the ducks that hatched in 1920; at least twenty-five ducklings remained after losing two. They dressed three ducks when the shredders came in mid-November. Eleven ducks were sold in Rockford at the end of the year.

May and Elmo kept close track of Fred Davis as he settled into his farming after his mother's death. Fred often came to call on Sunday evenings or stopped to talk to Elmo about one thing or another. Similarly, Elmo stopped by Fred's when he was in Cherry Valley.

Mama was fairly healthy and active throughout most of 1919 and 1920, although she was sick in bed for several weeks in early 1920. She attended her Gleaners auxiliary meetings and worked with the Red Cross until the circle disbanded. When Mr. Grow died in early May 1920, Emily was still too weak from her spring illness to attend the funeral. But she was well enough to celebrate her seventy-seventh birthday with May and Saidee Molander on June 30, 1920. She picked raspberries in July and grapes in October. She voted in November and finished a sweater for her granddaughter shortly thereafter. She found three eggs in mid-December and celebrated Christmas Day of 1920 at the Fitches, with May and Elmo. But Emily Lyford would die in 1921, not long after her seventy-eighth birthday.

In 1920, the Guilford community looked toward both the past and the future. May noted in June when Argyle's Willow Creek Presbyterian Church celebrated its seventy-fifth anniversary. The earliest Scottish settlers had founded the church in 1844. In December, Elmo attended a meeting at the Guilford Town Hall about joining Rockford. (Guilford Township eventually merged with Rockford in 1929.)

Ominously for the farm economy, farm prices were plummeting as 1920 came to a close. When the United States finally curtailed war relief credit to the Allied countries, foreign demand for U.S. agriculture began to evaporate. Certainly many farmers had anticipated the end of the wartime boom, but they could never have imagined how long it would be before agriculture would become prosperous again; nor could they have envisioned the scope of the trials to come.

CHAPTER 4

DOWN ON THE FARM IN THE ROARING TWENTIES

After the war and the postwar frenzy, Americans longed for "normalcy." They elected a new president in 1920, who promised to restore it. Warren Harding served from 1921 until his sudden death in 1923; then Calvin Coolidge came into the White House.

While a sharp economic recession blemished Harding's term, business prosperity was the hallmark of the Coolidge years. A Yankee from Vermont, Coolidge practiced frugality in an era of materialism and excess. He famously proclaimed, "The chief business of the American people is business." During his tenure, American business became ever more productive with the mass production of automobiles, radios, and new labor-saving electrical appliances. Consumers, bombarded with national advertising in magazines, newspapers, movies, and over the airwaves, responded enthusiastically. Abundant employment opportunities and the new availability of installment purchase plans encouraged consumers to buy now and pay later. By the end of the decade, businesses and consumers alike believed that a "New Era" of perpetual prosperity had been achieved. Herbert Hoover took over in 1929 before that vision was shattered.

Many of the images of the age—skyscrapers and speakeasies, bootleg whiskey and scantily clad women—had little to do with life on the farm. Farmers shrank to only 25 percent of the population by 1930, and the cultural divide between rural and urban areas grew. The "Coolidge Prosperity" did not extend to the business of farming. Farmers watched their farm values and profits fall while their urban neighbors reveled in the amenities of a new material world.

Still, the images of life on the farm in Guilford Township in the 1920s that sprang from the pages of May's diaries were largely happy ones. Trucks and tractors appeared on most farms, and roads improved significantly; radios connected Guilford farmers to the wider world. Farmers could handle more land; some expanded, and others, like Elmo, took more leisure time. May and Elmo took longer road trips, and by the end of the decade their social schedule was busy with Grange meetings and activities.

May's notes also reflect the return to normalcy in the 1920s that people had longed for. Family life fell into regular patterns again. Spring began each year with the digging of the horseradish and the return of the robins, blackbirds, meadowlarks, and bluebirds, and it ended with visits to cemeteries around Memorial Day. Summers were filled with making hay, Sunday drives, canning, and visits from relatives. When fall returned, the children stopped by on the way to and from school. Radio, books, and Elmo's fiddle made dreary winter days pass more quickly.

A story of low profits and financial distress in agriculture also creeps out of the pages of the farm ledgers May kept; only a few hints in her diaries help verify this unhappy tale.

From May's 1923 diary.

THE DEFLATED FARM ECONOMY

Before the end of 1920, the long period of rising farm incomes and farm-land values came to an abrupt end. Farmers produced at expanded levels to satisfy export demand during the war and early postwar years, but when demand for exports dropped off, farm prices collapsed amid surplus production. Other factors, such as the sudden contraction of government spending and the tightening of wartime easy-credit policies, combined to help push the entire U.S. economy into a sharp recession. Unemployment soared from less than 2 percent in 1919 to 12 percent in 1921, before recovery began in 1922.[1]

But while the manufacturing sector soon rebounded, agriculture did not. Land values fell, foreclosure rates increased, and many rural banks failed. The farm population began to shrink as the promise of agriculture faded.

Plunging Farm Prices and Recession in Agriculture

Farm prices in 1921 continued the plunge begun at the end of 1920. In December 1921, Elmo sold hogs for less than seven dollars per hundredweight; in 1919, hogs had sold at twenty dollars per hundredweight. The prices of some farm products, such as hay, held up a little better. Hay was selling at twenty dollars a ton in Rockford, down from the typical price of thirty dollars a ton during and shortly after the war. On average in the United States, farm prices fell by 44 percent from the peak in 1919 to 1921. Thereafter, farm prices improved only modestly throughout the rest of the decade, settling in the late 1920s about one-third below the wartime highs.

· The economics of farming deteriorated across the country, since consumer prices and farm wages were off less than farm prices. Consumer prices in the late 1920s were down only 12 to 13 percent from the wartime peaks. Although average farm wages in the United States were off sharply in 1921 and 1922 from wartime peaks, later in the decade farm wages rose. Immigration slowed substantially during the war, and after the war, beginning in 1921, increased nationalism inspired laws to restrict immigration into the United States sharply. In Rockford and elsewhere, farm hands became more difficult to find.

Early in the decade, Will Brockman, a young local man, worked for Elmo, and the two men caught up on many jobs that had gone undone during the busy war years. Will began in March 1922 and worked continuously throughout the rest of 1922, 1923, and most of 1924. His wages increased from $27.50 to $32 per month over that time. (John Pratt had worked for similar wages during 1912 to 1914.) During the winter months, Will cut wood. In between planting, cultivating, and harvesting, he spread many loads of manure on the fields. Elmo and Will also grubbed stumps in the wooded pasture, and they broke new land for planting.

In the latter half of the decade, Will moved on to other work, and Elmo paid higher wages for less reliable help. In 1926, Elmo had steady help for less than a month in July, and he got by with very occasional day help during the rest of the year. He drew many dozen loads of manure himself that year. Then in 1927, Elmo paid sixty dollars a month (plus board) for help from late March to late August. In 1928 and 1929, he had steady help only in July and August, from younger, less experienced men.

With bills for groceries and hired help relatively high and farm prices relatively low, May and Elmo's farm income no longer covered their farm and household expenses. In only three years from 1901 to 1920 had they dipped into savings from previous years to meet current expenses, but in six of the years from 1921 to 1929, expenses significantly exceeded farm income. By this time, however, May and Elmo had put capital aside that was earning interest, so their lifestyle was uncompromised. Not until the latter part of the decade did they take noticeable steps to reduce expenses.

Investments in Farmland

Even more damaging than the lower farm incomes was the steady decline of farmland values. In 1920, an average farm in Illinois, consisting of 135 acres with buildings, had a value of $25,289; a decade later the size of an average Illinois farm had grown to 143 acres and was worth only $15,553. All farmers watched the value of their land fall, but those who had bought land during the speculative land boom, during the war and early postwar days, found themselves struggling to make mortgage payments. Farm foreclosures during the 1913–20 period averaged only 3.2 per 1,000 farms each year. But during the depression of 1920–21, 453,000 farmers lost their farms—about 7 percent of all farms. Many more lost their farms before the decade ended: farms were foreclosed at the rate of 16.7 per 1,000 farms during the 1926–30 period. Those farms with hogs, corn, wheat, and cotton (whose production had expanded substantially during the war) were the hardest hit across the United States, and young farmers were the most affected.[2]

Fred Davis, for example, bought 40 acres (with farm buildings), adjacent to his father's estate, for twelve thousand dollars in February 1919. (Factory wages for a year's work in 1919 amounted to about one thousand dollars.) The sinking land prices by late 1920 were another unwelcome surprise little more than a year after his mother's death. Fred was in a position to put half the money down in 1919 (in cash and Liberty Bonds), and he paid off the mortgage in February 1924, one year later than originally anticipated. Working those 40 acres and the 260-acre farm his parents had left him, he paid off all his debts by 1926. But he never forgot that land prices could fall sharply. Others faced more bitter lessons.

Howard Fitch was the same age as Fred, but he had other siblings, both parents living, and a family to provide for. Elmo helped Howard with a barn raising on his "new place" in late 1917. In the early 1920s, the family stopped by to visit a number of times, and Howard and Elmo exchanged machinery and worked together. "H. Fitch" was also noted regularly in the farm ledgers. Elmo had loaned Howard six hundred dollars in 1919, and each year May recorded thirty-six dollars of interest paid. But in early 1923, Howard Fitch and his family moved off the farm and out of state; then Howard's father paid the thirty-six dollars of interest each year.

May and Elmo were in a relatively fortunate position. Without children, they had less reason to expand their farm, and timing also favored them. When May's mother died in 1921, Starr bought out May's share of the farm at a fair price. In 1922, May began keeping track of her own financial affairs in a small notebook. She held most of her inheritance in Liberty Bonds, and Starr was making payments on a note to her. Judging from her records, May's share of her parents' estate must have been valued at about twelve thousand dollars.

Many farmers, however, did try to expand in the 1920s, particularly those with sons interested in farming. By 1925, average farmland values in Illinois were already down more than 25 percent from the highs in 1920. Naturally, farmers began to look for buying opportunities. With improving road conditions and labor-saving tractors, farmers could handle more land. Starr bought a new "north farm" in 1926, which consisted of 172 acres of rolling land and some woods near Argyle, but he continued to live on the 160 acres he had bought with his father as a young man.

Joe Lyford took on the farm that had belonged to his grandparents. From 1923 to 1925 during the winter months, Joe studied agriculture at the University of Wisconsin, in Madison. When he began farming "his place" toward the end of 1925, Joe often had dinner at Elmo and May's and sometimes spent the night. Joe and Elmo began sharing work in addition to machinery and horses. Joe raised cattle and pigs over the winter, and he and Elmo helped each other take hogs to market. In May 1926, Joe was driving a "new roadster." Later that year, he brought home 130 lambs from Belvidere.

Late in 1927, Joe began hauling sand to build a new house on his farm, and within a few months, he took out a big loan from his aunt May. (His grandparents' house burned in 1924.) May counted the loads of lumber and brick that came from the train depot at Perryville and the number of carpenters and bricklayers that came each day to build Joe's house. In March, Joe bought a used Delco plant, and he and Elmo spent several days wiring the house and the barns for lighting. (Many well-to-do rural families used Delco plants in the 1920s to generate battery-powered electricity. Elmo and May continued to use kerosene lamps for another decade.) In mid-June, Joe married Marian Pepper, and the young couple soon moved into their new house.

Spending, Saving, and Investing in the 1920s

May and Elmo invested relatively little in the farm after the addition to the barn was finished in 1921. Elmo spent some time and about $145 fixing up the barnyard for cattle in 1922. He waited to buy a tractor until 1926. Indeed the biggest single purchase that May and Elmo made, according to their farm ledger accounts from 1921 to 1927, was a new "Buick Six" in 1923, for $1,180.

In the farm ledgers in 1920s, May began tracking the investments made with the substantial savings she and Elmo had accumulated with farming during the first two decades of the century. Although her records of investments and capital transactions were incomplete, it is clear that most of the savings was still in Liberty Bonds. Some savings were earning interest in the bank, and some were invested in personal loans, mortgage debt, and bank stock. Elmo received about $1,300 from inheritance on the Campbell side of the family in 1924, which became part of their joint savings, and May and Elmo owned two lots in Rockford during the 1920s. They bought one in 1925 for $1,607 and sold another one in 1926 for $2,000. After 1926, Elmo still "mows weeds on our lot," and May still recorded taxes paid on the lot.

May spent the interest from her inherited capital on her own personal expenses, including indoor help. These expenses she recorded in her small notebook. Beulah Heidenreich (who had first worked for May in 1919) worked from March 1921 until early 1926, at seven dollars per week throughout the year; now May spent more than Elmo did on hired help. May's other personal expenses included clothes, books, magazines, stationery, and birthday cards and gifts. In 1927, May and Elmo took a long road trip that May paid for from her interest income. That year May recorded $576 of interest earned and $553 of expenses.[3]

Thus, although the farm income was tight, May and Elmo lived comfortably though modestly during the 1920s; new cars were their primary luxury. Throughout much of the 1920s they owned both a Buick and a Model T; the latter saved wear and tear on the Buick.[4] After the purchase of the six-cylinder Buick in 1923, Elmo bought a used Ford truck in 1924 for only $225. About the same time, he traded in the old Ford that he had used as a utility vehicle and, for an additional $175, came home with a Ford coupe. Two years later, in 1926, he traded the Ford coupe for a new one. By 1928, the Buick Six was becoming less reliable, so Elmo traded the Ford coupe for a Chevrolet. At this point, they began to drive only one car in addition to the truck. (What became of the Buick is unclear.)

Grocery bills added up to larger numbers in the 1920s. Elmo no longer butchered pigs and had long since stopped butchering cattle on the farm. Lard, bacon, and pork were now frequent purchases, and store-bought "frankfurts" and hotdogs replaced homemade pork sausage. Grocery stores, many of them now "self-service" chain stores, had an increasing array of items for sale. Canned soup, vegetables, and new brand names appeared in May's expense records. On the other hand, milk, eggs, and potatoes still came from the farm; so did garden vegetables, apples, berries, and cherries; and home canning still helped stock the shelves for the winter months.

Farmers Fall Behind

May and Elmo enjoyed some of the new things that money could buy in the 1920s, but, in general, farmers lagged behind in a consumer economy that was racing ahead. Stable prices, rising productivity, and job opportunities enhanced urban prosperity in the 1920s. Industrial wage rates increased by 17 percent between 1922 and 1929, and since prices were stable, these wages bought more goods.[5]

As a group, farmers were already a minority; urban life had become the norm. Even by the time May and Elmo were born, the farm population had fallen to less than half of the U.S. total. But the farm population still increased in absolute numbers to a peak of 32.5 million in 1916; then it fell to 30.5 million by the end of the 1920s, constituting just 25 percent of the total population. Only 13 percent of the Illinois population lived on farms in 1930.

While the farm economy sputtered and farmland values fell, the automobile economy roared. By 1921, many Guilford farmers had owned a car for a decade already, but most middle-class families across America purchased their first set of wheels during the 1920s. In 1920, 33 percent of households owned cars; this figure soared to 78 percent by 1929. The availability of installment credit, a booming used-car market, and the shrinking price of the Model T all helped to make the dream of car ownership a reality. The basic Model T sold for just $290 in 1924; in the same year, 70 percent of new cars were sold on installment.[6]

Access to electricity was also creating a booming market for new appliances. In 1929, when electricity had reached 63 percent of the U.S. population, half of all households owned an electric iron. Refrigerators, toasters, and washing machines followed, all available for installment purchase. More than one-third of all households in America owned radios by 1929.[7] Many of these radios ran on batteries and belonged to farm families. But most farmers lacked access to central electric power for modern appliances. The Delco plants that Joe Lyford and others installed for battery-powered electricity were primarily for lights rather than appliances.

Trucks, Tractors, Horses, and Roads

Perhaps what best benefited farmers in the 1920s were the improved roads, which, combined with ever-improving automobiles and trucks, made a difference in the time farmers spent hauling crops and running errands. Elmo was among the many Guilford farmers who drove both a truck and a tractor by mid-decade.

Road Improvements

Federal aid to states for road construction more than tripled with the Federal Highway Act of 1921. It provided matching grants to build an interstate system of highways and improved farm-to-market roads. Also for road building, the federal government turned over to the states some twenty-five thousand heavy trucks and fifteen hundred caterpillar tractors as military surplus after the war. By the end of the 1920s, all states collected gasoline taxes to finance the construction of main roads.[8]

Counties, townships, and farmers, including Elmo, worked to improve rural roads. More than 25 percent of all U.S. automobiles were on farms in 1921, and 31 percent of all farms had automobiles. In the Midwest, however, the percentage of farms with automobiles was much higher. More than 70 percent of farms in Iowa and Nebraska and more than 50 percent of farms in Illinois, Minnesota, Kansas, and the Dakotas had automobiles in 1920. By 1930 nearly 80 to 90 percent of farms throughout the Midwest had automobiles.

Elmo spent much of the decade grading and plowing roads and lobbying for additional help to maintain rural roads. He was elected justice of the peace in 1922, but he spent more time working alongside the road commissioner as a member of the road committee. (He received no compensation for either role.) Road crews finally started work "on our Rockford road" in the fall of 1924. In early November, Elmo and Will hauled twenty-five loads of stone for the road that ran south past the wooded pasture, likely using Elmo's truck. During the big snowstorm of early April 1926, Elmo plowed roads. May noted a county snowplow ("tractor plow") for the first time in January 1927. She used the term *snowplow* for the first time in 1929. In that year the snowplow came around three times in January and February, but Elmo also plowed roads in between.

By 1929, road crews had graveled many of the roads in Guilford Township. In October 1928, "road men" began to gravel Bell School Road, and May gave regular updates on their progress. They approached from the south, and before Thanksgiving, the gravel had reached the schoolhouse at the north end of the road. Then the crew worked south again, with a second layer of gravel in early 1929.

Throughout most of the 1920s, however, automobiles were still getting stuck in Guilford's mud, and horses rescued the autos. One afternoon in March 1922, their horse Bonnie pulled Elmo out when he was stuck "between creek & corner coming home." Later that evening, she assisted another motorist stuck in the same mud. The mud hole that developed during the war, down by May and Elmo's wooded pasture, trapped motorists through 1924, although Elmo made several attempts to fix it with loads of gravel. In mid-March 1926, May wrote, "Roads awful. We stuck on way down & C. Larson pull us out. Coming home Mr. Lake pull us out by Samuelson's. Then Joe meet us with team by ¼ line & pull us home." In mid-March 1928, when Joe was building his house, the workmen came out in trucks, but for several days they could get no farther than where the gravel ended. So Joe and Elmo took teams of horses out to meet them.

Steadily, however, the supremacy of the horse declined. Motor vehicles were more convenient and safer for negotiating Rockford traffic, even though rural roads required horses. Increasingly May and Elmo took the car or the truck into Rockford. Sometimes, the horse and buggy would have been a better choice. One cold February day, May and Elmo took the car and had "8 punctures [on the] rough roads!"

On the other hand, local trips between farms in the township and down to Cherry Valley or up to Argyle were frequently made with horse and buggy or sleigh. Even in 1929, when the rural roads were graveled, horses and sleds came out in the wintertime.

Trucks and Tractors

By the end of the 1920s, about 13 percent of U.S. farmers had a tractor. A similar proportion had a truck. These numbers were higher in the Midwest, especially for tractors. By 1930, about 30 percent of farms in midwestern states, such as Illinois, Iowa, and Nebraska, had tractors; the farms of Kansas and the Dakotas had even more tractors. Trucks were adopted more quickly where roads were good, like in the northeastern states. In 1930, about 20 percent of farms in most midwestern states had trucks.

Farmers in Guilford adopted tractors and trucks relatively early. Already by 1921, many of the farmers in the area, especially the younger ones, had tractors. Trucks burst onto the scene right after the war and were common on Guilford roads by 1924. When Elmo bought his first truck, the Ford he purchased in April 1924, May had already mentioned truck agents, lumber trucks, oil trucks, gravel trucks, milk trucks, and other trucks stuck in the mud in the Guilford neighborhood.

Because Elmo paid less for this truck than the price of a basic Model T, one assumes it was a used vehicle, and perhaps not such a bargain. Already in August, the "band clutch" was going bad, and Elmo had to drag the truck home with a team of horses. More fixing was necessary in November, and in late February 1925 the horses pulled the truck home again on account of worn bands. In December the truck broke a wheel, which Elmo fixed. In May 1927, Elmo had a new engine put in for $110. In 1929, it needed a new radiator among other things. Still, the truck lasted until early 1931, when Elmo traded it in for another.

Reading the histories of agriculture in the twentieth century, one might conclude that nothing could have been more exciting than the purchase of that first tractor. But May's diaries shed doubt on that assumption. The arrival of Elmo's first tractor (a Fordson), in September 1926, appeared to have been a rather ordinary affair, certainly when compared with the arrival of the Maxwell touring car in early 1911. May mentioned the tractor directly in her diary only four times in the first eight months of its life on the farm. The purchase ($621.60) was recorded in the ledger; Elmo then sold his gang plow (for $17.50) and purchased a tractor plow for $100. Several days later, "Men bring out tractor in AM & Elmo plow sweet clover sod in PM." In early October, he used the tractor to pull the grader on the roads and also helped two men out of the mud. A few days later, he dragged the rye with the tractor. The next mention didn't occur till the following spring in early May: when the men were plowing with both horses and the tractor up by the schoolhouse, the tractor got stuck in the mud.

Similarly, only a few mentions of the tractor appear in 1928 and 1929. In the spring of 1928, Elmo "pulverize with horses as too wet for tractor." On another warm day in July, the men used the tractor to cut oats with the binder but had trouble with both the tractor and the binder. All of the mentions in 1929 save one referred to fixing the tractor or getting grease or oil for it. The following year, the tractor acted up more frequently; once that year, "Elmo plow and get kicked in mouth by tractor."

One could argue that May simply didn't share Elmo's enthusiasm for his tractor. After all, she had been recording "engine bother" of one kind or another for a good many years. Yet Elmo could easily have bought a tractor in 1920, when other neighbors were buying them, but he waited until 1926. Both Elmo and May were fifty-three years old in 1926, and perhaps some of the shine of new motor vehicles had worn thin; the younger men were more eager to own tractors. But perhaps too, the advantages of the tractor were not so clear. Few farmers saved much money using tractors in the 1920s.

The tractors produced in the early 1920s were not designed for either planting or cultivating corn, which reduced their usefulness in the Corn Belt. Tractors made more sense in the wheat fields of the West. Some Illinois farmers used tractors for drilling small grains and cutting with the binder, but many preferred horses for these jobs as well. Not until 1924, when International Harvester introduced the "all-purpose" Farmall tractor with a tricycle wheel design, which enabled the front wheels to go between the rows, did any tractor producer claim product utility in cultivating corn.

When Elmo bought a Fordson in 1926, he used it for those jobs considered suitable for tractors at the time: plowing, pulverizing, dragging, and roadwork. The tractor sped up the process and allowed him to get by with less hired labor. Tractors also withstood hot weather better than horses and could work long hours without rest—an important consideration when labor was scarce.

In 1925, Henry Ford's lightweight tractor, introduced during the war, dominated the market; 75 percent of all tractors produced in the United States were Fordsons.[9] But that changed quickly. The new International Farmall included several key features beyond the tricycle design. In addition to the classic belt power to run stationary equipment, the Farmall offered the new "power take-off" developed during the war. The power take-off eventually proved to be a major advance for powering implements that were pulled behind the tractor (such as corn pickers, hay balers, and combines). The Farmall also carried a unique steering-wheel brake control that enabled it to turn sharp corners. Shortly after its introduction, the Farmall became the most popular tractor on the market; by 1928, it drove Henry Ford out of the tractor market in the United States.

International had a huge lead over Ford in the design of farm implements to complement its tractors, and so did other farm implement manufacturers, such as John Deere and J. I. Case. (The latter finally bought out Rockford's Emerson–Brantingham Company in 1928.) International built almost 50 percent of the farm tractors in 1928 and almost 60 percent in 1929.[10] Throughout the 1920s, new equipment designed to run on the power

Planting corn with a Farmall tractor, Grinnell, Iowa, 1927. Courtesy of Wisconsin Historical Society (image 23647).

take-off was developed and introduced. But Elmo already owned a full line of equipment, much of it jointly with the other farmers in his group, and these stationary machines ran on belt power. The power take-off could be added as an accessory to the tractor, but Elmo didn't invest in one until 1936, when he bought a corn picker that required it.

Fred Davis was a generation younger than Elmo, he farmed about twice as much land, and he invested more aggressively in tractors and modern equipment. He bought the International Harvester Titan 10-20 and a three-bottom plow in September 1920. (For both he paid $1,110.) Early the next spring, he bought an eight-foot tandem disk to use with the Titan. This tractor was more powerful than the Fordson, its lead competitor until the Farmall was introduced. The Fordson had a lower price but pulled only a two-bottom plow. Fred also bypassed the Farmall, in 1927, and bought a Cletrac, crawling-track-type tractor. (The Cletrac did not become an industry leader, but it had advantages on hills and for pulling machinery originally designed for horses.) In 1928, Fred bought an International Harvester combine (for $1,351.25), when combine sales were just beginning to take off in the Midwest.

Titan tractor pulling P&O plow, Aurora, Illinois, 1921. Courtesy of Wisconsin Historical Society (image 41496).

A Slow Farewell to the Horse

Despite the mechanical advances, most farmers still needed horses. In 1929, tractor manufacturers boasted only 1,000 horseless farms in the United States—a small fraction of the 6.5 million farms at the time. Especially in the Corn Belt, farmers preferred horses to the new tractors for planting corn and cultivating it when it was young and fragile. Most farms had more than one man working in peak periods; thus, getting rid of all of one's horses would have necessitated at least two tractors.[11]

Younger men saw the down side of horses—the regular care and feeding they required and the baffling diseases they were subject to—but men of Elmo's generation took their care in stride and appreciated their advantages. Although a tractor could substitute for a four- or five-horse team, many jobs might require only one or two horses, and the team could be broken down and used in its component parts. Moreover, cold winter temperatures didn't keep a horse from starting, and horses could get into the fields sooner in wet conditions. Nevertheless, the numbers of workhorses on U.S. farms peaked at about twenty-one million in 1921 and over the decade fell to about seventeen million.[12]

May and Elmo also began to keep fewer horses and far fewer colts during the 1920s. Several of the horses on the farm during the Golden Age were

Charlie, Bonnie, Colonel, and Captain: May and Elmo's team in the 1920s.

still there. Bonnie often went home with the hired girl, and Colonel was responsible for breaking the hay track in the barn. During the 1920s, Elmo bought three horses, and he also acquired a colt when he took one old horse, bought only two years earlier, to the canning factory. During the Golden Age, May and Elmo had at least eight adult horses, compared with the 1920s, when they had no fewer than five.

FARMING IN THE 1920S

Although the transition from horses to tractors and trucks was the most noticeable change in farming methods in Illinois in the 1920s, it was not the only change. Markets and farming technology also changed, and farmers added new crops to their rotations, resulting in shifts in the mix of production.

Shifting Crops and Livestock Husbandry

Cattle prices improved relative to hog prices during the decade, probably explaining why cattle became May and Elmo's major farming focus in the 1920s. During the war, hog prices in May's ledgers were up to 30 percent higher than cattle prices. But after 1923, cattle and hog prices were approximately on a par; now cattle accounted for about 50 percent of farm sales, and hogs about 20 percent. Oats and hay became much less significant.

Beginning in 1922, Elmo and most of the men in his group bought feeder cattle to fatten. That year and the next, the men drove down to Decatur, Illinois, together to buy cattle and sent them home by train. In 1924 Elmo's group took their wives with them to a cattle sale in Peoria. Several other couples in the neighborhood came along too, and they all stayed overnight in La Salle on the way home. May and Elmo drove their Buick Six. Later in the decade, they bought cattle closer to home, in Durand, Roscoe, and Chicago.

Throughout the 1920s, the neighborhood men helped each other drive cattle to the Perryville depot when they were ready for market. After the men loaded the cattle onto the train, usually one of them went into Chicago with the load. Previously Elmo had sold his cattle to livestock buyers, such as the Popham brothers in Cherry Valley, or to the Schmauss Company, a packing house and meat market in Rockford. These buyers handled the shipping if required. But during the 1920s, shipping cooperatives were formed all over the country.

Area farmers also bought feeder pigs in the 1920s, so cholera outbreaks increased in Guilford. Every other year or so there was news of cholera and vaccinating hogs at one farm or another. Elmo first bought feeder pigs in 1927.

Some farmers fed lambs in the 1920s, but May and Elmo stuck to cattle, hogs, modest amounts of dairy, and chickens. Prices of eggs and poultry held up better during the 1920s than prices of either cattle or hogs. So Elmo put a new roof on the henhouse, May paid more attention to chicks born in the spring, and they sold more eggs and poultry. May and Elmo first bought commercially raised baby chicks in 1927.

Production of oats and hay declined across the country as motor vehicles replaced horses. Because Elmo fed more cattle after 1922, it is not surprising that he sold considerably less hay. But he sold no oats from his 1921 oat crop, nor did he sell oats again until early 1925, although he raised them for the horses.

New crops in the 1920s included alfalfa and other legumes, such as sweet clover and soybeans. Alfalfa is high in protein and other nutrients; it makes excellent hay, is good for grazing, and fixes more nitrogen in the soil than most clovers. The only catch is that alfalfa grows poorly in acid soils, so Illinois farmers needed to lime the soil. Sweet clover is similar to alfalfa and also benefits from lime.

Alfalfa first appeared on a few Illinois farms in the early 1900s; by the mid-1920s it overtook traditional red clover in acreage.[13] Elmo experimented with alfalfa in 1916 but didn't try it again until 1922; that time he applied lime first. By 1923, most of the farmers in Elmo's group grew alfalfa. From 1922 on, Elmo harvested alfalfa hay; in 1924, he and Will borrowed a lime rock spreader from Fred Davis and spent many days applying lime to the fields. Elmo began planting sweet clover in 1925.

Illinois farmers also experimented with soybeans in the 1920s, although markets for soybeans were not well developed. Many farmers planted soybeans as forage crops; others plowed them under as green manure or used them to make hay.[14] May recorded small purchases of soybeans from 1923 to 1925 during spring planting, noting the planting of the beans in the last year. She made no reference to their harvest or use, however. Soybeans finally appear again in 1930, when Elmo planted them in with the timothy grass, implying a forage use.

Without access to the orchards and berry bushes that May's parents had kept, Elmo paid more attention to such crops in the 1920s. He and Beulah set out strawberry plants in 1923, and by 1925 there were "strawberries to eat & give away." He also tended the blackberry bushes, thinning and mulching them; by mid-decade, the blackberries were plentiful. During the summer of 1926, Mabel Fitch helped can at least twenty-one quarts of strawberries, many quarts of raspberries and blackberries, and various jars of raspberry and blackberry jam. May and her hired girls also canned grapes, made grape ketchup, and gave grapes away to friends.

Elmo also began to raise bees. In June 1923, "Elmo get a hive of bees from larch tree," and within a couple of weeks he was fixing "honey boxes." Throughout the rest of the decade, May made occasional brief mentions of beekeeping operations. In October 1929, Elmo brought in fifty pounds of honey from the hives.

Farm Work and Productivity

Farming technology changed rapidly in the 1920s; new crops and techniques, trucks and tractors, better roads, and new farm equipment all presented farmers with options for change. Many farmers went out of business during the 1920s, so used equipment came on the market. Moreover, the soured farm economy pressured farmers to keep expenses down and produce more efficiently. During the 1920s, farm employment fell while output expanded, increasing by 24 percent per worker. Not since the mechanical improvements of the 1870s had productivity increased so substantially over a decade.[15] For the most part, farmers had automobiles and better roads, along with trucks and tractors, to thank for the improvements in productivity. The new vehicles saved time, and fewer horses on the farm meant more land could be devoted to market crops. When farm machines that ran on the new power take-off were introduced, some farmers bought, eager to try the new technology; others watched and waited.

Although Fred Davis bought a combine in 1928, most farmers in the area were still threshing. All through the 1920s, Elmo and his machine company threshed together with the same thresher and gas engine they had bought in 1914, when they built their company shed on the Breckenridge property. In 1926 when the old engine acted up, "they have to use smaller tractor as repairs not get there till late & when they think they have it fixed, something else give out." But the "big engine" was more powerful than the tractors the men had, so they fixed it and used it for several more years.

Elmo's group owned several other machines that stayed in their shed and were used by at least some of the men throughout the decade. These machines included the silo filler and the corn shredder bought in 1914 and

1915 and the stationary hay baler bought at the end of 1918. Although Elmo stopped filling silo for several years in 1925 and stopped shredding with the group in 1926, other members of the group still used these machines. Elmo used the hay baler throughout the decade, but not all the other men did.

Elmo experimented during the 1920s with how he handled the corn and what he fed his animals. In 1926 and 1927 he fed cornstalks, apparently without chopping. Then in 1928 he bought an old silo filler to use with his tractor to chop dry stalks in the winter months. He also husked corn every year, although one can't determine how much corn he husked. In the early 1920s, when Elmo both filled silo and shredded with his group, few days were spent husking. Beginning in 1921, the husking was done by hand again; the mechanical husker used during the war and early postwar years was not used.

Elmo bought equipment during the decade, but with the exception of the Fordson tractor and the tractor plow bought in 1926, the equipment he bought was designed for use with horses and simply replaced worn-out machines. After last buying a hay loader in 1907, he bought a new one in Cherry Valley in 1922 for ninety-five dollars. The next year, his corn planter gave out before the crop was planted. After trying to repair it with pieces of another old planter, he gave up and bought a new one. The old planter apparently predated his marriage. Later in the decade, he bought a hay rake at one sale and a manure spreader at another. In 1929 he bought a new cultivator for a hundred dollars.

Farming was frustrating in the 1920s, and May's records attest to it. May and Elmo invested roughly 8 percent of gross farm income in major capital improvements on the farm during the 1921–29 period. During the first decade of the century, they had rolled back almost a third of their gross income into the capital stock of the farm. Now they had other investments—Liberty Bonds, mortgages, and real estate in Rockford—and the farm did not pay all the household bills. The sharp reduction in farm labor, after Will left in 1924, also suggested that Elmo was frustrated with farming and looking for ways to cut costs.

Moreover, after the hustle of the war and early postwar years, the records indicate a feeling of semiretirement in the 1920s. Elmo had more time on his hands, particularly during the winter months. Although he had less help in the latter part of the decade (and put in many tedious days spreading manure, cultivating corn, and husking corn alone), he also had less help to keep busy. He spent more time fixing automotive vehicles, but the cars, truck, and tractor also saved time. He spent fewer winter days hauling crops to market; now most of his production went to market on the hoof. During February and March, Elmo went to many more farm sales, averaging eight sales each year.[16] Usually the only purchases on these days were gasoline, lunch, and perhaps a shave.

Many area farmers farmed more aggressively: Joe Lyford, Fred Davis, and several of the farmers in Elmo's group. In particular, they bought and fed more livestock. Fred's gross farm income during the 1921–29 period was typically more than twice that of May and Elmo's. Fred had less hired labor and a farm that was twice the size of theirs. (Fred also cut back sharply on labor in the late 1920s.) But appreciably higher profits did not always follow from these larger efforts in the poor agricultural economy.

THE ROAR OF THE 1920S

Down on the farm was not the most exciting place to be in the 1920s. Americans in general experienced dramatic cultural shifts, but much of the change took place in cities and towns. The automobile, modern appliances, and new plumbing fixtures all became available to the broad urban middle class when consumers learned to spend on credit. When a building boom swept the country, skyscrapers rose to new heights in urban areas. Women, having achieved the right to vote and the prohibition of alcoholic beverages, now turned to fashion, parties, and homemaking, largely letting politics go for the time being. But Prohibition hardly ended the consumption of booze; the law merely made the manufacture, sale, and transportation of alcohol illegal and, in the process, energized organized crime. Mass media, such as movies and radio, broadcast the sounds and images of modern life. The flapper with a cigarette, popping out of an automobile and entering a speakeasy in a city filled with bright lights and tall buildings, became the symbol of the age.

Bright City Lights and Tall Buildings

Scenes from all the major pageants of the 1920s played out in Rockford as well as Chicago over the decade. Perhaps nothing in the 1920s grabbed American attention so much as the 1927 flight of Charles Lindbergh across the Atlantic Ocean to Paris. About a year later, Rockford's own "Fish" Hassell and "Shorty" Cramer attempted to fly from Rockford to Stockholm, Sweden, by way of the Arctic Circle. The men became national celebrities after they ran out of fuel, landed on the polar ice cap, and were finally rescued weeks later.

Urban economic prosperity overflowed. At least one economist of the time called Rockford the "most prosperous community in the nation."[17] The value of manufacturing output more than doubled in Rockford between 1919 and 1929, and the number employed in those factories increased from about fifteen thousand to twenty thousand people. The population of the city of Rockford increased by more than 30 percent over the decade, to almost eighty-six thousand by 1930, with the entire metropolitan area expanding to include more than two hundred thousand residents.[18] Chicago's population increased by 25 percent, to nearly 3.4 million.

Manufacturers Bank Building, Rockford, Illinois, ca. 1923. Courtesy of Midway Village and Museum Center, Rockford, Illinois.

A building boom helped fuel the economy across the country and transformed cities with new structures. During the decade, more than four thousand private residences, valued at $15.3 million, were built in Rockford. The Rockford skyline was redrawn with the construction of new banks and office buildings, rising well above previous heights. First the Ziock and later the Talcott Building, both on State Street, laid claim to being the tallest office building in the city, each at thirteen stories. The twelve-story Faust Hotel, which boasted four hundred rooms and filled an entire city block, took center stage when completed in 1928. The Coronado Theatre, a movie house with interior details to rock the imagination, opened in 1927 amid wild enthusiasm.[19] Meanwhile, Jazz Age skyscrapers shot up on Chicago's Michigan Avenue.

May didn't mention these changes, although she did note when the barn on the old Purdy farm was torn down to make way for a country club. She and Elmo went into Rockford regularly for business, visits, errands, and grocery shopping. Elmo also went into Chicago regularly; his primary interest was with the Union Stockyards.

Although Cherry Valley shrank in size during the first two decades of the century, Belvidere, with the National Sewing Machine Company as a major

Farmers with trucks, Belvidere, Illinois, possibly ca. 1924. Courtesy of the Boone County Historical Museum, Belvidere, Illinois.

employer, held its own. National produced more than sewing machines; from 1903 to 1907, it had produced the Eldridge auto. In 1912, it began producing washing machines. By 1920, Belvidere was a town of 7,804 people, with businesses oriented to the needs of farmers, so Elmo visited it with increasing frequency. When he needed lumber, bricks, cement, tile, or fence posts he generally went to Belvidere. Likewise, chicks in the spring and tankage to feed the hogs came from Belvidere. The town had a train depot and fine grocery stores, and the Boone County Fair was still an important area attraction.

Taking to the Road

Rural areas were seemingly left behind in the 1920s, but some farmers took to the roads. May and Elmo's purchase of the Buick Six in 1923 sparked the usual thrill and increase in road trips, often with other family members. May and Elmo explored the whole state of Wisconsin, including the Door County peninsula. A book of road maps purchased mid-decade helped them plan longer trips. In 1927, they went to Niagara Falls and then traveled west the next year.

New enclosed automobiles and much better roads made inclement weather much less of a problem for motorists; travel by train and interurban diminished rapidly. The train trip to Wichita that May and Elmo made in 1921 was May's last trip by train. Elmo and the other farmers still took the train to Chicago to sell cattle, and Joe Lyford took the train to school in Madison in the mid-1920s, but May's references to the interurban were now rare. Already by 1924, streetcar lines in Rockford were being abandoned and replaced by bus routes. By the end of the decade, the interurban made its final trips to surrounding towns. The same was happening to interurban systems throughout the Midwest.[20]

May kept only brief notes on the trip to Niagara Falls in September 1927. But clearly long days were spent on the road. The first day they drove 179 miles and camped near New Buffalo, Michigan. The following day they drove 271 miles and camped in a farmyard near Windsor, Ontario; 235 miles the next day took them to a tourist camp overlooking Niagara Falls by nightfall. After leaving Niagara Falls they traveled through New York, Pennsylvania, down to Wheeling, West Virginia, and back through Ohio and Indiana. Several nights they stayed in private homes, and only once did they stay in a hotel. Nine days after they left, they arrived home, driving 352 miles on the last day.

In 1928, when May and Elmo traveled west in a new Chevrolet, May kept extensive notes in a small notebook. Most days they drove between 250 and 300 miles, camping in tourist camps before sunset, rising early to leave camp by 6:00 or 6:30 AM and then stopping for breakfast (and perhaps a shave for Elmo) in a town along the way. They left home on September 4 and returned September 20, logging 3,349 miles in total.

May described the scenery, the crops in the fields, the conditions of the farms, the quality of the roads, and the attractions along the way. The roads were mostly good—cement and gravel; she noted only two punctures along the way and no other car trouble. The scenery was beautiful and hilly through Galena, Illinois, and Dubuque, Iowa; the towns were perched high on the hills. Some of the farms in northern Iowa had rocks and boulders sticking up through the fields, and May noted "few tractors at work & many farm horses on roads." The conditions were drier than at home, and some corn showed hail damage. As they enter South Dakota, some farmers were fall plowing, "mostly with horses, 5 or 6 to plow." Later, after another day's drive through South Dakota, May wrote, "Country grows poorer, dryer, & windyer as we go on. Around Reliance (elevation 1780 ft) they cut corn with binder & rake with hay rake. It isn't but about 2 or 3 feet high, no ears visible, . . . immense fields all burned brown." That day they drove 327 miles, reaching Rapid City around dark, after seeing some of the Badlands. May wrote, "For nearly all day we have driven over hill & vale with roads stretching ahead as far as the eye can see."

During the next day they drove through the Black Hills, and May noted the beautiful colored rocks and the "spruce, birch, oak, and cedar trees." They saw the early stages of construction of Mt. Rushmore National Memorial. Elmo visited the Hidden City and Wind Cave while May waited. ("He enjoyed that greatly.") The scenery as they drove in the afternoon was "grand." They camped that evening near Hot Springs, South Dakota, on top of a mountain, "in *midair* in a cabin." Still the farms were not like those at home. Commenting on the country south of Hot Springs, May wrote, "Very few decent farm buildings did we see, mostly lonely cabins, with what machinery they had standing out." When they reached Denver, Elmo visited the capitol building and a museum, and May waited in the car, parked by the Capitol. She noted the irrigated lands around Greeley, Colorado, and the "fine crops of potatoes, alfalfa, beans, and sugar beets." On the road to Denver, she noted "many trucks loaded with vegetables . . . also a good many loads drawn by horses."

From Colorado, they headed toward Wichita, Kansas, where they would stay several days with May's cousins. Eastern Colorado was "rather desolate country" with "lots of rattlesnakes." After entering Kansas, they "pick up two Arkansas boys," who "rode standing on running board." They spent the next four days in Wichita before heading back through Salina, Kansas, where they looked up a cousin of Elmo's.

The trip home took them through eastern Kansas, Missouri, and central Illinois. Elmo took pictures of the monument to the World War I soldiers near Ft. Dodge, and May noted the good corn through central and eastern Kansas and "wonderful potato crops near Topeka." The next morning they visited the University of Kansas campus, near Lawrence, and went on to Kansas City—"a nice city, fine buildings and broad clean streets" (unlike Denver, which May found to be "a busy, smoky city, not pleasant to drive through"). Missouri was "the prettiest state yet, hills, creeks, woods & rocks." May also noted several fine herds of cattle in Missouri. When they reached St. Louis, they visited the zoo. Before heading home, they visited Springfield, Illinois, including the Lincoln statue in front of the capitol building and Lincoln's tomb. May wrote, "Over 6 times as many visitors at tomb in 1927 as in 1907."

Obviously, May and Elmo were not the only ones traveling during the 1920s. The country experienced a virtual explosion in the tourist industries, and tourist camps and cabin camps popped up along all the major highways. Many of those traveling were farmers. A survey of motor vehicles entering Yellowstone National Park in 1926 showed that farmers outranked any other profession by more than two to one. Overall, recreation spending tripled during the decade, although much of the spending went to movies, sports, and amusement parks.[21]

Radio Days

Along with automobiles, movies, and other forms of middle-class recreation, radio changed American culture in the 1920s. May rarely mentioned movies in the 1920s, but radio caught on quickly in Guilford. Returns of the November 4, 1920, presidential election made for the first commercial radio broadcast in the United States. Those who listened learned that Warren G. Harding would be the next president, hours before newspapers delivered the news. By 1924, 2.5 million radios appeared in American homes and businesses; by 1928, there were three times that many. Rockford was home to an early radio station; KFLV operated from a church on ten watts, beginning in October 1923.[22] Guilford farmers soon tuned in.

Charley Kleckner had the first radio mentioned in May's diaries, in January 1923. A week later both she and Elmo spent a Sunday afternoon with Charley and Mary, listening to a Chicago church service on the "radiophone." Soon several other neighbors had radios. Elmo dropped May at the Shaw's to listen to President Coolidge in April 1924. At the end of November 1924, May and Elmo put in a new radio as an early Christmas present for May. (The radio cost $166.)

For May, radio was a welcome alternative to reading books when she was home and Elmo was out working or away on errands. But May's library continued to grow and add bookcases through the 1920s. When May recorded the Christmas presents that she and Elmo gave to each other, several books were always included. They still spent winter Sundays at home reading together. Frequently they loaned books to or borrowed them from neighbors and family.

RURAL LIFE

The cultural transformations of the 1920s created sharp distinctions between rural and urban life, but as this happened, rural institutions became more vibrant. Across Winnebago County, young people found social life at Grange gatherings; and the Farm Bureau revitalized agricultural extension activities. As always, schools and family took central roles in rural life.

Grange and Farm Bureau

When Guilford Hope Grange celebrated fifty years of activity in 1921, the Grange was stepping into the spotlight on the rural social scene. Membership grew, new granges were organized, and a variety of events such as dances, plays, socials, Halloween parties, and picnics, besides regular meetings, added fun to rural life. The new Perryville Grange, for example, hosted dances in the 1920s to pay for Perryville's newly built hall. South Guilford Grange also organized in the 1920s. Although May and Elmo attended social events, they didn't join the Grange until 1927, when the whole neighborhood was involved.

The Grangers met every two weeks, either at the town hall or at the home of one of the member families. The meetings featured music and recitations in addition to various committee reports. Although both men and women attended the formal meetings, children were not allowed. They were banished to the upstairs or the back porch, and the mischief they made while there provided happy memories in later years. So did the ice cream and crackers served after the meetings were over.[23]

The Burritt Grange hosted the largest grange picnic in the area. The Trask Bridge Picnic, sponsored by the Burritt Grange, was first held in August 1911, in the township just northwest of Rockford. The first picnic attracted a thousand people, and from that point it grew much larger. As 4-H clubs took off in the 1920s, this picnic became the site for both 4-H kids and Grange members to exhibit projects. Political candidates came to announce their candidacy.[24] May and Elmo first attended the picnic in 1921, and thereafter, during the 1920s, if both of them did not attend the picnic, Elmo usually caught it on his own. The Trask Bridge Picnic replaced trips to most other fairs. Elmo went to the Boone County Fair twice during the decade and only once to the Elkhorn Fair. Not since the Golden Age had he been to a state fair.

Perhaps the most impressive thing about the new Winnebago County Farm Bureau was how quickly the men organized themselves. The new organization evolved from the local Farm Improvement Association, established in 1913. The formation of the national American Farm Bureau Federation in late 1919 was the direct impetus for change in Winnebago County. Before the first formal meeting on June 12, 1920, when officers were elected, Frank Reid came to get Elmo to join. Both Elmo and Fred Davis paid fifteen dollars for three years of dues on that same day. Membership as of the first formal meeting was 947 farmers. In August, the group hired the farm adviser for the county extension service.[25]

The emergence of the Farm Bureau coincided with the precipitous drop in farm prices, and almost immediately, the Farm Bureau Federation became a major national voice for farmers. Care was taken to preserve the educational nature of the relationship between the farm adviser and the local branches of the Farm Bureau, but politics was often on the minds of both farmers and farm advisers. From the beginning, the Farm Bureau attracted educated, commercial farmers, who were interested in the services that farm advisers could provide. In Winnebago County, this included most everybody.

Elmo attended formal Farm Bureau meetings only once or twice a year. Beyond advocating for better roads, the Winnebago Farm Bureau also promoted the use of hog cholera serum and the testing of cows for tuberculosis. An insurance company was formed, and at the end of the decade, a committee looked into the establishment of a farm supply oil business.

Home Bureau, the female counterpart of the Farm Bureau, was not organized in Winnebago County until the late 1930s, but the Guilford Gleaners women's auxiliary was still going strong. The Gleaners provided assistance to victims of the floods that devastated the lower Mississippi River Basin in April 1927 and, closer to home, to the victims of the tornado that struck the southeast side of Rockford in September 1928.[26]

Bell School

Bell School remained a pillar of rural life in the northeast corner of Guilford Township, and a few improvements were made to the old one-room schoolhouse, built back in 1869. Starr and his neighbor, Mr. Seele, built a shed at the school in late 1922, and in 1929, May and Elmo stopped by to check the progress on a new garage. In 1928, the schoolhouse boasted modern septic toilets ("which did not always work so well"), but the building was still lit by two gasoline lamps and heated by a large stove in the corner. Within a few years a new bubbler replaced the pail and dipper that the children drank from throughout the 1920s.[27]

The yearly Christmas entertainment, school social, sporting competitions, and school picnics were among the events that May and Elmo either attended or kept track of. As the 1920s progressed, most of Starr's children moved up through the grades and on. Schoolchildren and neighbors continued to drop in after school to visit with May, and she and Elmo both remained active in school administration. May was elected secretary when the PTA was first organized in 1926.

Family Life Moves On

After May's mother died in July 1921, few family events caused major ripples in the lives of Elmo and May; family life marched forward at a measured pace. The young people in the family grew into adults. Many loved ones died—aunts, uncles, cousins, and neighbors. Holiday celebrations fell into regular patterns: New Year's Day was celebrated at Starr's, and May and Elmo hosted Thanksgiving for all of Starr's family. (Annetta would come early and stay all day to help with the meal.) On Christmas Day, May and Elmo joined Florence and Ed Fitch and their family. May also corresponded regularly with many relatives, including her cousins, Kate and Puss, in Wichita, and Elmo's sister, May Purdy, now in Tacoma, Washington.

Starr's boys were all doing farmwork throughout the decade. Joe was the first to marry, after beginning to farm his grandparents' farm in 1925, when he finished his agriculture schooling in Madison. The Lyford boys, like many area farmers, did not attend high school, preferring to advance their vocational training on the farm. Brown's Business College, in Rockford, provided another alternative, like the agriculture school in Madison, to further professional education without the time commitment of high school classes. By September 1929, Walter (Starr's second son) was investing in his own farming equipment; Elmo went with him to buy an old corn binder from Mat Ralston. Stanley was the youngest boy; he turned fourteen in 1929. All of the boys worked with Elmo occasionally, when an extra hand was needed. Usually they worked on their home place and the new "north farm," and other times, they were up the lane, helping Joe.

Annetta and Emily Lyford, however, both attended high school. Annetta graduated from high school in 1924 and then entered training in the fall to become a nurse. In June 1929, Annetta was working on her first private case. Emily began high school in 1926. Annetta, in particular, often stopped by to see May and Elmo. She brought flowers or berries or perhaps a rose bush from Aunt Alice's garden in Rockford. Occasionally Annetta and Emily worked for May and Elmo, especially when they had threshers to feed. Frequently, when May and Elmo were out for a drive, the girls came along.

Most of the Fitch children were college bound in the 1920s, and so was Marion Whittle. Marion went on to get her master's degree in home economics. Mabel Fitch was already in college in 1919 and 1920, when she worked summers for May. According to May's notes, Mabel graduated in 1926, presumably with an advanced degree. Elsie Fitch entered Rockford College as a freshman in 1922 and later attended the University of Iowa.

Fred Davis farmed as a bachelor throughout the 1920s. He stopped by regularly to see May and Elmo, and they stopped in frequently on the way to Cherry Valley, perhaps with a pumpkin pie or some such. Sometimes Elmo went down to pick apples or crabapples with Fred, or Beulah canned plums for him. Fred borrowed Elmo's buzz saw on a regular basis, and Elmo borrowed Fred's lime rock spreader and his cement mixer. And when other cousins were in town, they got together. After May Purdy's husband died in Tacoma in September 1928, Fred went out west to visit.

Both Elmo and May enjoyed generally good health during the decade, although May had more trouble with her eyes. She left short gaps in her diaries in 1925 and 1927 when she couldn't use her eyes to write. She also had numerous teeth taken out and had them replaced at the dentist's. In 1922, May weighed eighty-eight pounds, but her weight fell to only seventy-seven pounds in 1929. At that time, Elmo weighed two hundred pounds, and they were both fifty-six years old.

BOOM AND BUST IN 1929

By early 1929, the business prosperity of the 1920s had begun to run amok. A speculative bubble inflated on Wall Street in 1928 and 1929, after years of solid gains for stockholders. At the same time, a variety of weaknesses lurked in the shadows of an economy that was still surging forward. Business prosperity in the 1920s was real enough but not so evenly distributed. Although wages rose, they failed to keep pace with the increased profits of industrialists. Those at the top with money to spare turned increasingly to speculation on stocks. As the market soared in 1928 and 1929, so did the demand for brokers' loans; brokers loaned money to their customers to purchase stocks on the margin. Many ordinary people of moderate means were thus enticed into the market.

Meanwhile, the overall economy was beginning to falter. Agriculture had lagged since the decade began, and farmland values were still falling. May and Elmo now drove only one car, a Chevy, instead of both a Buick Six and a Ford. Other farmers also considered capital expenses carefully. The building boom earlier in the decade had resulted in oversupply, and the market for cars was also nearing saturation. Many consumers had been buying on credit, but the spending spree could not continue indefinitely.

For most of 1929, however, the stock market soared and the mood of the country was exuberant. The increase in wealth, occasioned by the boom in stocks, produced another spurt in consumer spending. When the stock market peaked in early September 1929, May and Elmo were planning to add a modern bathroom to their house. In early August, May had mentioned that the Whittles were fixing up their house ("ready for polishing woodwork"). On September 3, Florence and Ed Fitch were also "all torn up fixing house." When Elmo and the mason laid the foundation for the bathroom addition in the second week of September, stocks had already begun to wobble.

The new bathroom would have a modern septic system and hot running water. Up to this point, few comments described water systems or plumbing in the house. When May and Elmo were married, a sink and a new pump were put in to provide pumped water in the kitchen at least. There were two wells on the farm: a "house well" and a "stock well" (the latter near the barn, for livestock). Both wells had pumps. In addition, a cistern collected rainwater for washing, and the cistern had a pump. (Once in 1915 a mouse got stuck in the pipe to the cistern pump. Despite his efforts, Elmo could not get it out, and they could pump no water for almost two months.)

May never mentioned an outhouse or chamber pots in her diaries, but these were surely the technologies in use on the farm until the fall of 1929.

Before the twentieth century dawned, towns like Rockford had municipal water systems, and inexpensive sanitary fixtures were available for urban homes. Few farmers, however, had yet gone to the trouble and expense of installing septic tanks. In 1919, only about a quarter of midwestern farmers had running water in their homes, and some 90 percent used outdoor privies.[28]

Throughout mid-September and early October, the stock market drifted downward while Elmo and his cousin Thad Davis worked on the addition for the bathroom. The hired man dug the hole for the new septic tank and later helped with some painting and wallpapering. On September 25 (May's birthday), the plumber brought out the new bath fixtures. By early October, all the digging was finished and the septic tile was laid. May used one of her rare exclamation points on October 15 to describe the progress: "Men think water system is finished and turn on water at night. Flood bathroom!" But after some additional work on the system the next day, everything seemed to be in working order. (Out-of-pocket expenses for the bath and remodeling came to $586.)

Despite the downward drift in stocks, brokers' loans were still strong on Wall Street, and optimism maintained an upper hand until the week beginning October 21. That Monday, the ticker tape fell behind for the first time amid heavy volume, and people began selling, not knowing how fast prices were falling. As stock prices fell during the week, brokerage clients, who had borrowed money to buy shares, were forced to sell to meet margin requirements. The first big rout came on October 24, Black Thursday. The market bounced back on Friday, but Monday was another down day; the Dow lost 13 percent of its value early in the day. On Tuesday morning, October 29, sellers jammed brokerage houses all across America. They dumped sixteen million shares that day and sent some stocks down 50 percent from September highs.

May did not mention the stock market troubles, although she had recorded dividends on bank stock throughout the 1920s. She and Elmo had weathered financial panics. The Panic of 1907 disturbed the farm sector little. The Panic of 1893 and the depression that followed had been the worst in their memory and the worst of that century. The year they were both born, 1873, was also a year of financial panic.

The stock market recovered substantial ground on October 30 but later fell to a new low by mid-November, giving up most all the gains of the previous two years. About that time, Elmo was finishing husking corn by hand, without hired help. Meanwhile, industrial production and residential construction both fell sharply as the year ended.

CHAPTER 5

DEPRESSION, DROUGHT, AND THE NEXT GENERATION 1930–1934

The economy tumbled downward, picking up speed as it fell. On the farm, the Depression was compounded by drought, which gripped much of the East and the Midwest in 1930 and then intensified as it moved farther west. The drought peaked in Illinois in 1934, with huge crop losses.

For the most part, however, on the farm was a better place to be than on the street. Despite plunging farm prices and worsening drought, people on midwestern farms had food to eat and work to do. Although nearly a million farmers across the country lost their farms to foreclosure in the early 1930s, these farmers were in the minority. Even those who suffered foreclosure often continued farming the same land as tenants.[1] Most farmers carried only light debts or none at all and had little fear of losing their livelihoods or their homes in these uncertain times. The populace in the 1920s had fled farms and streamed into cities; Rockford grew by more than 30 percent. But during the decade of the 1930s, the population of Rockford actually shrank while farms and rural areas welcomed hard-up family and friends.

The feeling of normalcy that had pervaded May's diaries through most of the 1920s was gone in the 1930s. Around every corner was something unexpected. Banks failed, dust blew, floods raged, and crops failed. Tragedy struck in May and Elmo's family and in the neighborhood. Other surprises were joyful ones: at every turn, another of Starr's children was either getting married or having a baby, and Fred Davis also married in 1932.

1930, THE ECONOMY SPUTTERS AND CROPS WITHER

In the early months of 1930, few imagined that the country was headed into a long period of deep recession. For farmers who had already endured economic trials in the 1920s, the problems of the Wall Street speculators were unlikely to elicit either sympathy or fear. President Hoover and business leaders spoke confidently of the future, and the stock market staged an impressive recovery. But as the year progressed, the anticipated recovery was always around the next corner, and over the summer a drought parched many areas of the country.

The Stock Market Recovers

Optimism was the order of the day when the year began, even if the undertone was decidedly cautious. Consumers cut back on spending, business was off, and so was employment, but things would get better. January and February might be dark and dreary, but spring would come. During the first three months of the year, some stocks recovered more than half of their losses.

Guilford farmers were moving forward. In early January, the "Farm Bureau farmers are looking at cattle." A week or so later, Elmo went into Chicago at the invitation of a farm equipment dealer. Joe and Marian Lyford were modernizing their farm with a new milking machine that ran on power from the Delco plant, and Marian also had a new electric iron.[2]

Transportation was still improving, roads and airports in particular. When Elmo went into Chicago, the concrete road was not even slippery, although the roads in Rockford were. ("Cement worn bare by traffic.") May remarked on other concrete roads newly built in the county and noted that the snowplows were doing a good job that winter. In early March, airmail began arriving through the Rockford airport.

Delivery trucks were saving farmers the trouble of driving into town. A "Perryville man" delivered coal in mid-February. The "oil truck" came around in the spring with gasoline for the truck and car and kerosene (as well as gasoline) for the tractor. The Jaeger Bakery truck came for the first time in mid-March.

Various distractions brightened the winter months, including Grange meetings, Gleaners auxiliary meetings, and Mother and Daughter Club meetings. Joe and Marian stopped over regularly. May and Elmo were also on a kick with the card game "500" that began with a game at Starr's on New Year's Day.

May and Elmo made no spending adjustments on account of the financial slump, but, for the most part, they continued to live frugally. Beulah had worked year-round in the early 1920s; now she was coming about once a week to help May, at two dollars per visit. (Additional payments for wash were recorded every two weeks.) This was no different, however, from the situation in 1929.

For May and Elmo, the gap between total expenses and farm income over the last three years had been large; forty-four hundred dollars of interest income had helped cover their expenses. There was no farming surplus in 1929 to cover the water system or May's hired girl. The interest and dividend income on their lifetime savings amounted to $863 in 1929, and May's interest income on her inheritance came to $678. The returns on this capital exceeded farming profits for 1929,[3] allowing them the luxury of hot water and indoor plumbing while still living within their means.

So despite the uncertain outlook, Elmo went to an auto show on March 20 and came home with a new Chevrolet Coach. (He received $325 on the 1928 Chevy he traded in and paid an additional $326 for the new model.) And come Sunday, May and Elmo took the new car up to Durand to call on the Campbell cousins.

Warm Winds Blow and Prices Fall

Spring arrived on schedule in early April. The ground was still too frozen to work on March 29, when Elmo's new pulverizer, designed for tractor use, was delivered. On April 3, he began to work the ground and sow the oats.

The promised economic recovery, on the other hand, was nowhere in sight. Producers had cut production, and commodity prices were falling. The stock market began to drop sharply in April, and by the end of June it was testing the November lows. May noted that a "tramp" came by in early April; later that month, the Jaeger Bakery truck was no longer making rounds. On June 9, a man came by looking for work.

Elmo did the spring fieldwork himself. When he planted corn in mid-May, he had a new fertilizer attachment on the corn planter, and May recorded purchases of fertilizer for the first time. The chemical fertilizer didn't replace manure, however; Elmo had already spread many loads in April.

The steady help situation was similar to last year. Mabel Fitch began work in mid-May, and George Minet started work in the third week of June. George had worked two months the previous summer at the same rate, thirty-five dollars a month with board. This year he started two weeks earlier and finished up again at the end of August. Mabel worked this summer at seven dollars per week and stayed on through mid-September.

Although wages were stable, cattle prices were down from last year. Joe sold cattle on May 16 for $11.25 per hundredweight. Then when Elmo took cattle into Chicago on May 20, the cattle sold at only $10.00 per hundred-weight. Cattle had brought $13.10 per hundredweight in 1929.

By early June, it was dry and dusty, warm and windy; much of the country, especially in the East and the Midwest, faced drought that summer. Winnebago County was north of the worst area of drought. Rains were scarce in May, but June brought welcome rains. The heat arrived in mid-July with only a little break before it continued, even hotter, through the first week of August.

The lack of rain through much of August helped to speed the threshing along, and crop yields were not severely affected that year in Winnebago and Boone counties. More rains arrived in September to help the corn.[4] Even so, Elmo would buy $61.67 worth of ear corn the next year when he ran out and still needed feed for livestock.

Other troubles matched the drought and falling farm prices that spring and summer. Various family members had health problems, and May's aunt Augusta died. But those seasons brought pleasures too. Joe and Marian were expecting a baby. May was pleased when the lilacs and the pansies bloomed in May and when Elmo found kittens in the barn in June. She and Elmo attended barn dances at the Seeles' in early June and hosted a Grange meeting in July. In August, as usual, the canning, threshing, and feeding of the threshers captured attention on the farm.

New Life, Smallpox, and Late Summer Travels

Smallpox struck in late August. Marian was in the hospital after giving birth to a daughter, and, over several days, Joe took meals with May and Elmo and May noted that he wasn't feeling well. Finally, Joe was "all broken out," and the next day, "Dr. pronounce Joe has smallpox." Then a quarantine sign went up at Joe's, Elmo and May went to get vaccinated, and Joe's hired man came to board with them. Soon Walter Lyford was also diagnosed with smallpox, and he stayed with Joe under quarantine. Two weeks later Joe and Walter were pronounced well, and the quarantine sign came down the next day, but before Marian and the baby could come home, the house underwent a flurry of cleaning and scrubbing.

Joe and Marian had scarcely settled back home when May, Elmo, and Annetta took the new Chevrolet out to Wichita, Kansas, to visit May's cousins. They left for Kansas in the early morning of September 22, drove most of the way through Iowa, and then spent the night in a private home in Carroll. The drought was worse in Iowa than in northern Illinois. May wrote, "Very dry, especially in center & western part. Lawns & pastures brown. Corn nearly all dead from drought. Much of it not well eared. Almost no tractors on farms, or trucks. . . . Hot wind." The next day they turned south and drove through Nebraska and Kansas, logging 395 miles; they stayed overnight with Davis cousins in Salina, Kansas. Of that day's travels, May wrote, "Not quite so hot, but very windy. Southern Nebraska & northern Kansas not as dry."

After arriving in Wichita, they witnessed a strange windstorm on September 25. May described the day: "Hot AM & most of PM. Thermometer drop 41° in late PM & eve. Awful wind & sand storm." Later that night, Elmo caught the train to Tacoma, Washington, to visit his sister and niece, while May and Annetta remained with their Kansas relatives. When Elmo returned on October 5, they traveled back to Illinois, driving through the Ozarks, St. Louis, and on to Springfield, where Annetta and Elmo toured the Lincoln home and the capitol.

The Economy Slumps Further

By late October 1930, the dismal economic news was becoming harder to ignore, with the numbers of unemployed spiraling upward. Before the 1929 crash, only 3.2 percent of the labor force lacked work, with about 1.5 million people looking for jobs. By the end of 1929, twice as many were unemployed, and the numbers of jobless doubled again before the end of 1930. One reason was clear: industrial production was plummeting. By the end of 1930, the index of industrial production was down 35 percent from the peak in mid-1929.[5]

Like the economies of other industrial cities, Rockford's economy began to crumble. The total value of residential building permits was 60 percent lower in 1930 than in 1929. Late in 1930, a county-organized work program that employed people to work on county buildings and roads began to supplement direct relief provided locally by the Rockford Public Welfare Association.[6] Many who were unemployed left town in search of opportunities elsewhere.

Area farmers also felt the effects as farm prices dropped precipitously throughout the year. The wheat farms of the plains were not affected by the drought, and a bumper crop sent wheat prices to the lowest levels in thirty years. World wheat markets were also glutted, so large grain purchases by the newly established federal Farm Board failed to slow the price decline. Even though the corn crop was reduced by more than 20 percent, corn prices fell, and livestock prices were down sharply. Over the course of 1930, the prices of farm products in aggregate fell by about 30 percent.[7]

Bank failures increased dramatically late in 1930 and grabbed national headlines. These failures had been high in the 1920s, particularly among small banks in rural areas; almost 7,000 banks failed during the decade. In 1930, however, 1,345 banks failed, and 564 of these failed in November and December alone. Among them was the prestigious Bank of the United States in New York City.[8]

The banks that remained solvent struggled to shore up their financial positions by calling in loans and restricting lending. Farmers who were heavily in debt had trouble getting bank loans renewed; whether their collateral was land or crops, the value of it was tumbling. Most farm loans were short-term; even mortgages, at the time, were not more than three to five years in duration. Under normal circumstances the loans would have been renewed, but at the end of 1930, banks were increasingly jittery.[9] Just before Thanksgiving, Joe's bank refused to renew his note for six hundred dollars; he sold a boar and six sows to help generate cash.

Other farmers in Guilford were also short on cash. Joe's hired man was having trouble getting back wages owed from the tenant farming Bert Shaw's farm, and Joe was helping him handle the lawsuit. The tenant farmer couldn't come up with the cash, so in early December, Elmo went with Joe, his hired man, and the constable to the Shaw farm to retrieve some payment in kind. Then before Christmas, Joe hosted a sale so his hired man could sell the chickens, grain, and machinery confiscated in payment for the back wages.

The Hawley–Smoot Tariff Act, signed into law over the summer, hadn't done farmers, or the world economy, any good either—just the opposite. Ironically, the bill began with the intent to help farmers, but major industrialists all jumped on board, seeking tariff protection for their goods. The result was a bill bad for all, and bad for farmers in particular. Even though over a thousand leading U.S. economists signed a letter to the president requesting his veto, Hoover approved the bill in mid-July. With world demand for U.S. agricultural products already waning, the tariff act increased the price of imported goods and provoked swift retaliation from trade partners. The net result was a sharp decline in world trade, exacerbating the world depression in general and the situation for farm exports in particular.[10]

Still, by and large, the mounting economic woes of the world had yet to dampen spirits in the Guilford community. The Guilford Hope Grange held the traditional Halloween party on October 31, with an orchestra to keep things lively. Bell School hosted a Halloween social the same week. May and Elmo attended both functions, and they also went to the play (*The Empty House*) that the Grange performed. The Grange earned more than $140 in profit from four performances.[11]

The Lyford holidays were especially joyful this year with both the new baby and a newly married couple. Thanksgiving was at May and Elmo's as usual. When Joe and Marian hosted Christmas Eve, many presents were exchanged. They still had the tree decorated with electric lights, put up to host the recent Grange Christmas party for more than seventy people.

1931–1932, the Tumble Downward

Although spirits in Guilford may have resisted the economic gloom, by early 1931 there was no question that times had changed. The decade of prosperity had ended, and the 1930s were turning out to be not at all what the 1920s had promised. The headlong plunge of the economy accelerated through 1931 and 1932. Drought moved deeper into the country's heartland, damaging crops and threatening groundwater levels in many areas. And, although most residents of Winnebago County remained patient with President Hoover throughout these trials, when offered a choice in November 1932, voters across the country asked for new leadership.

Despite the ferocity of the economic crisis, however, it did not overwhelm life. By the end of 1932, almost 25 percent of the nation's workforce was unemployed, but 75 percent had jobs, although they were earning less than previously. Most who lived through these years were at least as likely to remember the kidnapping of the Lindbergh baby in March 1932 as they were to remember the bank failures. Despite drought through much of the country, in northern Illinois, well-timed rains brought crops to fruition and reminded farmers of nature's resilience.

Changing Times

By early 1931, women's fashions signaled profound changes afoot and were making the best of the generally dire turn of events. Hem lengths had begun to drop with the stock market at the end of 1929. Eveningwear swept the floor in 1931, and daytime dresses were dropping well below the knee again. Moreover, the waistline had moved back up to its proper place, and boyish figures lost their charm. Femininity and curves were back, even as fashion magazines discussed the "return to statelier morals and manners."[12] In early January 1931, May went to see Belle Davis (Elmo's cousin by marriage) about "making my new green dress." She stopped again in two weeks to have the dress fitted, and before the end of the month, it was ready. Although Belle had been sewing for May for several years now, this dress caused a hint of excitement not present in earlier mentions of clothing. Women of May's generation must have been particularly pleased to see styles change at this time.

National sentiment was also turning sharply against prohibition. The issue ranked top among concerns of the day, far above unemployment. A government report released in January concluded that the noble experiment had failed to control the abuse of alcohol and that its primary effects had been to enrich the underworld, corrupt police forces, and diminish respect for the law. Proponents of repeal of the Eighteenth Amendment pointed to the opportunities for tax revenue that legalization could bring.

Cities had suddenly lost their allure. No longer the place to be, cities were where millions of workers were being laid off. For the first time since 1921, the U.S. farm population increased in 1931, by about 300,000 people. Farms absorbed another 1.5 million people over the next two years, before the tide turned the other way again.

A cousin, Walter Seele, moved in with the Guilford Seeles during the summer of 1932 and worked for Joe and Marian throughout August. He husked corn for Elmo in November. Over the course of the decade, however, population grew more in small towns than anywhere else. While the population as a whole increased about 7 percent, the rural nonfarm and small village population increased by 14 percent.[13] During the 1930s as workers were laid off, the population of Rockford fell by more than 1 percent. On the other hand, the Cherry Valley suburbs grew when Fred Davis began to build houses along some of the road frontage of his farm. May first mentioned Fred's houses in mid-February 1931, but Fred started work on one house at least as early as the summer of 1930. Invoices for building materials found in his personal papers mark the date.

At some point before the summer of 1930, Fred decided that the house his parents had built in 1893 could easily serve as two houses. So with the help of a carpenter and perhaps some extra hands, he cut off part of it and moved it across the road and south a ways. It wasn't long before there were other houses. Some he moved from area farms, and others were newly built. They were not grand, but Fred had no trouble renting them. Having sold twenty-eight acres along the Kishwaukee River in 1929, which he'd rented as a "beach resort" since the early 1920s, Fred had some capital to work with.

Before the end of the Depression decade, he had a dozen rental houses.[14] Fred built the houses in part to satisfy a demand for cheaper housing by former Rockford residents; the rural lots were big enough for a garden and a cow. Fred also told the story that he hired a man at the train station to help bring sheep home from the depot. The man turned out to be an out-of-work carpenter, so the houses began. In any case, for almost every year from 1930 to 1941, his papers include invoices for building materials and checks to carpenters.

As times changed, at least one trend of the 1920s continued: the importance of the truck on the transportation scene increased, resulting in the further decline of Chicago's once central role as a livestock market. After almost eighty years of sending livestock to Chicago on the train, Guilford farmers trucked their livestock to Chicago in the spring of 1931. Crowded conditions in Chicago, even before the turn of the century, had encouraged meatpackers to set up plants farther west. But the rail lines to Chicago's stockyards continued to provide advantages to meatpackers there. During the 1930s, however, the output of the stockyards began to decline, and packers increasingly located elsewhere.[15] May noted a severe fire in 1934 that burned at least half of the stockyards, marking the beginning of the end of the Union Stockyards.

For many farmers across the country, the Depression slowed the transition from horses to trucks and cars. As the recession deepened in the early 1930s, the number of trucks and cars on farms in the United States fell,

Life as a bachelor:
self-portrait of
Fred Davis, ca. 1923.

but in 1930 and 1931, the number of trucks on farms was still increasing. In mid-January 1931, Elmo traded his old truck for another used one. (He was credited with $60 for the old truck and paid another $325 for the new used truck.)

Elmo used his new truck several times in 1931 to haul pigs into Elgin, where they were sold. In early July, when he sold thirty steers in Chicago, he hired a trucker from Belvidere to help out. The truckers provided two trucks, Elmo also borrowed a truck from Fred Davis, and he may have used his own truck as well. The truckers finished loading the cattle in the middle of the night, and Elmo drove into Chicago with them. He paid the truckers fifty dollars for the service.

The number of horses on May and Elmo's farm dwindled in the early 1930s. Joe and Elmo often borrowed a team of horses from each other for those relatively few times when extra horses were needed. Elmo sold little hay these days and negligible oats during the 1930s. He also sold a colt in early 1932. Nevertheless, after Charley died in mid-1932, May and Elmo went to a horse sale and bought another horse.

The Banking Crisis and Other Economic Woes

Banks toppled at an evermore alarming rate in 1931, and as they did, depositors withdrew their savings from those that remained solvent, forcing them into more precarious situations. Wave after wave of bank failures struck across the country as the months passed. By the time the avalanche came to rest in 1933, more than nine thousand banks had closed their doors, which was more than a third of the banks in existence at the beginning of 1930.[16]

May first mentioned bank failures when Rockford banks began to fail. On June 15, 1931, she noted that the Manufacturers' and Security banks closed their doors. In fact, three banks closed their doors on that fateful Monday, and they never resumed business. (Both the Manufacturers' National Bank and the Security National Bank had built new buildings during the boom of the 1920s.)[17] Coincidentally, Rockford civic and business leaders had planned a prosperity parade for June 15 to launch a weeklong jubilee to inspire consumers and to celebrate the end of the Depression. The spectacle in town was considerably more than organizers had bargained for. Those who witnessed it long remembered the incongruity of the marching bands and cheerful banners amid desperate groups of depositors gathering around the city's banking institutions. They told of a band playing "I Can't Give You Anything but Love, Baby" as it passed one of the closed banks.

May also noted the failure of two other venerated Rockford financial institutions. The Rockford National Bank, established in 1891, was the biggest
bank in Rockford, relied on by many Rockford businesses. Its building was
increased by four stories to reach eleven stories in 1922. After the stock market crash in 1929, the Rockford National Bank installed eight-foot letters
calling itself "The Big Strong Bank." It failed in February 1932. The Forest
City National Bank failed two months later.

Of the eight banks that existed in Rockford at the beginning of the
decade, only two survived the Great Depression. The Third National Bank,
where May and Elmo did their banking, was one of them. Third National
was established in 1854, and throughout the 1930s, George C. Spafford, son
of the bank's first president, was at the helm. Spafford also helped to steer
the Cherry Valley State Bank through the Depression without failing. Fred
Davis did his banking there.

The banks that failed in Rockford eventually returned a portion of the
deposits to each of the depositors, after they liquidated and sold their buildings. But the immediate repercussions for the local economy were severe.
Even those who were not directly affected by the failures were frightened
and withdrew deposits from other banks or limited their spending. Elmo
purchased a safe within two weeks of the time those first three banks failed.

Throughout 1931 and 1932, the picture was similar across the country and
indeed around the world. Some say that the weakened state of Europe, as a
result of the war, and attempts to maintain the international gold standard
were more important factors in the Great Depression than the U.S. stock
market crash. In any case, international finance was in chaos; many countries, including Britain, were forced to abandon the gold standard by the
end of 1931. But the United States still clung to the standard.

In the meantime, the U.S. economy went down, down, down. Investment fell to almost nothing; indeed, any new investment was overshadowed
by depreciation on existing buildings and equipment. Production fell by
about 30 percent from 1929 to 1932. Prices, wages, and salaries were all
falling too. By 1932, roughly 12.5 million people were out of work, nearly
a quarter of the nation's workforce. May noted "welfare" men cutting brush
along the road in early June 1932. By that time, local relief funds were ex-
hausted, and the State of Illinois was providing funds to county relief
efforts. The Dow Jones average hit bottom in July 1932, after suffering a
90 percent loss of value from the peak in September 1929. Stock dividends
were also drastically reduced.[18] No one escaped the destruction of the economic decline.

On the Farm in 1931 and 1932

Farmers across the country were hard hit as a group; farm prices were still falling further and faster than the prices of all other commodities. While commodity prices overall fell 25 percent from 1930 to 1932, the prices of farm products fell by 45 percent. Although wheat had taken the most dramatic drop from 1929 to 1930, Corn Belt crops now led the plunge. Hog prices were off 62 percent from 1930 to 1932; corn and cattle prices were off 45 percent. During the war, Elmo sold hogs at twenty dollars per hundredweight; in 1932 he sold at less than four dollars. Hog prices and many other farm prices were down to levels not seen since the 1890s. The Farm Board failed at its attempts to support the prices of wheat and cotton and abandoned the effort in 1932.[19]

The low farm prices made it extremely difficult to pay back loans taken when prices were high. Thus, farm foreclosure rates, already high in the 1920s, climbed, while land values dropped further. From an average foreclosure rate of 16.7 per 1,000 farms during the 1926–30 period, farm foreclosures climbed to 28.4 per 1,000 in 1932. The risk of foreclosure was severe but selective; only those farms that were heavily mortgaged were at risk. In the United States as a whole, 42 percent of farms carried mortgages in 1930, and most of those were manageable. Of those farmers who were indebted, about a third had a high ratio of debts to land value and risked default. Those states with the highest percentages of farms mortgaged (55 percent or more) included Iowa, Wisconsin, the Dakotas, and Idaho. Relatively few mortgaged farms were found in the Virginias, Kentucky, and Tennessee. Illinois was closer to the nation's average.[20]

The impact of weather on farming was also selective, and the drought that scorched the East and the Midwest in 1930 was now shifting west. In 1931 and 1932 much of the country was affected by conditions drier than normal. Excessive heat accompanied the drought, and the random arm of nature tagged counties scattered across the map for severe crop losses. In other counties, rains arrived just in time to deliver harvests. The Great Plains, however, were beginning to bake, and by early 1932, small dust storms, like the one May and Elmo saw in Wichita in 1930, were becoming more frequent.[21]

In Guilford, these years brought dry winters and hot summers; the oat yields were light, but the corn was not too bad. Blizzards in March both years added needed moisture. In June 1931, Elmo lost two pigs from the heat, and one of Joe's horses collapsed. Mid-July 1931 held another spell of extreme heat, and in August, May noted that the house well was so low that water could not be pumped into the house. In early November, the cornstalks were too dry for the mechanical corn picker. The next year was drier still, especially in the spring and summer. The corn crop came through all right, but the hot, dry July days made for a short crop of hay.

The drought conditions and low farm prices drove some farmers to desperation and rebellion by mid-1932. The Farmers' Holiday movement was ignited in certain counties of Iowa, good farming counties afflicted by drought and foreclosure.[22] The farmers staged strikes to demand the cost of production for their goods. They hijacked milk trucks and dumped the contents into the ditch. They came to mortgage foreclosure sales with guns and hangman's nooses and turned them into "penny auctions," in which goods were sold to activists and neighbors for pennies, rather than for serious bids, and then were returned to the farmer the next day. Other farmers around the country—in Nebraska, Minnesota, and the Dakotas—emulated these techniques. Such demonstrations attracted attention in the newspapers but involved relatively few farmers.[23] The "sheriff's sale on the Sword farm" that Elmo attended in September 1932 took place as planned. Elmo spent six dollars on a "machine." Despite the conventionality of some of the area's sales, dairymen in Guilford organized in protest. Joe went to milk meetings in the spring and summer of 1932; on June 28 he took the train to Chicago with two hundred other dairymen. But Elmo had refused to sign the petition that Joe circulated a month earlier.

If there was a bright spot in the farming situation of the early 1930s, it was the availability of good help. Especially in late 1931 and 1932, people who used to work for Elmo kept stopping by. If they weren't looking for a job themselves, they likely knew someone who needed one. But May and Elmo were still economizing on help. Elmo often helped with the housework, especially when May's once-a-week help couldn't make it. In April 1931, when Elmo couldn't find help at short notice to spread the lime rock, May drove the horses for him, two days in a row. Those who worked for Elmo and May in the early 1930s included family, close friends, and neighbors. With cheaper help available for corn husking, it was done by hand again.

Willis Seele began working for Elmo in June 1931, at thirty-five dollars a month with board. The Seele farm was across the road from Starr's farm, and Willis grew up with the Lyford boys; he was twenty-one years old in 1931. Last year's boy had also worked for thirty-five dollars a month, but Willis was an experienced farm boy. Farm wages were heading lower with everything else. Across the country on average, farm wages fell 45 percent from

1930 to 1932—the same decline as farm prices.[24] In 1932, Willis worked for thirty dollars a month. Given how much other prices and wages were falling, this wage cut for Willis was more like a raise.

While farm income was much lower, along with dividends and interest income, May and Elmo's financial position remained sound. May received close to $5,000 from Aunt Augusta's estate in 1931, some of it in the form of International Harvester stock. But May kept that money invested, and she and Elmo continued to live within their income. The interest and dividend income that May recorded in the farm accounts fell from $854 in 1930 to $637 in 1932. Gross farm income fell from about $3,000 to just less than $2,000 over the same period. (The latter was the lowest level of farm income since 1909; but in 1909 farm income covered expenses.) Similarly, May and Elmo's total expenses, including hired help, fell from $4,195 in 1930 to $2,830 in 1932. The interest on May's loan to Joe made up for the income shortfall with some to spare.

May and Elmo reacted to the economic crisis by keeping a watchful eye on expenses but nevertheless made some interesting purchases. In 1931, all of May's remaining teeth were removed, and she was fitted with a set of false teeth for two hundred dollars. (The removal of the teeth coincided with the purchase of a new lounge for $12.50, to recline on while putting ice on the jaw.) In addition to the new truck in early 1931, Elmo bought a new manure spreader in 1932 but otherwise invested little in the farm, except for the cattle and pigs he bought to fatten. In late 1931, however, Elmo brought home a load of lumber and two loads of old bricks from the silver plate factory, apparently shut down. Then he and Willis tore down the old milk house and built a tank shed with the old materials. Elmo also gathered up all the old iron in the spring of 1931 and took it into Rockford to trade for three dollars. And he continued to court the farm equipment dealers, attending a "tractor talk" in early 1931 and a "reaper movie" later that spring.

Despite the severity of the farm situation in 1931–32, few went hungry on Illinois farms. May and Elmo still raised chickens and sold eggs, and May also saved eggs in the water glass, as she and her mother had done during the war. From 1929 to 1932, May and Elmo sold no milk or cream; dairy prices were too low. But Elmo still milked for home use. As always, he raised potatoes to last until the new potatoes came, and the garden provided many other fruits and vegetables.

The garden produce received much mention during these years of economic uncertainty. May noted when Elmo set out the cabbages and tomatoes in 1931 and when the first lettuce, onions, and radishes were ready for the table in the spring. There were cherries to pick at the end of June, and the new potatoes were ready shortly thereafter. The first beet greens came in mid-July, and string beans came at the end of the month. By then, apples and blackberries had also appeared. The Kleckners had strawberries to share in 1932, and May and Elmo had grapes both years for friends and neighbors to come and pick. Marian and Joe shared rhubarb and early cherries. In 1931 Mabel canned all sorts of home produce: apples, cherries, pickled beets, jams and jellies, grape juice, tomatoes, green tomato pickles, and forty-three quarts of peaches from two bushels. When packing summer's harvest into jars, it was difficult not to feel blessed, even if farm prices were sinking to levels not seen in more than a generation.

May and Elmo felt relaxed enough about their finances to take road trips in the early fall of both 1931 and 1932, although theft had become a concern. In 1931, they took a week to drive down to Mammoth Cave, in Kentucky, with cousins from Durand. On their return, they drove on through Tennessee and saw Chattanooga before turning toward home. In 1932, May and Elmo made a quick trip to Wichita to see Kate and Puss and their families, returning home within five days. Both years, Willis stayed at the house while they were gone. In 1931, May noted that Elmo crawled in through a window when they arrived home and found everything OK. Never before had May mentioned such security precautions or fears.

Other Things in Life

During these two years when banks failed, farm prices crashed, and the economy crumbled, somehow other things in life provided as much drama and distraction. The joy of having a new baby in the family, just up the lane on the farm where May grew up, must have been for her the most powerful ingredient of these years. Marian and her baby, Joanne, stopped in at least weekly, and May could watch the baby as she grew. On her first birthday in late August 1931, May sent up a cake and presents, including material for a dress and a toy cow. Sometimes Elmo also stopped up with presents—a little pair of rubber boots, for example. May also sewed for Joanne, and just occasionally Marian left the baby with May when she was out. In mid-April 1932, Marian and Joanne brought spring wildflowers to May. Before she was two, Joanne was outside with her father, "helping" care for the pigs and the cows.[25]

Grange activities provided other happy distractions. The Grange participated in the Seventh Street Fall Festival, a Swedish harvest celebration in

Rockford, in both 1931 and 1932. They decorated a storefront window with harvest produce and won first prize in 1931.[26] May used another of her rare exclamation points in 1932 to note how "good!" the Grange play was. There were baseball games between the Grange and the 4-H club at summer picnics. And, of course, the annual Halloween party was a gay affair.

May and Elmo completed thirty years of marriage in 1931, and several things besides May's teeth coming out reminded them that they were growing older. Elmo was quite sick in early 1932. He was so dizzy when he went out to work one day that he fell over. But Annetta and Russell came to help out, and Elmo was better within a few days.

Tragedy struck in July 1932, when Elsie Fitch was killed, at the age of twenty-eight, in a head-on collision with another car. Elmo, in particular, helped Florence and Ed through the aftermath of that, which included a trial postponed several times.

But that summer also held joyful family news. After living as a bachelor for thirteen years after his mother had died, Fred Davis finally married the young postmistress in Cherry Valley, Emma Enders.

Hoover Disappoints and Roosevelt Rises

Not long before Elsie's death, both the Republicans and the Democrats held their party conventions in Chicago. The Republicans had no surprises up their sleeve; they chose President Hoover as their candidate, despite his

Joanne Lyford, 1931.
Courtesy of JoAnne Reid.

role as scapegoat for the dreadful state of the economy. The Democrats had more at stake and several serious contenders for the nomination, but the popular governor from New York, Franklin D. Roosevelt, was the front-runner. When he wrapped up the nomination, Roosevelt broke with tradition to fly to Chicago, accept the nomination, and rally his supporters, promising to give the American people a "new deal."

By the time Fred and Emma were married, the presidential campaign was heating up. Hoover was at a clear disadvantage in several respects. For the last three years he had promised recovery around the corner, only to have things get worse rather than better. The shantytowns that had sprung up along roadsides and in the outskirts of cities—"Hoovervilles"—bore his name; so did "Hoover blankets," the newspapers that homeless people used to keep warm when sleeping on the streets. Whereas Hoover was somewhat shy, soft spoken, and ill at ease on the campaign trail, his opponent was charming and self-assured, a natural leader untarnished by the failed economy. Roosevelt also had the clear advantage on another key issue: the Democratic platform had endorsed the repeal of Prohibition, whereas the Republican platform was murky on that issue. Prohibition was a hot button issue of the day, and by this time most voters favored repeal.

In other respects the party platforms had as many similarities as differences. Both candidates promised to maintain a sound currency. Neither politician was clear on what he would do for the farmer, although both spoke of the need to control crop surpluses. Hoover promoted his firm belief in "rugged individualism" (which some had renamed "ragged individualism"), whereas Roosevelt vowed to help the "forgotten man." Among the ideas that were beginning to form the basis of the New Deal were federal relief, financial reforms, public works programs, unemployment insurance, and generally a shifting of responsibility from the local to the federal level.[27]

After the votes were cast on November 8 and counted the next day, May noted the "sweeping Democratic victory" with some disappointment. Only a few days earlier, President Hoover came through Rockford and spoke from the train; fifty thousand local residents, including Elmo, went to hear him speak. As usual, May and Elmo both voted in the election. Although Hoover lost to a national landslide of electoral votes for Roosevelt, the incumbent carried Winnebago County.[28]

Most voters in Winnebago County shared Hoover's deep respect for the value of self-reliance and voluntary action to solve problems at the local level. The Guilford community was accustomed to taking care of its own. When, in December 1931, disaster befell the Baxter family, the whole neighborhood dropped off clothes and food at Elmo and May's for several months to share with the family. When barns burned, all the men in the neighborhood went to help. But most voters countrywide shared Roosevelt's desire to try something, anything, that might help to get the country back on its feet again. Marian Lyford cast her vote for Hoover, despite the financial problems that she and Joe were facing. She and Joe had also gone to hear Hoover speak, but the crowd was already so large when they arrived that they couldn't get close enough to hear.

By the time of the election, Joe and Marian were running three weeks late with their interest payment to Elmo and May. The pig sale they held on their farm in early November didn't result in the kind of bids they hoped for, so they called it off. But life continued to make demands. At the next Grange meeting, Joe was elected the new master, and Marian also became an officer; they were to go to the state grange meetings in Bloomington in December for three days. Just after Thanksgiving, May recorded the full payment of the interest due from Joe. Marian noted in her diary that day that Aunt May and Elmo came with a shirt and tie for Joe and three dollars for her, to help get ready for their trip to the state grange.

1933, THE DEPRESSION BOTTOMS

The year that Roosevelt took office, 1933, was a pivotal date in history. At the end of 1933, Will Rogers predicted hopefully that historians would label it as "the year of the big switch, from worse to better."[29] In that year, unemployment reached a new high of fully 25 percent of the nation's workforce, and national output reached a new low.[30] The New Deal administration began in the spring with a flurry of activity and a rush of hope, even as the foundation for peace in the world developed serious cracks. During the summer and fall, Americans flocked to Chicago to marvel at the World's Fair.

Waiting for the New Deal

May gave little indication in her diary of the tension building before Roosevelt's inauguration. She noted the books she was reading, including two that she read aloud to Elmo: *Oil!* by Upton Sinclair, and Nordhoff and Hall's *Mutiny on the Bounty.* Elmo went to many farm sales and regularly visited Mat Ralston, who had been sick. May noted when Elmo traded two bushels of potatoes plus one dollar to a magazine agent for a year of the *Saturday Evening Post.* In mid-January, Elmo sold eighteen hogs at only $3.15 per hundredweight—even less than the year before. In early February, May and Elmo began selling cream again; the weekly sales were minor: only one to two dollars worth. Elmo put together a hay deal, however, that was a relative boon. A livestock producer bought fifteen tons of hay for $128, delivered to Roscoe. The price was $8.50 a ton—less than a third of wartime prices.

Across the United States, however, the crumbling banking structure had everyone on edge. Hoover blamed the rising panic on uncertainty over the incoming president and, in particular, whether Roosevelt would stick to the gold standard. If not, well, it might be better to exchange one's dollars for gold now, and Europeans were doing just that. As gold fled the country, panicky Americans continued taking their money out of banks and putting it in safety deposit boxes and other places for safe keeping.

By mid-February the entire banking system was near collapse. Nevada had declared the first banking holiday during the previous October—a twelve-day breathing spell to save some banks from going under. Beginning again in early February, state after state declared a banking holiday. On March 2, ten more states declared bank holidays after six states had done so the day before.[31] That day, Elmo went to see the movie *State Fair,* starring Will Rogers, at the Coronado Theatre in Rockford.

It's difficult to overestimate the impact of Will Rogers in the early 1930s, especially among farmers. Everyone loved him. Raised on a ranch in the Oklahoma Indian Territory, Will Rogers was part Cherokee and all-American. Attracted to rope tricks early on, he joined a Wild West show in South Africa to finance the wanderlust of his youth. When he added jokes to his rope tricks, his career took off on Broadway. By 1920 Rogers was a syndicated humorist. In the early 1930s, he was on the radio, on the lecture circuit, in the new "talkie movies," and in newspapers read by forty million readers. Although much of his humor was at their expense, he counted the nation's top politicians among his friends. He wrote for the popular *Saturday Evening Post,* and his daily one-paragraph column appeared on the front page of the *Rockford Morning Star.*[32]

The warmth and humor of Will Rogers helped displace the pain and uncertainty of the Depression for millions. He confronted the critical issues of the day with wit, compassion, and keen insight into human character. On October 29, 1929, Rogers referred to Wall Street's debacle as "wailing day" and quipped, "There is nothing that hollers as quick and as loud as a gambler. . . . Now they know what the farmer has been up against for eight years."[33] He kidded in the spring of 1930 about women's skirts coming down to cover their knobby knees and then joked about Hoover asking his help in "restoring confidence." ("Course I haven't been buying anything myself. . . . I want to give the other folks a chance to have confidence first. . . . There is none of the Greedy Pig about me.")[34] He voiced people's concern when Japan invaded Manchuria and when the Lindbergh baby was kidnapped. He covered both the Republican and the Democratic conventions in the summer of 1932 and on returning home quipped, "Flew down here to recuperate from one straight month of speeches. Heard a mule braying a while ago out at the farm and for a minute I couldn't tell who he was nominating."[35]

During these first few weeks of 1933, Will Rogers followed the progress of Japan deeper into China and deplored the rise of Hitler in Germany. He poked fun as Congress voted to repeal the Prohibition amendment. And he waited with Americans everywhere to see what kind of leader Roosevelt would be: "Well we are all getting ready for the new deal. We don't know what kind of hand we will get, but we want it even if its just duces."[36]

Finally, Saturday, March 4, arrived—the day of Roosevelt's inauguration. That morning, banks closed in New York and Illinois, the financial strongholds of the country. The collapse of the banking system was virtually complete. May noted the closure of the Illinois banks, which were expected to open within three days. She listened all morning to the inauguration ceremonies over the radio, along with Americans across the country.

The voice of the new leader rang clear and resolute over the radio: "This great nation will endure as it has endured, will revive and will prosper. So, first of all, let me assert my firm belief that the only thing we have to fear is fear itself—nameless, unreasoning, unjustified terror which paralyzes needed efforts to convert retreat into advance." He went on to condemn "the money changers [who] have fled from their high seats in the temple of our civilization," and he promised "action, and action now" to wage war against the economic foe.[37]

These confident words were followed by decisive action the next day. Roosevelt called Congress into special session on Sunday and proclaimed a national bank holiday to allow banks to be examined and the solvent ones to be reopened gradually. He also took the first step away from the gold standard by forbidding dealings in foreign exchange and the export of gold.

The banks remain closed for several days while Elmo hauled hay to Roscoe and attended to other business. May's concern was evident when she noted on March 8, "Banks not open as predicted." On March 9, however, Elmo got into his safety deposit box at the bank. The next morning, with the end of the bank holiday still uncertain, Rockford merchants offered scrip certificates in the newspaper, which could be cut out and used in exchange for merchandise at sale prices. The paper also recorded "a day of tumbling, swift-moving developments such as Washington had not seen since the troubled times of the world war."[38]

The Hundred Days

Roosevelt's confident and inspiring inaugural speech, followed by swift action, went over well in the depression-weary country. On Sunday, March 12, the president spoke again over the radio in the first of many "fireside chats." Clearly and persuasively he explained how the reopening of the banks would proceed and that everyone could do his or her part to help things go smoothly. When the banks began to reopen the next day, deposits exceeded withdrawals. The bank holiday was a success; the panic was over, and hope was restored.[39]

Most administrations begin with a bit of a honeymoon, but in Roosevelt's case, the Congress and the country submitted entirely to his will. Will Rogers put it this way, "The whole country is with him. Even if what he does is wrong they are with him. Just so he does something. If he burned down the Capitol, we would cheer and say, 'Well, we at least got a fire started anyhow.'"[40] Roosevelt took advantage of the moment and pumped an unprecedented mass of legislation through Congress in the "hundred days" between March 9 and June 16. The whirlwind of activity resulted in bills to put people to work, provide emergency relief, reform banking and financial markets, prevent foreclosures on those unable to meet mortgage payments, and authorize "fair trade" codes for business under the National Recovery Administration. The NRA also shortened both the workday and the workweek, to spread employment around, and launched programs to stimulate buying. As Republicans had predicted, Roosevelt abandoned the gold standard in an attempt to inflate the currency, boost the economy, and help debtors pay back loans.

Of course, the legislation also included something for the farmer. Farm credit was reorganized, and provisions were made for refinancing farm mortgages and extending loans. The rate of interest on Land Bank loans was reduced to 4.5 percent. Further, the Agricultural Adjustment Act (AAA) was passed with the intent of raising farm prices by inducing voluntary crop reduction. In the process, the Farm Board, established by Hoover, was abolished and its authority reassigned. Hoover's Reconstruction Finance Corporation, chartered in early 1932, continued to lend money, however, to farmers and other businesses.[41]

In the short run, the result of all these actions was a boom (as businesses raced to produce before the new "fair trade" codes took effect) and a run-up in prices, including farm prices. The index of industrial production rose each month from April to July, and speculators drove up stock prices and commodity prices. Although employment failed to improve, the feeling emerged that a corner had been turned.[42]

On the farm, though, March had been a little slow, marked by Mat Ralston's death, cold temperatures, and quite a bit of snow. Elmo delivered the last loads of hay to Roscoe and shipped fifteen pigs by truck to Elgin to sell at $4 per hundredweight (up from $3.15 in mid-January). Elmo was a pallbearer at Mat's funeral.

The pace picked up substantially in early April. On April 8, a Mr. Smith began working for Elmo two or three days a week, fixing and painting. Mr. and Mrs. Smith had stopped by in mid-February to talk about a mortgage. May and Elmo had put up the money for the loan, but the Smiths were unable to make the mortgage payments, so Mr. Smith began to work off the debt. By early May, a Mr. Olson had joined Smith, and the two of them repaired the barn; then they painted both the barn and the granary.[43]

Of course, the spring fieldwork needed to be done, and Elmo was also called for jury duty. So he ran back and forth among fieldwork, jury duty, and helping with carpentry and painting. He did most of the fieldwork himself, since Willis didn't start again until mid-June. Then to top it off, May and Elmo hosted the April 28 Grange meeting at the town hall. Elmo hadn't been so busy since the frantic war years.

Although life was busy and the house was full of people that spring, it was not too busy to buy a new car. The Chevrolet agents were out at the end of March to "give Elmo a little ride." They returned on May 11, when Elmo was flush with cash, having just sold nineteen steers the day before in Chicago. (The steers sold at only $4.85 per hundredweight but nevertheless generated about $850 in cash.) Elmo parted with $521 and the old Chevy to buy the demonstrator vehicle.

The Heartland Bakes

Even before the Congress of the Hundred Days adjourned on June 16, the temperatures had started to soar in the Midwest and the Plains. While Roosevelt tried everything for the ailing economy, administering "in quick succession all the tonics on the shelf,"[44] nothing in his medicine chest could check the scorching heat or the deepening drought. The hardest hit

areas were farther to the west, in the Dakotas, Kansas, and across the southern plains. The dust storms intensified with dry and windy conditions
during the spring of 1933, but such storms still attracted primarily local
attention.[45]

In Guilford, June 1933 was hotter than any June on record. The wet
month of May had soaked the earth, and it developed a hard crust on top.
On June 20, May wrote, "98° at noon, no sign of rain & oh! So dry & dusty,
though Willis say he turn up moist earth when cultivating." Rain that was
"hardly enough to lay dust" followed the next day.

Late June held several more 100° days, and as a result, the June hay crop
and the yields of small grains were poor. But rains came just in time to help
the corn. Then hard rains came on July 2, damaging the rye ready to harvest. The barley was "very short" that year; when threshed it yielded only
twenty-two bushels per acre. (Good years for barley would be thirty or
thirty-five bushels per acre.) The oats were "poor and short like most grain
this summer" and yielded twenty bushels per acre, about half of the yield of
a typical year. Both temperatures and rainfall moderated in July and August.

If the year was not memorable enough already, another tragedy etched
this threshing season firmly into the collective memory of the community.
On a day in early August, Elmo and the other farmers in his group were
threshing grain at Floyd Ralston's. (Floyd had taken his father's place as a
member.) Floyd had married just the year before, and a healthy baby girl
was born to him and his wife that day. But word came early the next morning that Floyd's wife had died. Threshing stopped until after the funeral.

When threshing was done in the late summer of 1933, many Guilford residents (but not May) flocked to the World's Fair in Chicago. The fair had
opened on May 27 and ran through mid-November that year amid such
success that it returned the following year for an encore. At least a few Guilford residents, including Elmo, Joe, and Marian, went into Chicago more
than once to see the spectacular sights. Elmo and May also took an eleven-
day road trip up through Wisconsin, Michigan, Canada, and to the Adiron-
dacks and then came back through Vermont and Gettysburg, Pennsylvania.
After getting a good start on the corn husking, Elmo went into the World's
Fair again on October 18.

The New Deal Honeymoon Ends

As the leaves began to fall, "Republicans that have been hiding in the trees,"
according to Will Rogers, appeared from the shadows and voiced dissent.

One Republican, Rogers wrote, "climbed right out on a sycamore limb in plain view (brazenly mind you) and started chirping."[46] These comments appeared in Rogers's October 11 column—a date as good as any to mark the end of the New Deal honeymoon. By this time the business boom of the spring was fizzling. The stock market had already taken a dive back in July, and the downward trend in commodity prices, begun at the same time, continued into the latter part of the year. Ever since July, the index of industrial production had been moving steadily lower.[47]

Friction had developed surrounding centerpiece New Deal programs, such as the NRA and the AAA. The business and financial communities, in particular, were losing confidence in the administration. By then, the NRA Blue Eagle symbols appeared in most factory and shop windows in the country. While some lauded the new cooperation between industry and government, others called it state socialism; Henry Ford refused to sign the automobile code.

The AAA had already attracted negative attention in its attempts to limit farm production. In a desperate move to jumpstart the program and lift prices, the AAA began to plow under cotton growing in the fields in August and to slaughter six million young pigs and breeding sows in the month of September. Only a fraction of the pig slaughter was made available for relief food, the rest used only for grease and fertilizer tankage. The papers reported that well-trained southern mules balked at trampling the cotton while pulling the plows to destroy the crop. And the public's outrage at the slaughter of baby pigs, as many went hungry, was no surprise. So far, however, the AAA had failed to relieve much pressure in the Farm Belt.[48]

Back on Bell School Road, May was surprised at the corn yield that year, despite the extreme temperatures and dry weather in June. Nevertheless, gross farm income was even less than in 1932, only $1,699, down from $1,984 the year before. Interest and dividend income, recorded in the farm ledgers, was also down to $378 from a high of $863 in 1929. The lack of the Smith mortgage payments accounted for only part of the difference.

May's income on her personal accounts was down too, since Joe and Marian had fallen behind again on interest payments. The strain on family relationships began to build.[49] On July 3, Joe paid part of the interest that was due in April, and he had been trying, without success, to negotiate a lower interest rate with Elmo. Joe paid the balance of the back interest on October 19, but on that day another payment of $225 was due and was left unpaid. Marian noted that Joe looked into the possibility of a federal loan.

Federal loans now offered rates below the 6 percent he had agreed to when he built his house.

With the corn crop safe in the crib and the house well pumping water again after a dry spell, nature played another wild card in mid-November. It was the first of the storms that became known as the Great Black Blizzards. May noted on November 12, "Cold & middle PM, cloud came up & wind blow dust hard all rest of day and most of night." The cold wind blew the dust all the way from South Dakota, where fierce winds had ravaged farms the day before and left drifting mounds of sand and dust. The storm moved through Chicago and farther east, dropping dust and darkening skies all the way to Albany, New York. Francis Seele came the next day to dust May's books.

1934, Climax to the Farm Crisis

On midwestern farms, the drought dominated 1934. From November 1933 to June 1934, very little moisture fell on Guilford farms. The scene was similar across the country's richest agricultural areas; crop production in the country was cut by about one-third.[50] Ironically, early in 1934, farmers in Guilford signed up for the Corn–Hog Program, one of various programs under the New Deal Agricultural Adjustment Act designed to limit farm production. In the end, it was the drought, not the AAA, that limited farm production. Farm prices rose, however, as the program intended, for those farmers lucky enough to have crops to market.

The drought was not the only event to make it a memorable year. Many recall the year for the midwestern bank robber John Dillinger, who was declared public enemy number 1 by the FBI and gunned down in Chicago. The Cherry Valley State Bank installed bullet-proof glass in the teller's window, and little boys learned to play cops and robbers with cap guns that mimicked machine guns. The shoot-outs between real cops and robbers on city streets continued through the mid-1930s.

Rockford hit a new low in residential building permits in 1934. In 1929, the city had issued 368 residential building permits for buildings with an average value of about forty-three hundred dollars each. Only six permits were issued in 1933 and only two in 1934.[51] Rockford, however, also celebrated its centennial in late May, and the economic depression did not dim its plans for the celebration. It featured a week of parades, pageants, concerts, and sports.

Wedding Plans and Corn–Hog Meetings

Family tensions were mounting in early January. May noted the traditional New Year's Day dinner at Starr's with "all the children & grandchildren home." But Marian noted that Joe and his dad paid a visit to Aunt May, at her request a week later, to discuss the overdue interest. May recorded a partial payment of twenty-five dollars that day.

Starr was worried about Joe and Marian's financial situation and was also concerned about seeing that the rest of his boys were set up in farming. Walter was farming the 172-acre "north farm," and, like Joe, he was surely burdened by debt. Franklin had also recently married, and Russell was planning to wed Marian's sister, Marjorie, on February 24.

Marian was caught up in excitement before her sister's wedding. She hosted an announcement party for Marjorie two weeks before the wedding and was busy varnishing floors and making new curtains before the party. Joanne was to be the flower girl; she and Marian practiced walking slowly with her basket. Of course, there were new dresses for everyone, including a blue silk dress for May. The wedding came off without a hitch. But the unpaid interest on the loan was still causing tension in the background.

Meanwhile, most of the farmers in the neighborhood, including Elmo and Joe, were attending the "Corn–Hog meetings" at the town hall. The first

Marjorie and Russell Lyford, 1934.
Courtesy of Carolyn Wheeler.

meeting was on January 13. Marian noted, "The government is to pay us for raising less corn and hogs. I hope it helps us." Then just days before Russell's wedding, Elmo and Joe each worked on Corn–Hog papers and signed up for the program.

The popular secretary of agriculture, Henry A. Wallace, had announced the program the previous October and encouraged farmers to participate. Wallace's respect among the agricultural community and the pitiful state of hog prices undoubtedly pulled in farmers otherwise skeptical of New Deal programs. Wallace, from Iowa, was an ex-Republican turned New Dealer. His father was secretary of agriculture under Presidents Harding and Coolidge, and he edited the influential *Wallaces' Farmer* magazine.

Because of the critical links of corn and hogs in the marketplace and at the feed trough, their production had to be limited in tandem to improve prices successfully. Instead of selling their corn in the market, producers were to store it on the farm and take out a government loan, at 4 percent interest, for the corn valued at an agreed price above the current market price. Such borrowers also agreed to limit the acreage planted to corn and the number of hogs produced.[52] All across the Corn Belt, county extension agents and committees of farmers held informational and sign-up meetings in January and February. By March 1, seventy-two thousand Illinois farmers had signed contracts.[53]

In mid-March, the loan friction surfaced again in Marian's diary. Marian noted that Joe was about to pay some interest on the loan when Starr came up to advise him not to do so at the 6 percent rate. After some back and forth and some discussions with a lawyer, Elmo agreed to lower the interest rate to 5 percent. But Joe was not yet satisfied; federal Land Bank loans had been reduced to 4.5 percent under the New Deal administration. Marian made only a few more entries in her diary after that point, but the friction over the loan undoubtedly continued throughout the spring and summer. May recorded back interest paid at 5 percent in mid-April; then another overdue payment lingered through the summer.

Hot and Windy, Dry and Dusty

The drought and the dust storms, however, were at the root of much of the tension that farmers felt in 1934. The months of November 1933 through March 1934 bestowed little more than half an inch of precipitation each month. The dust began to blow in mid-February. On March 6, May and Marian each commented on a strong wind, full of dust. By this time, severe dust storms were increasing in frequency in the Great Plains and beginning to cause alarm throughout the country. May noted that the house well was dry by mid-April.

Harry Shipe started working for Elmo in April, and by mid-month the men were pulverizing the dry earth and sowing the oats and barley. Harry began full-time on April 5, at twenty-eight dollars a month. The rate was lower than the thirty dollars per month that Willis had worked for the year before, but Harry had a longer contract; he would work at that same rate through mid-November. May also had a new girl (Beulah Johnson) who would work for her from the end of April to mid-November at three dollars per week, down from the five dollars per week that Mrs. Martell had worked for the year before. Mr. Smith and Mr. Olson painted again this spring but put in far less time than in 1933. The mortgage payments were still running behind.

Harry and Elmo planted the early potatoes, the alfalfa, and the sweet clover before the end of the April, but still there was no rain to speak of, and the temperatures were starting to rise. When George Pepper and Tom Garrett came to appraise the land contracted to the government on May 1, Elmo was putting in the garden and setting out the cabbage plants. A week later, still with no rain, the men were planting corn.

The second Great Black Blizzard blew through Illinois on May 9–10. On May 9 the wind came up and "blow hard, carrying dust in clouds." The next day, "Sun hardly shine all day because of pall of dust through air." It was the worst dust storm since the Armistice Day blizzard in 1933, blowing dust all the way to the East Coast and beyond before it was through.

Elmo and Harry continued to plant corn on May 9 and 10, despite the dust and drought. Rain finally came during the afternoon and evening of May 12, just enough to "lay the dust." The next day was Sunday, and May and Elmo took a drive with Fred and Belle Whittle, noting some areas that had had a bit more rain than their fields had.

The temperature soared again after a few cool days, and warm winds dried out the soil further. On May 20, Rockford began its centennial festivities, but the heat and the dust sent May and Elmo home early. The next day hard winds and dust ushered in a shower by evening, enough to "wet down at least an inch."

After that latest rain, Harry and Elmo began to replant corn in cooler weather, "though not tear up first planting in doing it." Elmo soaked some seed corn to plant in by hand south of the barn. By Memorial Day the temperatures were soaring again. The month of May had had the hottest days on record and had yielded less than three-quarters of an inch of rain for the crops.

June began with a sudden shower in the midst of another very hot day— 106° in the afternoon with blowing dust. "Rain helped but want more." Elmo and Harry were cutting a field of rye to use as hay; then they plowed and replanted the ground with sweet corn and soybeans. Some days May reported a "few drops of rain," and June 8 brought another "good shower" that "wet down over an inch." Elmo and Harry made hay out of a very short crop of alfalfa. On June 18, Elmo sold cattle in Chicago; he went in on the truck with the shippers. Many other farmers were doing the same, for lack of feed and hay. There was a "big run of cattle, so ours not sold when he left."

Finally, on June 20, "a fine shower, rain came down in sheets . . . wet down 6 inches in the field." Elmo went to Rockford for cabbage and tomato plants and seed potatoes. June 22 brought a little more rain in the morning; the men planted potatoes and picked cherries for a cherry pie. The cherries were "small, but good." Elmo and Harry continued planting potatoes the next day "where others not come up," and May noted "lots of corn in neighbor's fields planted early just coming up." Elmo had corn up too, but some fields were full of chinch bugs.

Thereafter, the rainfall was more respectable. Summertime rainfall levels of four to five inches a month are not uncommon in northern Illinois. In 1934 in Rockford, June, July, and August brought 2.5, 3.4, and 2.5 inches, respectively—well below average but gladly received, nevertheless. The temperatures, on the other hand, were well above average in June and July, with high temperatures averaging in the low 90s.

On July 9 and 10, Elmo took advantage of some showery days to plant more soybeans where the chinch bugs had eaten the corn. Elmo was only one of many farmers in the Midwest planting soybeans in 1934 to take advantage of a growing season shortened by drought.[54] Some farmers, like Elmo, would use the soybeans for animal feed, substituting for failed barley and corn, but commercial demand for soybeans was also growing rapidly by this time.

July's hottest weather arrived just as the oats and barley were ready to be cut. The men started cutting what little barley there was on July 18. At first they used the horses, despite the heat, but then switched to the tractor. May recorded 108° by 2:00 PM on July 24. It was on a Sunday in the middle of this hot spell that the notorious Dillinger was gunned down coming out of an air-conditioned Chicago movie theater. May and Elmo spent part of

that day at Rock Cut State Park, reading under a tree, while the temperature soared to 104° in Rockford.

Threshing began in early August. The yields were dismal—by far the
worst May had ever recorded: "oats 14 bu per A, barley 6 bu, and rye 6¼ bu
per A," about one-fourth the usual yield. On the other hand, May was
pleasantly surprised in July with "quite a few apples."

Although drought-related notes fill May's diary, other bits of information
also surface. Beulah Johnson, May's hired girl, was busy with 4-H meetings
and Grange meetings, and Joe and Marian hosted four barn dances over
the summer. When agriculture secretary Wallace was at Camp Grant on a
Sunday in mid-August, May and Elmo went to hear him speak.

Travels, Harvest, and Starr's Stroke

Right after threshing in late August, May and Elmo started out on their
most ambitious road trip thus far, to Tacoma, Washington. They traveled
with Fred and Belle Whittle, to visit May Purdy and Belle's sister, Bertha,
and her family. They logged more than five thousand miles to Tacoma and
back, averaging four hundred to five hundred miles a day when on the road.
May made few notes of the journey, but she did note the "dried up country" through Iowa and South Dakota.

Starr Lyford, ca. 1934.
Courtesy of Sharon Waugh.

The travelers had spent three days in Tacoma when a telegram arrived from Annetta to tell them that Starr had had a stroke. Only a week earlier, Starr had married off his youngest daughter, Emily, to a promising young farmer. With Russell's marriage in February, Starr managed to see all five of his boys set up in farming. During the next several years, the nursing skills of his oldest daughter, Annetta, were put to good use in taking care of her father.

The drought was finally dowsed in November, with almost eight inches of rain coming primarily in the latter half of the month. Heavy snow followed in December. Almost all the crops were affected by the drought that year, although some that were planted late did well. May recorded a "*good* crop" of late potatoes, not enough to sell at harvest, but enough to sell leftover potatoes the next spring. Elmo harvested the dry soybeans to use as feed for cattle during the winter; he and Harry mowed and raked the beans and stacked them in the barn. They also cut dry beans and cornstalks in mid-October for the livestock. The corn yield was diminished throughout the state. Illinois turned out the lowest corn yield since 1901—only twenty-two bushels per acre.

May and Elmo's gross farm income, however, was up somewhat, to $1,919 from the Depression low in 1933 of $1,699, primarily because the cattle brought higher prices in 1934. May and Elmo also received a government check that year for the first time. The first Corn–Hog benefit payment, of $82, arrived on September 20, about nine months later than the AAA program had intended.[55] The issue of the interest rate on the loan to Joe was also finally settled that fall. As of the October payment date, the interest rate was lowered to 4 percent, and the interest was then paid monthly.

With the strain of the drought, the loan difficulties, and the stroke, the year had undoubtedly been exhausting for May and Elmo, for Joe and Marian, and, perhaps most of all, for Starr Lyford. For the first time in many years, May and Elmo even missed the Grange Halloween party. In early December, after the snow had already started to fall, Elmo went to see another Will Rogers movie while May spent the afternoon with Florence Fitch. A few days later, Joe and Marian attended the state grange meeting in Peoria, and then George Pepper came to count pigs for the Corn–Hog Program. Except for holidays undoubtedly rearranged on account of Starr's stroke, the year ended uneventfully.

CHAPTER 6

FITS AND STARTS
IN THE LATE
1930s

W hen the drought ended in 1934, the Depression decade took a
turn for the better in the Guilford community. The Depression
was not over for agriculture, nor was the drought on farms farther west. But, helped along by the drought, the New Deal farm programs,
and slow improvements in the overall economy, farm prices improved.
Although drought and severe crop losses returned to Guilford in the summer of 1936, these events were bounded by wet weather in 1935, 1937, and
1938. Some crops were spoiled in the wet years, but others did well. Guilford farmers, like many farmers across the country, invested in new tractors and machinery in the latter half of the 1930s. Before the decade ended,
they began planting hybrid corn. Still, farm income lagged below farm and
household expenses for May and Elmo throughout the 1930s.

Despite all the efforts of the New Deal, the Depression also lingered in
the country as a whole. Roosevelt launched a second round of New Deal
programs beginning in 1935, even as key programs of the Hundred Days legislation, such as the NRA for industry and agriculture's AAA, were declared
unconstitutional. Eight million people were put to work under the Works
Progress Administration (WPA), created in 1935. The WPA improved roads,
bridges, and culverts; it repaired and remodeled schools, laid storm sewers
and sidewalks, and built dams for flood protection. In early 1935, more than
eight thousand families in Rockford and Winnebago County were on relief.
By the following spring, about half of those families were employed by the
WPA. As the local economy improved, the numbers employed by the WPA
shrank from 4,153 in early 1936 to 1,365 in early 1938.[1] Other major thrusts
of the Second New Deal included the passage of the Social Security Act and
the establishment of the Rural Electrification Administration.

Although in May 1935 the NRA was declared unconstitutional (for excessive federal intervention in private affairs), Congress restored the rights of

labor to organize and bargain collectively. In the late 1930s, union membership soared, and strikes became common again. Many strikes turned violent, including a steel strike on Memorial Day 1937, on Chicago's south side. In March 1938, May recorded a strike riot at Belvidere's National Sewing Machine factory.

Meanwhile, the economy began to improve, picking up slowly in 1935. Farmers' renewed purchase of tractors and machinery contributed to the economic pickup, and so did increased car sales. By 1936, the recovery looked real; the index of industrial production was up sharply, and the stock market showed impressive gains. Retailers in Rockford sold products worth forty-two million dollars in 1936, about twice the total in 1933. Local car dealers sold more than four thousand new cars. Many industries in Rockford, including tool-and-die makers, machine-tool producers, and small contract manufacturers, were strongly linked to the auto industry; others served the aviation industry.

But although production began to increase sharply, employment improved only modestly. The number of unemployed fell from twelve million in 1933 to eight million in 1937. Fourteen percent of the workforce remained unemployed. If those employed in government make-work programs were counted with the employed, the unemployed in 1937 still made up more than 9 percent of the workforce. The improvement was significant, but unemployment remained very high by historical standards.[2]

Then in the summer of 1937, the stock market fell again, and industrial production collapsed suddenly. Millions of workers were laid off, and unemployment returned to 20 percent of the labor force.[3] Critics called it the Roosevelt Recession. May noted that several men came by looking for work one day in early August.

While the economy zigged and zagged, headlines in Rockford papers focused attention on other disappointments of the late 1930s: the untimely death of Will Rogers in an airplane crash in 1935, the German dirigible *Hindenburg* exploding and burning in 1937, the loss of Amelia Earhart and her navigator in the South Pacific on a round-the-world flight two months after the *Hindenburg* incident. The story that sold the most newspapers, however, was undoubtedly that of the British king Edward VIII, who abdicated the throne in 1936 for the love of an American divorcée.[4]

During all of these years, anxiety about increasing aggression in Europe and Asia grew while Americans voiced determination to stay out of war. Italy invaded Ethiopia in 1935. Civil war broke out in Spain in 1936. Japan moved farther into China in 1937. Germany seized Austria and Czechoslovakia in

1938. The Nazi persecution of the Jews was made plain when the Nuremberg Laws were passed in 1935; and in 1938, German attacks on Jews became even more deadly. The isolationist sentiment, so strong in the United States at mid-decade, slowly began to erode while outrage built. By the time Germany stormed into Poland in September 1939, and Britain and France responded with declarations of war, Americans were ready to help but still determined to keep their boys at home. In the final months of 1939, all eyes in America were fixed on Europe. In 1935, however, the dust storms in the West and the bizarre weather in the rest of the country still commanded the attention of U.S. farmers.

NATURE'S EXTREMES

During the mid- to late 1930s, the display of natural force was nothing short of astonishing. Severe drought, extremes of cold and heat, hurricanes and other violent storms, heavy snows, torrential rains, and plagues of grasshoppers visited the country during the latter part of the 1930s.

A drought unmatched in previous history precipitated the development of the Dust Bowl in western Kansas and the adjoining corners of Colorado, Oklahoma, New Mexico, and Texas. The devastation, however, occurred primarily because wheat fields had expanded into areas ill suited to crops. The Homestead Act of 1862 had stimulated extensive settlement of the Great Plains. Later, strong demand for wheat during the Great War, along with the increased use of tractors, encouraged the expansion of wheat fields into marginal lands. The remaining pastures became subject to overuse. When drought struck in the early 1930s, these fragile lands turned to dust and began to blow away. The dust storms of the Great Plains were at their most intense during the spring of 1935, when the term *Dust Bowl* was first used. The storms continued to increase in frequency, if not intensity, in the plains through 1937 and finally ended when abundant rains arrived in 1940 and 1941.[5]

Guilford farms were wet in 1935, even while May remarked on the dust that blew in from the West. On April 27, she wrote, "Cloudy early, but sun shine after breakfast through a peculiar light which from what we hear on radio, must be dust from Oklahoma dust storm." The next month brought more heavy rains; at the end of the month, May wrote, "Ground thoroughly soaked now surely, rye tall as man's chin." Just a few days later, she noted, "Cool west wind, but sunny. Dust in air from another Colorado dust storm. Floods in Nebraska." June, July, and August also averaged more than six inches of rain each month. It was too wet for the barley and the alfalfa but fine for the rye, oats, corn, and the apples. It was so cold and wet in May that Elmo had to replant some corn, and thirty-five chicks succumbed to heavy rains in mid-June. In early July, a big rain took the bridges out in Freeport; by mid-September, a former oat field had turned into a "duck pond." But the oats, threshed in August, yielded fifty-three bushels per acre this year, up from only fourteen bushels per acre the year before.

The next year, 1936, was striking for its seasonal extremes. In January and February the snow drifted so badly that sometimes the snowplows didn't come; at other times they did and got stuck. The Lyford boys used teams and sleds for their milk routes when their milk trucks were stuck in drifts or frozen up. The temperatures fell so low that Elmo couldn't read the thermometer many mornings. One of these mornings, Joe's thermometer read 26° below zero. These low temperatures lasted for days at a time and returned again and again. The vehicles often didn't start, Elmo used his team to pull cars out of the ditch, and, on one occasion, he picked up the mail from the Browns' on horseback. Most often, however, he used his truck for transportation. Once May wrote, "Elmo get stuck by school bridge coming back because he forgot to take shovel. Had to walk home for it." In early January, the young folks took the sleighs and cutters out for sleigh rides.

February had the coldest average low for any month on record: 0°. January was not much better. Snowfall for the two months was 36.5 inches. When the temperature finally rose, the roads flooded. February 22 dawned with a temperature of 10° below zero; two days later the temperature was 46°. May wrote, "Water at our corner about 1 ft. deep."

The weather in 1936 continued to surprise. March, April, and May were rather dry, although nine inches of snow fell in early April. The month of May was unusually hot and windy; June was cooler with more rain. Then July was dry again with "scorchingly hot" days. On July 7, the corn wilted when the temperature rose to 101°. July 11 was "hottest day Rockford ever has had, 108° in shade, 105° here." A Sunday drive the following day failed to refresh: "Oh, such a hot day, hotter riding in hot wind than indoors." Elmo and the hired man worked through these hot mornings, rested part of the afternoon, and then worked past dark in the evening. On July 15, the *Rockford Morning Star* reported nine heat-related deaths in Rockford, bringing the death toll from heat to twenty-five during nine days of temperatures in excess of 100°. The newspaper reported a new all-time high of 112° on July 14.

Grasshoppers arrived with the scorching heat. "Grasshoppers do not seem to have hurt oats, but are eating corn leaves some," noted May on July 14.

This was her sole comment regarding the grasshopper plagues. Grass-hoppers reached "an unbelievable peak" in 1936 in the country as a whole, according to one historian. Nationwide, crop losses from grasshoppers in 1936 reached $106 million.[6]

Although August and September were unusually wet again, the corn yields suffered in Illinois that year. Thunderstorms in August knocked down corn. And when the men filled silo in the fall, the cornstalks were short, and it took many acres to fill the silo.

Early the next year, the great Ohio River flood topped national news. By February, floods were spreading devastation from West Virginia to Louisiana. The damage was the worst in U.S. history. Half a million people fled their homes, and nine hundred lost their lives.[7]

Northern Illinois also struggled with flooding in early 1937. January and February were relatively mild with more rain and ice than snow. By February 21, the rivers and creeks were booming locally, and Belvidere was "flooded above the park." Warm, heavy showers on June 13 left four inches of rain, the "creek on rampage," and Elmo's truck became stuck in the mud when he went out to survey the crops. The wet weather contributed to rusty barley, but the oats yielded more than fifty-two bushels an acre again this year after lower yields in 1936. The corn was also good, but the potato crop was poor.

Wet and unsettled weather persisted in northern Illinois in 1938. A full-blown blizzard struck on April 6, after the rose bushes had already leafed out. The next morning, "all roads into Rockford blocked except to Madison this morn, 45 autos stuck on New Milford Road." There would be no apples and few cherries this year. The summer was unusually wet; June, July, August, and September each yielded more than five inches of rain.

Weather conditions calmed down for Illinois farmers when the 1930s came to a close. The rains moderated in 1939. Warm temperatures and gentle showers one night in mid-May provoked the following comment from May the next day: "Thunder & look showery at times through day—grand weather to grow things!" Nevertheless, rust afflicted the small grains in 1939, and the oats and barley yielded only twenty and ten bushels per acre, respectively. But hybrid seed, combined with good conditions, boosted corn yields substantially in 1939.

THE NEW DEAL ON THE FARM

The pressure on farmers, inflicted by drought and economic depression, was lifting by 1935. In the Guilford community, most farmers were thankful primarily for rain, but the New Deal programs also played a role in the improving farm situation. For the country as a whole, cash receipts for farmers had increased by 64 percent between 1932 and 1935, from a low of $4.7 billion to $7.7 billion.[8] Farm prices in aggregate had also increased by 64 percent. Both prices and income continued higher in 1936 and 1937, until prices fell by about 20 percent when the Depression returned with renewed vigor in 1938. Farm prices stayed at these lower levels through 1940.

The aggregate figures, however, masked sharp swings in the output and prices of individual crops. In 1932, for example, U.S. farmers sold 587 million bushels of corn at an average price of 32 cents a bushel. The drought of 1934 reduced corn sales to only 170 million bushels—less than a third of the output in 1932—but the price of corn more than doubled to 82 cents a bushel. In 1936, the drought continued to affect corn sales, which had rebounded a bit to 245 million bushels, and by this time the cumulative effect of crop shortfalls resulted in a price increase to $1.04 a bushel. The 1937 crop swelled with abundant rains; 595 million bushels reached the market this year, and the price of corn fell by 50 percent from the year before.

Because of the severe droughts, it is difficult to know if government efforts to limit production helped to improve prices, but most analysts have said that, except in the case of cotton and tobacco, the drought was the overwhelming factor in agricultural price increases.[9] The general improvement in the economy until 1937 also contributed to healthier markets for meat and grain. For May and Elmo, gross farm income in 1935 and 1936 averaged $3,375, almost double the Depression low in 1933. Since the prices of other products were also rising, expenses were higher too. Nevertheless, the picture for net income improved in these two years.

Government benefit payments, for all farmers, increased from $131 million in 1933 to $573 million in 1935. In 1935, benefit payments represented 7.4 percent of cash receipts for production. May recorded Corn–Hog payments of $82 in 1934, $129 in 1935, and $41 in 1936. For May and Elmo, the 1935 payments were less than 5 percent of gross farm income for the year. In 1938, 5.25 million farmers received benefit payments totaling $482 million. Almost half of those farmers received payments of $40 or less, another third received sums in the $40 to $100 range, and a small percentage of AAA farmers (fewer than 2 percent) received payments in excess of $1,000.[10]

The benefit payments were only part of the subsidies for agriculture during this period. Price support loans and interest subsidies also benefited farmers. Moreover, during the drought of 1934, the government purchased more than eight million head of cattle to keep prices from plummeting in regional markets. Low-income farmers realized few benefits from the AAA and commodity loan programs but received other forms of relief. Drought relief was available to those suffering the worst of conditions. In February 1935, approximately one million farm families, three-quarters of them tenant farmers and farm laborers, received some form of relief grants. As things picked up for agriculture, these numbers fell rapidly. New Deal programs also bought up submarginal farmland to return to the public domain and attempted to resettle the destitute farmers in productive communities.[11]

Most significantly perhaps, the New Deal had helped reduce the burden of debt on farmers by mid-decade and, with it, the fear of foreclosure. By 1935, many farmers had refinanced loans at lower rates, either through New Deal programs or privately, as in the case of Joe Lyford. Other farmers had defaulted and returned their farms to the creditors. In most cases, the farms were then resold at lower prices with less debt. Farm foreclosures peaked in the United States at 38.8 per 1,000 farms in 1933, then fell to 21.0 per 1,000 by 1935, and continued downward. By 1939, foreclosure rates were 13.5 per 1,000 farms, lower than in the late 1920s. Farm values slowly began to recover in places such as Illinois, making it easier for farmers to manage debt.[12]

The New Deal for agriculture evolved as bountiful harvests followed awesome dust storms. The Great Black Blizzards of 1934 and 1935, which moved dust from the Great Plains all the way to the East Coast, understandably shocked the nation. Conservation initiatives that had simmered on the back burner moved to the forefront of activity. The Soil Erosion Service, established in 1933 as a temporary agency within the Department of the Interior, was shifted to the Department of Agriculture and made permanent in the spring of 1935, when the dust storms were at their peak. The renamed Soil Conservation Service worked together with the Civilian Conservation Corps on numerous projects to control wind and water erosion: ditches and dikes, channels and terraces, and thousands of acres of trees planted.

When the Supreme Court declared the AAA unconstitutional in January 1936, Congress acted quickly to pass the Soil Conservation and Domestic Allotment Act within a month. The AAA had paid farmers to reduce acreage in the name of limiting production, and the new act paid farmers to do the same in the name of conservation. From the perspective of the Supreme Court, the most objectionable piece of the AAA of 1933 was that the benefit payments were financed by a tax imposed on the processors of primary agricultural products. Under the new legislation, the benefits were paid out of the general taxes, sidestepping the Court's objection.

The crafting of the 1936 legislation at top speed, however, later required its recrafting as the Agricultural Adjustment Act of 1938. Nevertheless, for the most part the legislation of 1938 incorporated the new conservation objectives and the key elements laid out in 1933: agreements to limit the acreage cultivated and availability of commodity loans at price support levels. If the market price fell below the price support level, the farmer could default on the loan and forfeit the crop. These building blocks put together in the depth of the Depression had long-lasting effects on agricultural policy.

What did Guilford farmers think of all this innovative New Deal farm legislation? Certainly, they were not all of one mind, but May and Elmo Davis were not enthusiastic, particularly in the months prior to the 1936 presidential campaign. Like most other farmers, Elmo had signed up for the Corn–Hog program in 1934. He attended another Corn–Hog meeting in January 1935, and George Pepper came by on "Corn–Hog business" in June and December 1935. May recorded three Corn–Hog payments in 1935 and another payment in April 1936. On the other hand, May noted with bold letters when the AAA was declared unconstitutional in January 1936. When Mr. Garrett came in October of that year to "see if Elmo want to have land measured for government check," May recorded Elmo's negative response. Although Elmo stopped by at two "conservation meetings" at the town hall in the spring of 1938, he did not sign up for the farm program again until 1941.

May followed the election campaigns closely in the fall of 1936, making frequent notes in her diary. In mid-September she and Elmo attended the Cherry Valley homecoming and found a Democrat speaking in the rain, with few there to hear. Throughout the month of October, she and Elmo listened to the candidates over the radio in the evening—Franklin Roosevelt, Al Smith, Frank Knox, and Alfred Landon. She mentioned Landon, the governor of Kansas and the Republican nominee, several times. He swung through Rockford on the campaign trail on October 9, and May and Elmo went to hear him speak. Later in the evening, they also heard him speak over the radio.

On the evening of November 3, May and Elmo listened to the election returns, after having the radio fixed earlier in the day. The next day, May reported that both Roosevelt and Horner (the incumbent Democratic gubernatorial candidate) won with big majorities. For the first time since 1912, Rockford failed to support the Republican candidate, and Democrats also prevailed in Winnebago County.[13] These sweeping Democratic victories are what prompted May's comment, "What can't be cured must be endured."

Despite Roosevelt's 1936 landslide, strong anti-Roosevelt sentiment was common among conservatives and among many farmers in Winnebago County. Elmo attended a Republican rally at the town hall in early November 1938, and after the midterm election, May remarked on the Republican gains. Her irritation with Roosevelt also surfaced regarding the movement of Thanksgiving from the last Thursday in November to the fourth Thursday of the month. Although the change extended the Christmas shopping season, it upset the holiday schedules of businesses, government, and schools and generally irked conservatives.

Both the Farm Bureau and the Grange supported the New Deal farm programs at the national level, although neither was a leading force in their design after 1933.[14] Records of the Guilford Hope Grange in the mid-1930s refer to regular communications concerning bills before Congress and updates on the progress of the Rural Electrification Administration. But at least as much attention was devoted to plans for oyster suppers, pancake suppers, the Seventh Street Fall Festival exhibit, and plays to raise money. Elmo continued to participate in the Farm Bureau and also participated in the Winnebago Service Company, the cooperative established by the Farm Bureau in the early 1930s. It provided fuel and other farm inputs to patrons.

Off the Land and on the Road

Just when things were looking better for most farmers in the latter half of the 1930s, the popular media were broadcasting images of the many thousands of farmers forced off their land in the Dust Bowl and the equally many sharecroppers "tractored off" their land in the South. Additional hundreds of thousands of unemployed joined their ranks on the highways heading west in dilapidated Model Ts or hopping freight trains from town to town in hopes of finding greener pastures. The images were irresistible. Perhaps a million people in total looked to the road for refuge during the darkest years of the Depression decade.[15]

Some have estimated that as many as 350,000 fled the Dust Bowl and crossed into California by way of Arizona during the four years that began midsummer in 1935.[16] Many of these refugees hoped to find work as migrant labor on large commercial fruit and vegetable farms. Their genuine stories of misery inspired "reporters and magazine writers by the score, playwrights and novelists, preachers and poets."[17] John Steinbeck immortalized their tale in *The Grapes of Wrath* in 1939.

Half the farm families in some counties of the Dust Bowl abandoned their farms,[18] but Dust Bowl historians have emphasized the tenacity of those who survived the winds and dust. Donald Worster noted that for every farmer who left, two others stuck it out, and he described how Americans, through newspapers, magazines, and movies, were exposed to an "extreme slice of reality, the most sensationally barren parts of that land." Douglas Hurt agreed that Steinbeck's novel tells the story of a minority; "the vast majority of the people," he said, did not flee the Dust Bowl.[19] Moreover, the Dust Bowl per se was confined to western Kansas, southeastern Colorado, the far northeastern corner of New Mexico, and the panhandles of Texas and Oklahoma, areas responsible for a limited portion of the nation's agricultural output in the best of weather conditions.

The "Okies" from the Dust Bowl were not the only sorry farmers on the road in the mid- and late 1930s; the "Arkies," sharecroppers from Arkansas and their neighbors from the cotton fields of the South, traveled with them. Ironically, it was the New Deal that helped to push many southern sharecroppers, tenant farmers, and farm laborers off the land. The AAA encouraged farmers to limit their production; in fact, it paid them to produce less. At that same time, tractors were becoming increasingly useful. Many large southern landholders took advantage of this by accepting the AAA payments, using them to buy tractors, and then getting rid of the sharecroppers and laborers they no longer needed. The AAA intended for landlord and tenant to share the benefit payments, but the landowners found many ways of maneuvering around this intent. Between 1930 and 1940, the number of sharecropper families in the South fell by one-third when 235,000 families left the land. Broadway's *Tobacco Road* played continuously from December 1935 for almost four years, then went on the road.[20]

To city dwellers, the plight of farmers looked worse than it was for the majority. During the worst Depression years on the farm, the early 1930s, farms provided refuge for unemployed city cousins. The farm population increased from about 30.5 million in 1930 to 32.4 million in 1933, even while banks foreclosed on hundreds of thousands of farms. Then with the Dust Bowl and repercussions of the New Deal in the South, hundreds of thousands were forced off the land. As things improved in the latter half of the 1930s, farmers bought tractors, and the trend toward fewer and larger farms continued, further reducing the farm population. Subsistence farmers lost their land to foreclosure, and the federal government bought up submarginal land, reinforcing the trend toward larger, more productive farms. Nevertheless, in 1939 farms supported a population of 30.8 million, still somewhat larger than the farm population of 1930.

May and Elmo were surely curious about the media coverage of the plight of the farmer. In late September and early October 1935, they traveled through Arkansas, Oklahoma, Texas, and New Mexico to see what was going on. As on previous trips, they spent most nights in tourist camps. May noted the quality of the corn as they drove through Illinois and the presence of more soybeans farther south. Through Arkansas she remarked on the many Negroes, cotton fields, and oil wells. After driving through Texas, May commented on the dust ("1st day wind has blown") and the heat. In New Mexico, they saw Carlsbad Caverns. Then they circled back to Wichita to visit May's cousins. They passed through Amarillo, Texas ("flat, sandy spaces"), and entered Oklahoma again, visiting the capitol in Oklahoma City. On the return trip, Elmo bought cattle in Kansas City, shipping them back to Rockford on the train. They drove 451 miles the last day to reach home, ending a sixteen-day trip.

Other farmers in the Guilford community were also on the road in the mid- to late 1930s. Fred and Emma Davis went east in 1935 and then west in 1936. They camped with a trailer pulled behind the car. In 1935, they visited Niagara Falls and then went into Canada, heading up through Montreal,

Fred Davis's family travels, New Brunswick, 1935.

Quebec, and into New Brunswick. In 1936, they saw Yellowstone National Park in Wyoming, Glacier in Montana, and the redwood forests in California. They also stopped in Tacoma, Washington, to see May Purdy and the other cousins there. The Frank Reid family visited Yellowstone in 1935. In 1938, Frank sent Elmo a postcard of the San Francisco–Oakland Bay Bridge and noted having driven 693 miles the day before.

May and Elmo were on the road again in 1938 and 1939. In the first year, they returned to Wichita, by way of Iowa and Nebraska, to visit May's cousins. On leaving Wichita, they went southwest to Tulsa, Oklahoma, and then to Fort Smith, Arkansas, and Memphis, Tennessee. The last day they drove 517 miles home from Dyersburg, Tennessee. In 1939, May and Elmo took another long trip out west but left no record of it.

MODERNIZING THE FARM IN THE DEPRESSION ERA

Although the Depression lingered throughout the decade, it did not halt the modernization of agriculture in the latter half of the 1930s. Sales of tractors and farm equipment picked up quickly beginning in 1935. Major innovations pushed the mechanization of agriculture several big steps forward. Sales of farm machinery from the largest eight companies swelled from $85 million in 1932 to $373 million in 1936.[21] The increasing use of soybeans and the new hybrid corn dramatically increased the productive capacity of the average Corn Belt farm, and the Rural Electrification Administration helped make electricity more available in rural areas.

Tractors, Corn Pickers, and Combines

The severity of the Depression on the farm in the early 1930s kept many farmers from buying a tractor, just when it was developing into a truly efficient machine. The tractor had taken a big leap forward when International Harvester introduced the all-purpose Farmall in 1924. In the country as a whole, the number of tractors on farms climbed steadily until 1932 but then fell for two years when farmers, overwhelmed with debt, lost their tractors. In 1934, approximately six thousand fewer tractors were found on farms than in 1932, and the proportion of tractors to farms was one to seven. But from 1935 to the end of the decade and beyond, the number of tractors on farms shot up. By 1940, the ratio was one tractor for every four farms in the United States. In most midwestern states about half of all farms had tractors, and many had more than one.

As always, Guilford farmers were eager to test the new tractors, but Elmo was not first among them. Despite the appearance of tractors in Guilford in 1919, Elmo put off his first purchase of one, the Fordson, until 1926. Although Elmo courted the International dealer from the early 1930s on, he didn't buy another new tractor until July 1938, when he spent $1,040 on an International Farmall F-20 with rubber tires. One of the first things Elmo used his new tractor for was to cultivate corn, but it was also powerful enough to run the threshing machine later that summer.

While most farmers in Guilford drove Farmall tractors in the late 1930s, other farm machinery companies were gaining market share. Fred Davis bought a new Allis-Chalmers WC with rubber tires in 1934 for $825 and then bought the smaller Allis-Chalmers Model B in 1938 for $440. John Deere began producing a popular Model A in 1934, available with rubber tires; the McLartys and the Molanders had John Deere tractors.

All these tractors were much more efficient than the tractors of the early 1920s. They came with a power take-off to power trailing corn pickers, mowers, and combines and a power lift to raise and lower attached equipment. The new rubber tires, introduced in 1932, sold many tractors. In 1937, 43 percent of the tractors produced were equipped with rubber tires. By 1940, 85 percent of the tractors produced had rubber tires. The new rubber-tired tractors drove at higher speeds—between 2.5 and 5 miles per hour in the field,

Anne Davis, Fred and Emma's daughter, with an Allis-Chalmers tractor in background, ca. 1937.

considerably faster than horses or early tractors. New gear ratios allowed speeds of up to twenty miles per hour on the road, allowing the tractor to do the work of a truck, especially for short hauls. The higher speeds also facilitated access to more distant fields, which allowed farmers to expand their acreage. A smoother ride was another important consideration; steel wheels had subjected both the tractor and the farmer to constant pounding and jarring. The rubber tires meant less wear and tear on both tractor and driver. Also, the newer tractors lasted longer, and fuel efficiency was improved.[22]

By 1938, Fred Davis had abandoned his horses,[23] thus his need for two tractors. But most farmers, including Elmo, had horses at work in their fields, alongside their tractor. A survey of 847 Corn Belt farms in 1936 reported no farms that used tractors only. Fifty-seven percent used horses and one or more tractors, and the remainder used horses only.[24] Elmo used horses to dig potatoes, plant corn, cultivate corn, husk corn, and pull wagons loaded with crops in from the fields. More often than not, Elmo used the horses while the hired man drove the tractor. On the other hand, Elmo finally took the old buggy apart in 1939. Even on the country roads, buggies were no longer suitable.

Elmo's horses were often found cultivating both before and after the purchase of the 1938 Farmall. The development of the rotary hoe, however, allowed farmers to use early model tractors to remove small weeds. With increasing frequency since 1933, Elmo had been using his 1926 Fordson tractor with a borrowed rotary hoe to cultivate corn and beans. (He bought his own rotary hoe in 1938.) The blades of the rotary hoe would penetrate only the surface of the soil and, when pulled quickly across it, destroyed the tiny weeds without damaging the more deeply rooted corn or beans. The young corn or beans also recovered easily when bruised by the wheels of the Fordson. The new Farmall, on the other hand, was designed for use with the traditional row cultivators, which dug deeply and eradicated larger weeds. Much of the time, however, when there was cultivating to do, both Elmo and the hired man were in the fields, one of them using horses. May and Elmo bought three horses in the mid- to late 1930s.

Until mechanical corn pickers took over, corn husking required horses. The well-trained team pulled the wagon, while the farmer walked behind, husking the corn and throwing it against the bangboard, from whence it fell into the wagon. By 1938, however, an estimated 43 percent of the Illinois corn crop (and 35 percent of the Iowa crop) was gathered with mechanical corn pickers, pulled through the fields with tractors. Sales of corn pickers increased from 1,845 in 1935 to 16,044 in 1938.[25]

On May and Elmo's farm, the evolution from hand husking to machine picking took twenty years and then some. Elmo first bought a mechanical corn husker, designed for use with horses, at a Fitch sale in 1916 for thirty-six dollars. He used it briefly during the war while labor was scarce but abandoned it in the early 1920s. During the late 1920s, neighbors with corn pickers harvested some of Elmo and May's corn, but these newer machines were still problematic. Labor was plentiful in the early 1930s, so Elmo went back to husking by hand. In 1936, he bought another used corn picker and added a power take-off to his tractor to use it. He had it up and running for an out-of-pocket cost of $112.55 plus $9 for the power take-off. The men still "open the fields" by hand, and the machine broke frequently. Elmo still struggled with the used machine in 1939, but he also went to look at the new corn pickers in neighboring fields. He used his machine with its frequent breakdowns until 1941.

As the days of husking by hand neared their end, nostalgia built for this dreaded but character-building chore, and farmers held husking contests. Not until the later 1930s did May mention such contests, when several occurred locally. Joe and Marian Lyford also attended a state husking contest in November 1936.

Dramatic change in Corn Belt farming was also set in motion by the "baby combine," introduced in 1934. The Allis-Chalmers "All Crop" combine weighed only twenty-eight hundred pounds and cut a swath five and

Allis-Chalmers tractor and combine, ca. 1940.

a half feet wide. The price was right, and farmers rapidly adopted it. Not only was it suitable for oats, rye, barley, and wheat, but it also harvested soybeans. Other farm machinery producers rushed to come out with comparable products. By 1939, 80 percent of combines sold cut a swath of five to six feet or less.[26]

The number of men threshing in Elmo's machine group began to shrink in the late 1930s when some members bought combines. Frank Reid had an Allis-Chalmers combine in 1936; he harvested May and Elmo's beans with it that year. The other men contended with the threshing machine bought back in 1914; it broke down almost daily, and the threshing proceeded slowly. In March 1937, May recorded an expense of $164 for a threshing machine; this year and the next saw fewer breakdowns. Finally, Elmo bought an Allis-Chalmers combine in July 1940 for $550; the Lyford boys—Russell, Stan, Franklin, and Joe—all used it that year. By then at least one farmer in the neighborhood had a small International Harvester combine at work in the grain fields.

The big threshing dinners also slowly began to fade from the scene. Combining grain required far fewer men. One man could drive the tractor to pull the combine, although others were still needed to haul grain in from the field. Now that the men could travel quickly in their cars and trucks, sometimes they even went out for dinner. The first time May sent a crowd of working men out for dinner was on her sixty-third birthday, in 1936. Fifteen men were at the farm, filling silo. The day before, Mrs. Johnson helped May and her hired girl get dinner for the silo fillers. But on May's birthday, the fifteen men had their dinner up in Loves Park, a suburb of Rockford. After managing meals for threshers for thirty-five years, most of that time without the ability to walk, May retired from the job. Later that week, the Browns also sent silo fillers up to Loves Park for dinner.

Soybeans, Hybrid Corn, and the Biochemical Package

The new combines, corn pickers, and updated tractors arrived just in time to take advantage of synergy with the increasingly popular soybean and the new hybrid corn. The production of soybeans took off in the Corn Belt in the mid-1930s, in part because small combines were on hand to harvest them. In the 1920s, soybeans were grown as a forage crop, but in the drought of 1934, the dry beans were mowed and then stacked in the barn to replace corn for feed. Frank Reid's Allis-Chalmers combine made the 1936 harvest of the dry grain much easier.

The drought first prompted many farmers to plant soybeans, but new varieties and markets encouraged them to continue. The commercial use of soybeans to crush for oil increased from about 3 million bushels in 1933 to 9.1 million bushels in the drought year of 1934. By 1939, this commercial demand exceeded 57 million bushels. Elmo sold just two bushels of beans in 1935 and fed the rest, but in 1937, he sold close to two hundred dollars worth of beans, about 7 percent of gross farm sales. Finally, the New Deal also encouraged Corn Belt farmers to plant soybeans, which were classified as a soil-conserving crop.

Although the New Deal hoped to limit the production of corn and thereby boost prices, the widespread adoption of hybrid corn by 1939 frustrated this goal. Acreage planted to hybrid corn jumped from just forty thousand in 1933 to twenty-four million in 1939. Experimental results in Iowa and Illinois prompted many farmers to try the new seed. By 1936 an Iowa station reported that hybrid corn could outpace traditional varieties by 30 percent. In that year, 10 percent or more of the corn acreage in northern Illinois and northeastern Iowa was planted to hybrid corn; within four years that percentage increased to eighty-eight.[27]

May first noted a purchase of hybrid "seed corn" in early 1937, and by 1940 both she and Elmo were believers in the new seed. In 1937, Elmo used the new seed for only part of his corn crop. He also shelled seed corn from the previous year's best ears and, in late 1937, saved corn again for next year's seed. Hybrid corn quickly ended that practice. Hybrid seed is bred each year by cross-fertilizing two different varieties of corn. Farmers soon learned that the seed was well worth the cost. For the corn crops of 1938 and 1939, Elmo bought increasing amounts of hybrid seed corn. He also attended a "hybrid corn meeting" near De Kalb, Illinois. In late June 1940, May was pleased with the corn crop: "Best corn more than knee high. All good."

The new corn pickers' invasion of the neighborhood during the same three years was not a coincidence. Hybrid corn was developed with the mechanical husker–picker in mind. The ears had stronger shanks so that they wouldn't fall off so easily when jostled by the machine in the dry weather. Moreover, the plants all matured at the same time and were uniform in height. On the other hand, the stronger shanks of the hybrid corn made husking by hand an even tougher job.

Along with the hybrid corn came an increasing use of commercial fertilizer to push the corn to its potential. The herbicides and pesticides for corn and beans that would revolutionize Corn Belt farming after the next war had not yet been developed, but May noted minor new uses of pesticides for Canada thistles, fruit trees, and roses.

New biochemical developments also affected the dairy and livestock industries. The Farm Bureau initiated efforts in the 1920s to eradicate bovine tuberculosis, which yielded success by the 1930s. May and Elmo had their cattle tested for tuberculosis regularly throughout the decade. Some area dairymen were undoubtedly experimenting with artificial insemination. By 1939, seventeen associations of dairymen had formed for that purpose in ten states.[28]

Rural Electrification

Modernization on the farm, in the late 1930s, extended into the farmhouse. After the establishment of the Rural Electrification Administration (REA) in 1935, millions of farmers hooked up to central electric power sources and, for the first time, turned on electric lights. In most cases, cooperative organizations were formed to apply for loans, at low rates, to set up the power lines and finance some appliances. At the beginning of the decade, only 10 percent of farms across the country had access to central power lines; by 1940, 25 percent of all farms did.[29]

In 1935, farmers in the Guilford community already had a variety of power sources, including windmills and gasoline engines to pump water, tractors with belt power to power a wide range of machinery, and batteries to run their telephones and radios. Some had Delco plants to generate power on the farm, primarily for lights, although Joe and Marian also ran their milking machine and iron on the power generated by the Delco plant. Even before the Delco plants of the 1920s, some of the finer farm homes, such as that of Starr Lyford, built in 1913, were equipped with gas lights. But May and Elmo and most others still used kerosene lamps for light and cellars and wells to keep food products cool.

Local farmers near the main roads had been hooked up to central power since the mid- to late 1920s. The farms along State Road from Rockford to Chicago, south of May and Elmo, had central power, and so did Fred Davis, down near Cherry Valley. Farmers had to pay from fifteen hundred to eighteen hundred dollars a mile to bring the line to the farm.[30] The McLartys and the Molanders, whose farmhouses were just across the road from each other, a mile south of May and Elmo, were the "last to get it in 1932."[31]

There the central power line ended, until 1937, when the REA began to make headway in rural areas across the country. On February 13 of that year,

Elmo went up to Caledonia on electric business with Charley Kleckner and Floyd Ralston. May mentioned several other "electric meetings" early that spring and more business in Caledonia. She also noted that Elmo measured the distance "from Rob Watson to our driveway, 1.3 miles." By April 21, the electric contracts were at Floyd's, and Elmo took them around to the neighbors to the east to get them signed.

Finally, on the last day of 1937, two "electric men" came to leave the wiring and other materials; they returned the next day to wire the barn. ("Test by attaching to car.") Within another couple of days, they finished wiring the house as well. May recorded a seventy-five-dollar check and a twenty-five-dollar cash payment for the hookup. A week later, the men returned with some electrical appliances for May and Elmo to look at. They decided to keep the electric oven, the iron, and a few other items ($20.50 for the oven and $2.20 for the iron). Later, after the electricity was turned on in early June, May began to note the $1.10 monthly installment payments on the oven, in addition to the $6.25 monthly electric bill.

In the meantime, May and Elmo began shopping for a Frigidaire and a new radio. They waited until June to purchase the Frigidaire (for $102.48) from Sears Roebuck. At about the same time, Elmo converted the hot water system to electricity (for $57.22), but not without a leak up in the attic and plaster falling onto the kitchen table! But May was pleased later in the year with how nicely the bread baked in the new electric oven. In early 1939, May and Elmo also bought an Electrolux, after the agents dropped in to demonstrate the popular vacuum cleaner. By that time, Elmo had bought several electric motors, and he and Ivan Seele had wired the steer shed and the pig house for electricity as well.

The REA had its critics, but the electrification program pleased many farm families and businesses that sold appliances. Some have said that making electricity more available to farmers was the greatest contribution that the New Deal made to agriculture. Electricity facilitated modern farming techniques in addition to indoor plumbing and refrigeration. Most of all, perhaps, access to modern appliances gave farm wives a big lift.

THE DEPRESSION FARMING EQUATION

In the end, the Depression decade both punished and blessed farmers in northern Illinois. As the decade neared its close, farmers still cut corners to make ends meet, but rapid modernization reduced the drudgery and enhanced the quality of life on the farm. Despite New Deal efforts, prices were still low, but, absent drought, corn yields were up, and the soybeans were also looking good. Farmers employed less outside labor than they used to, but both family members and city cousins riding out the Depression still ate well.

Farm Labor and Productivity

Despite the drought at mid-decade, U.S. farm production expanded in the 1930s. Farmers produced more food to keep up with a growing population, and they did it with less labor input. Productivity (output per man-hour) increased by 25 percent, just as it had in the 1920s.[32]

Many factors contributed to the increase in productivity. The new farm programs encouraged farmers to limit production, so some of the least productive land went uncultivated while farmers devoted more attention and more fertilizer to improving yields on their best land. Expanding fields of soybeans, which were a high-yielding crop, increased overall production in the Corn Belt. The switch to hybrid corn boosted yields by about 20 percent on average. Moreover, with more farmers buying tractors and keeping fewer horses, more land could be devoted to producing crops for market rather than feed for horses. The acreage thus reallocated was substantial; raising feed for an adult working horse required between three and five acres.[33]

The shift to a more mechanized agriculture, with more efficient tractors, combines, and corn pickers, also reduced the amount of manpower required to produce and harvest the crops. Even though the number of family workers increased on Corn Belt farms in the 1930s, the number of hired workers fell by more than enough to compensate.[34] Early in the Depression, the average size of Illinois farms suddenly began to shrink again, reversing the trend toward larger farms begun at the turn of the century. The lack of opportunity in urban areas backed up population on farms; with more people trying to farm, the average size of a farm shrank from 143 acres in 1930 to 137 acres in 1935. But by 1940, the average size of an Illinois farm was back up to 145 acres, as many farmers expanded and others looked for opportunities elsewhere.

May and Elmo, however, did not expand their farm acreage in the 1930s, nor did they cut back on hired help as they had in the 1920s. By 1935, May and Elmo were both sixty-two years old, and May was less able to care for herself and do housework. Moreover, good help was still easy to find, and wages were relatively low. Elmo had paid sixty dollars a month with board for his hired hand in 1927; Harry Shipe worked for half that in 1935.

Consumer prices were also lower in 1935, but only about 20 percent lower. As the farming situation improved in the latter half of the 1930s, Harry came back to work at forty dollars a month in 1937, after working on a neighboring farm in 1936. Even at forty dollars, Harry's experienced help came at a bargain, relative to labor costs in the 1920s.[35] Through most of the late 1930s, Elmo's hired men worked eight months of the year or more, and May had help full-time year-round. The wash went out weekly to Mrs. Rosene.

Elmo found work to keep his hired men busy, and he spent more time on other business and activities. He and May had more money loaned out on mortgages, and Elmo had business to do in town. Some years, he went to quite a few farm sales, and he performed in the PTA fundraising plays. He also spent time fixing old machinery. In 1935, Elmo and Harry worked on the cattle shed, fixing the roof and putting in a new cement floor. May and Elmo also redecorated and fixed up their house in 1938 and 1939. In 1939, Elmo and his hired man tore down the old icehouse and built a new chicken house and later worked on fixing fences.

The biggest extra project came in 1937, when May and Elmo decided to build a house with a garage on their lot in Rockford. Emmanuel Larson, from Cherry Valley, was the carpenter hired for the job, but Elmo and Harry helped with the construction project in between farmwork from mid-June until mid-October, at which point the new bungalow was rented out. Early the next year, even while the house was occupied, Larson and Elmo built a new room upstairs, and then in March, Elmo and his hired man put in sod and sowed grass seed. A new tenant moved in during the fall of 1938, so there was also more painting to do between tenants.

Making Ends Meet

In the late 1930s, May and Elmo had little trouble making ends meet, but farming did not provide as it had in the Golden Age. The value of farmland in 1940 was still less than half of what it was in 1920, whereas consumer prices were only about 30 percent lower over the same period. The commodity loan programs looked to "parity" prices as a goal—prices that would return farmers to the favorable ratio between farm prices and farm costs that had existed from 1910 to 1914. In reality, however, loans were made at prices somewhere between 52 and 75 percent of parity, depending on market conditions for the particular crop. Market prices in 1935 and 1937 were quite favorable because of the severe droughts in 1934 and 1936, and farm income at the national level briefly rose slightly beyond Golden Age parity levels. Then prices fell with the Roosevelt Recession, and farmer parity fell to about 77 percent of the Golden Age standard.[36]

Gross farm income for May and Elmo went back up to levels of the late 1920s, leaving behind the dismal levels of 1932 to 1934. Farm and household expenses also increased and continued to exceed farm income but by less than they had in the early 1930s. Expenses increased in part because prices increased but also because May and Elmo could afford to spend more. Not only had farm income partly recovered, but also interest payments on loans and mortgages were now paid more regularly. Interest and dividend income recorded in the farm ledger fell to $378 for 1933; in 1936 these payments were back up to $720, still about $100 short of levels in the late 1920s. May kept a separate record of the income on her inheritance, until joint investments in Elmo's ventures made that too complicated. She nevertheless carefully recorded the regular monthly payments that Joe Lyford made on his loan from her.

Smith and Olson, who had worked off mortgage payments by painting May and Elmo's barn and other buildings in the spring and summer of 1933, put in only about ten days work in 1934 and just two days in 1935. Eventually, in the summer of 1937, May and Elmo foreclosed on that mortgage, and when the matter was finally settled late the next year, Smith continued to live in the house as a renter.

May and Elmo continued to diversify from farming investments, which they had begun to do in the 1920s. Nevertheless, they bought the new tractor and other equipment, so farm investment added up to more than it had in the 1920s. Still, a larger share of their total portfolio was now invested off the farm. By 1939, most of this off-farm investment was in real estate and mortgage debt. There were also the personal loan to Joe, smaller amounts in other personal loans, and a few shares of stock. The Liberty Bonds had all been cashed in and reinvested.

Cattle sales continued to account for most of farm income (close to 70 percent) throughout the 1930s, but subsistence crops, such as chickens, potatoes, and milk, were no less integral to the farming operation. In 1935, Harry Shipe regularly took part of his wages in potatoes and eggs, and May noted when Elmo traded "4 roosters for some repair." Every year in the 1930s, May and Elmo bought chicks in the spring, as many as a hundred or more. After the new brooder house was built in 1939, May counted the chickens when they landed on the dinner table, as her mother had done in her diaries, for example, "54th chick for dinner" in mid-November. That fall, she and Elmo also gave away many chickens.

Although the new supermarkets of the 1930s offered more and better fruits and vegetables, the garden still played a central role on the farm. The groceries that May recorded in the late 1930s were similar to what she recorded in the 1920s, with a few new brand names and perhaps more produce. May's diary notes in the summertime still conveyed the same sense of abundance (when the rains were good in 1935 and 1937), not only from their own garden, but from neighborhood gardens as well. Mary Kleckner and her son Ralph brought over raspberries in early July 1935 and took home peas. Ed Fitch brought plums in early August and took home apples. May did less cooking, however, and Elmo spent more time in the kitchen. On Sundays in the late 1930s, May and Elmo made a habit of going out to "get Elmo's dinner."

Despite some unexpected health care costs, May and Elmo were easily able to live within their income in the late 1930s, but like other farmers all across America, they adjusted their lifestyle to the changing times. Although tractors increased rapidly on farms in the late 1930s, not so automobiles. In the United States as a whole by 1940, the number of automobiles on farms only barely regained the 1930 level. Elmo drove both a Ford coupe and a Buick in the early to mid-1920s. Throughout the 1930s, he drove a Chevrolet, although he traded for a new one every three years. He cut wood for fuel in the wintertime; he also helped Ed Fitch get wood while Florence helped May with housework. Friends and neighbors helped one another cut costs in all kinds of ways; for example, Elmo traded dynamite (plus ten dollars) for a horse in 1936.

FAMILY AND COMMUNITY

Family and community life in the latter years of the Depression decade was no less turbulent than in its early years. As May and Elmo moved into their middle sixties, many more close friends and relatives died, but these years were also full of joy. May and Elmo were nearly grandparents to a great many children born in the late 1930s.

The Lyford family grew explosively when babies were born to the several couples who had married in 1933 and 1934. All of the new Lyford parents stopped in regularly with their babies and growing children. Joe and Marian's daughter Joanne was also growing up. Joanne was five years old in 1935, and she came down the lane by herself frequently to visit May when the weather was nice. Sometimes she would bring spring wildflowers. After she started school in 1936, she would stop to tell May about her day. May was thrilled in 1939 by the "grand birthday surprise party" that the Lyfords threw for her on her sixty-sixth birthday. Maggie, Annetta, and all the young mothers and their children came, and so did many other cousins and new in-laws.

Starr Lyford was much less able than Elmo and May to enjoy his grand-children, since he never fully recovered from his stroke in 1934. Annetta sometimes brought him by to see May, however. Starr Lyford died peace-fully in August 1938, at the age of sixty-six. May noted the beautiful service, the lovely flowers, and the "many friends . . . there to honor him."

The Lyford boys all farmed, as their father had hoped, until Walter moved off the "north farm" in 1939 and became a carpenter. Walter was unable to keep up with his debts, so in March 1939, Russell and his family moved to the north farm. Russell and Stanley had begun farming together when Russell married, and they continued to do so. Stan and Viola lived on the old home place. Franklin continued to farm the forty acres that he and Marie had bought just after they married in 1933. Franklin also drove a milk truck, as did Walter, through most of these years.

Annetta worked as a nurse on private cases, and when she was off duty, she was usually found taking care of her father, keeping track of one or more of her nieces and nephews, or caring for another family member, including May. When May had another ulcer on her eye in the spring of 1936, Annetta

Lyford family, 1935. Starr and Maggie are seated in front. Courtesy of JoAnne Reid.

was the nurse on duty for much of the time. For about a month, May stayed in Rockford with the Fitches, and after she came home, Annetta came every morning and evening to change the dressings on her eye, put in eyedrops, and monitor her progress. She helped out again when the eye trouble returned early the next year and May went into the hospital for an operation. In between times, Annetta brought wildflowers to May in the spring or peonies in the early summer.

Fred and Emma Davis kept busy with their rental houses, in addition to the farming and their children. Fred and Ben Garrett continued to build more houses, and Emma took charge of the decorating. When a plank broke and Fred and Ben fell from the scaffolding on the latest house, May wrote, "Fred broke arm, skinned face, bruised many places & hurt foot, but out walking about." Fred and Emma would come up to May and Elmo's for young cherry trees to transplant or to bring fresh pork, lamb, or gingerbread. Fred borrowed the buzz saw, and Elmo borrowed an old cultivator. Elmo helped get Fred's cows out of the corn and fix fence; Fred came up to help diagnose a problem with the new electric oven. Fred's daughter, Anne, vividly recalls how Elmo carried May into the house whenever they would come to visit.

May and Elmo spent most of their holidays in the late 1930s with the Fitches, and after Ed Fitch died in late 1935, they kept close track of Florence and her daughter Mabel. Then Florence had a heart attack and died in 1939, and Mabel also died two months later. Lee Fitch had moved to Moline with his young family, so Elmo helped Lee get ready to sell the farm that Florence and Ed had still managed ever since they moved to Rockford back in 1916.

Despite all the activity with these closest family members, May and Elmo also kept up with many other relatives. They always kept in mind the older ones who were failing in health and appreciated a visit. May and Elmo still exchanged Christmas boxes with May's Kansas cousins every year, May wrote regularly, and if May and Elmo didn't make it out to Kansas, Kate or Puss and their husbands would come for a visit. Almost every year, Elmo worked at the Davis Cemetery with his cousin Thad Davis. When May and Elmo got together with Belle Davis, it was often related to a dress that she was sewing for May. Fred and Belle Whittle were also mentioned regularly for visits, drives, dinner, or returning borrowed books.

If it wasn't family stopping by, it was friends and neighbors. Myrtle Dorn stopped by with peonies or other "beautiful flowers" to brighten May's day. Mrs. Shaw might come by with a book, such as *Gone with the Wind* in early 1937. Jimmy Reid came by with gladioli before he and his folks left for a trip west in 1935. Frequently when May and Elmo were out visiting, they missed someone else who had stopped by to see them.

The Kleckners, of course, were particularly close friends, and they were always back and forth to each other's homes. May and Elmo had watched their many children grow up, go away to school, and start families of their own. May noted that Kenneth fell from the hay wagon in 1935. Harold was back home from school at the University of Illinois that year. Clarence was mentioned stopping by with his own family before the end of the decade. When twenty-one-year-old Ralph suddenly took ill in June 1939, May gave updates on his condition in her diary. When he died within two weeks, May and Elmo went all about the neighborhood to organize flowers for the funeral.

The McLartys were also practically family. The McLarty girls—Alice, Frances, and Luella—were now young women, and they stopped by regularly to see May, even though they had graduated from Bell School. Their father, Earl, had been active in the PTA since the 1920s. He and Elmo bought chairs and built some tables for the school in 1938.

May and Elmo also attended many other community gatherings in the late 1930s. From 1935 to 1939, Elmo went to thirty funerals, and May went to seven. The PTA at Bell School hosted potlucks and Christmas programs. May was especially active in the Guilford Gleaners auxiliary in 1935 and 1936; when she was in bed with her eye ulcer in 1936, the ladies of the Gleaners give her a "card shower," sending twenty-eight cards. Although May and Elmo did not attend many Grange meetings in the late 1930s, they did attend Grange social events, including, of course, the annual Halloween parties. May stayed home with the hired help in 1939 but noted, "Elmo mask and go to Halloween Grange party." Rural life continued to be full for May and Elmo even into their later years.

CHAPTER 7

ANOTHER GREAT WAR FUELS CHANGE

When Germany invaded Poland on September 1, 1939, May and Elmo were out west on a trip, and May left a gap in her diary until they returned on September 7. Except for a brief mention of Red Cross soliciting in late 1938, May made no reference to the violence in Europe and the increasing tension in the world until April 9, 1940: "War news bad. Germany has taken over Denmark." In May, she made other mentions of war news; on May 16 she wrote, "As war news are so discouraging, we can only hope & pray."

Backed by a treaty with the Soviet Union, Hitler quickly overwhelmed Poland in 1939. On April 9, 1940, Germany stormed through Denmark and within a month had begun an advance into Belgium, the Netherlands, and France. On May 16, when May recommended prayer, Roosevelt urged Congress toward military preparedness saying, "These are ominous days—days whose swift and shocking developments force every neutral nation to look to its defenses in the light of new factors. The brutal force of modern offensive war has been loosed in all its horror."[1] While Americans prepared for Memorial Day (Elmo went "to see about flags for cemetery"), British and French troops under German siege evacuated from the beaches of Dunkirk, protected by the British navy. By June 4, more than 330,000 of those troops had safely reached England. Even then, German tanks were moving toward Paris, and France fell before the end of June.[2] During these spring and early summer days of 1940, May recorded many evening trips to Rockford for the latest newspaper.

May's diaries and farm ledgers, however, add far less insight to World War II than they did to the previous world war. In part, this is so because Elmo had cut back further on farming and rented pieces of his land to younger neighborhood farmers. In addition, however, May's health was failing; her handwriting was very shaky much of the time. Sometimes she repeated herself in the same diary entry or gave other evidence of confusion. Gaps due to illness were more frequent, even though others, especially Elmo, often wrote for her and kept the ledgers. Elmo was also laid up with a bout of rheumatic fever for much of the latter half of 1941. No diary has been found for 1943, although May kept the ledger all through 1943 with some help from others, and Elmo helped her keep a diary in early 1944. The information in the ledgers is less reliable during these last years of May's life, and the notes in the diaries are more focused on family.

That is not to say that the war years were in any sense dull for May and Elmo. In late 1940, they built another house for rental, this time in the country, on a piece of their farmland across the field from their farmstead. In early 1941, they purchased an additional eighty acres of nearby farmland. In 1943, they bought another house in Rockford. Meanwhile, war contracts flooded into Rockford factories, and the farm economy produced for the war effort.

LENDING HELP TO WAR IN EUROPE

Through 1940 and 1941, Britain held out, waiting, in the words of Churchill, until "the New World, with all its power and might, steps forth to the rescue and liberation of the old."[3] Britain survived German air attacks on London and other cities in September 1940, and Hitler learned that he would not quickly overpower Britain. Meanwhile, despite a continued reluctance to send men to Europe's aid, America began to build its "arsenal of democracy."[4]

Soon after war broke out in Europe, at Roosevelt's urging the United States acted to reposition itself to help and to ready its defenses. Amid the isolationism of the mid-1930s, the U.S. Congress passed the Neutrality Acts prohibiting the sales of munitions and other goods to belligerent countries. These acts were amended in late 1939 to allow the sale of goods to those countries able to pay in cash and provide their own transport. This "cash and carry" policy clearly favored the Allies, who controlled the Atlantic, but as the German advance continued, it became clear that the Allies would run short of cash. After Roosevelt's reelection, he pushed for the Lend–Lease Act, which Congress passed in March 1941. Under this act, he was authorized to sell, lease, or lend supplies to "any country whose defense the President deems vital to the defense of the United States."[5]

Roosevelt's Republican opponent in 1940, Wendell Willkie, ran an energetic campaign but also helped to unite Americans in preparation for possible war. Like Roosevelt, Willkie favored helping Britain, and he criticized

Roosevelt for lack of military preparedness. Both Roosevelt and Willkie favored the Selective Service Act, which passed Congress in the fall of 1940 and required males between the ages of twenty-one and thirty-five to register for the draft.

The stimulatory impact of the war in Europe was felt early on in Rockford. Already in 1939, the orders began arriving in Rockford factories—just as they had in the last war—and the Great Depression finally ended in this city. After a low of $23.4 million in 1933, Rockford retail sales climbed to $59 million in 1940. Bank deposits more than tripled, from $9.8 million in 1933 to $34.2 million in 1940. Cincinnati, Ohio, was the only city in America that built more specialized machine tools to manufacture munitions than did Rockford when the new decade began. In 1934, 10,971 workers had jobs in 106 industries in Rockford; by mid-1941, these same industries employed 18,538 workers. Several industrial companies were already building additions to their plants in that year.[6]

Contributing to Rockford's renewed prosperity was the reactivation of Camp Grant in the fall of 1940. On October 16, National Registration Day, 16.5 million Americans, including Elmo's hired man, signed up for the draft, and within two weeks the first numbers were drawn. Before that time, the rebuilding had already begun at Camp Grant. More than six thousand civilians worked to erect some five hundred new buildings on the thirty-two-hundred-acre camp south of Rockford, at a cost of nine million dollars. Since the last war, the camp had been used for National Guard encampments, but it was soon to become the army's principal medical training facility and the nation's largest reception center for recruits. Before the end of 1940, Annetta Lyford was working at Camp Grant as a nurse. By mid-1941, once again men in military uniforms crowded Rockford streets.[7]

The economy also finally picked up in the country as a whole. Defense spending increased more than tenfold from 1939 to 1941 on an accelerating trend. Other government expenditures were directed toward assembling a bureaucratic apparatus to help manage the war effort. Unemployment fell from 17.2 percent of the workforce in 1939 to around 6 percent by late 1941, and average weekly factory earnings rose by 25 percent from 1939 to 1941. With more people working and earning higher wages, consumers spent more on goods they had lacked during the Depression years, and producers responded to satisfy demand. Overall the economy produced 25 percent more goods and services in 1941 than in 1939.[8]

Large stockpiles of grain and cotton, however, removed the need for farmers to respond promptly to the winds of war. Indeed, the first impact of the outbreak of war in Europe was a significant drop in U.S. grain exports. Agriculture also held large reserves of labor in 1939. But as the U.S. economy recovered, consumers demanded more food, and when the Lend–Lease Act went into effect in the spring of 1941, the Department of Agriculture was already forecasting shortages and taking steps to stimulate production with guaranteed prices. From 1940 to 1941, farm prices rose by 22 percent, and farm wages increased even more sharply.

Perhaps in anticipation of impending war and the rising prices and shortages of goods and labor sure to come with it, Elmo and May made several significant moves in the latter half of 1940. Elmo bought his Allis-Chalmers combine not long after France fell. Then in the second week of September, Elmo and his hired man, Fred Crocker, fenced off part of the pasture, between the creek and Spring Creek Road, and began digging the cellar of the new rental house. Elmo hired Ben Garrett to build the house, but Elmo and Crocker provided much of the labor. When May and Elmo went to look for masons in Cherry Valley and Loves Park on September 23, everyone was reported to be busy.

The work on the house moved along quickly, however, in the pleasant fall weather. Despite tightening labor markets, Elmo was able to find help. Within a few weeks, the project was attracting substantial attention in the neighborhood. On one particularly beautiful mid-October Sunday, "a number of people come by to look at beginnings of house in AM and Elmo there talking with them till nearly 11:30." Since the new house was close by, Elmo could help with the husking and get back over to the house to put the masons to work on the chimney. And he could help unload the bathtub from Sears Roebuck and then go out to help combine the soybeans. Crocker and his wife (who had been hired with him to help May) both stayed on into January. Elmo and Crocker worked on the house whenever they had time in between other chores. At the end of January, the house was rented to George and Mary Andersen, who planned to move in at the end of March.

Before the end of 1940, Elmo also made initial contacts to buy eighty acres of farmland from the Breckenridge estate, less than a mile to the east. May and Elmo had money to invest, because, in October, Joe Lyford had paid off the loan he had taken out from his aunt May back in 1927. Moreover, farmland looked like an attractive investment. Land prices had begun to rise, but they were still far below the highs of World War I, when Fred Davis had bought forty acres (with buildings) for twelve thousand dollars. In late January 1941, May and Elmo paid fifty-eight hundred dollars for the eighty Breckenridge acres.

These ambitious projects were, however, interrupted by the deaths of several close family members, including Fred Whittle and, tragically, the two-year-old son of Franklin and Marie Lyford. Then in 1941, sickness became a major theme for May and Elmo. May had pneumonia already at the end of January and was unable to attend her cousin's funeral. She was in bed all through February, and the few entries in the diary that month are in Elmo's hand. He also kept the ledger. Among other things, he recorded the oxygen tanks that May required and charges for the nurse who came to assist. In late April 1941, May had another ulcer on her eye that was "cured" in an office visit. May was sick again in early June for a week, when she made few diary entries.

But May and Elmo's lives were most affected by a case of rheumatic fever that he came down with in mid-July. Of course, many helped make sure the farmwork got done: the Lyford boys, Fred Davis, Charley Kleckner, and Willis Seele. Another young couple was working for May and Elmo that year, so the men in the family and close neighbors such as Charley and Willis helped to supervise the hired help and took care of other business for Elmo. Annetta provided support in her capacity as a nurse, and another nurse was later hired. George Andersen, who was now renting the new house, dropped in repeatedly; he brought an electric fan to add comfort in the summer heat. Indeed, the stream of visitors never ended; the Lyford wives and their children, Fred Davis and his family, Belle Whittle, the McLartys, the Kleckners, and the Seeles all stopped by regularly, and many others came to call as well.

Both Elmo and May were confined to the house, however, through most of the late summer. Finally on September 10, Elmo was outdoors and was given a ride over to the "80" to see the progress that Willis had made clearing brush and building the new fence. (Shortly after May and Elmo had bought the new acreage, a note in the ledger stated that it was rented to Willis for four hundred dollars a year for 1941–43. His improvements to the property paid for part of the rent.) May didn't get out of the house until a week later, when the doctor told Elmo that he might drive the car again but could not yet work.

Elmo was still weak through the fall and early winter months, and this apparently prompted May and him to purchase a wheelchair. May noted a few times that one of her nephews put her in the car before she and Elmo went for a ride. The wheelchair was ready for pickup in late November, just before Elmo went into the hospital for an operation on his eye. For the last week his eye had been giving considerable trouble with pain and blurred vision. May was quite worried about the operation, and afterward she noted

Elmo and May Davis, ca. 1942.

with a rare expression of emotion, "Elmo's eye coming fine. Dr. says, will have sight! Thank God." He stayed in the hospital for more than a week, then was home just a few days when the Japanese bombed Pearl Harbor on December 7. May noted, "Japanese declare war on U.S."

AMERICA GOES TO WAR AGAIN

The surprise attack on Pearl Harbor devastated the fleet of U.S. battleships anchored there and killed some twenty-four hundred sailors, soldiers, and civilians; in the wake of the attack, all remnants of isolationism vanished. Evening extras of the *Rockford Morning Star* anticipated Roosevelt's request for a declaration of war. Camp Grant was put on alert, and Rockford factories filling military contracts doubled their guard.[9] When war was declared on Japan, European Axis powers responded by declaring war on the United States.

The United States shifted into overdrive for the war effort. Military spending increased from $6.3 billion in 1941 to $76 billion in 1944. By 1944, military spending accounted for more than one-third of national production; in 1941, even after accelerating sharply from 1939 levels, it had represented only 5 percent of national production. Those serving in the armed forces increased from 1.6 million in 1941 to 11.4 million in 1944. After Pearl Harbor, the age of the draft was expanded to all men between the ages of eighteen and forty-five years. Despite the shifting of these millions into military service, however, an almost equal number entered the civilian labor force to take their place. Many of these new workers were women, young people, older folks, and others who had given up looking for work during the Depression. The civilian labor force dropped only slightly from 55.9 million in 1941 to 54.6 million in 1944. Unemployment essentially vanished, and manufacturing output increased by 60 percent between 1941 and 1944.[10]

This extraordinary effort placed severe strain on the economy. Labor shortages became acute; wages and prices rose. To ensure that goods were allocated to critical needs rather than to those willing to pay the highest prices, the government intervened massively with wage and price controls, subsidies, and rationing. The voluntary sacrifice programs of the last great war were insufficient for the immense demands of this war. To pay the price of war, the federal government once again borrowed from the people by issuing war bonds and also changed tax rates and collection systems. Interest rates were still at record lows when the country moved from Depression to war; long-term rates were only 2.5 percent. Despite these low levels, Americans

bought $157 billion worth of bonds—more than was sold to financial insti-
tutions. Income tax rates were increased, and other special taxes were levied.
In 1943, income taxes were first collected on a pay-as-you-earn basis, chan-
neling the money to government spending needs more swiftly.[11]

May gave brief indications of war on the home front in 1942. She recorded
bond sales, daylight savings time (beginning on February 9), reminders to
file income taxes, and mentions of sugar and gas rationing and of the sewing
machine loaned to the Red Cross. She noted that Elmo did much of the
canning during this war, with some help from hired girls. May and Elmo
attended farewell parties for the many young men in the neighborhood who
went off to war. May and Elmo continued to go into Rockford frequently
in the evening for the late edition newspaper.

War bond purchases were recorded regularly in the farm ledgers during
these years, but they were modest relative to those bought during World
War I. May and Elmo's total purchases of war bonds from 1942 to early 1944
amounted to only $850 in face value. They were not the only farm folks
to moderate their purchases of war bonds this time around. Other farmers
across the country noticed the low interest rates on the government bonds;
many opted to pay off debt, buy land, and accumulate bank deposits rather
than investing heavily in government debt as they had during World War I.[12]
May and Elmo put surplus cash ($5,500) into the purchase of another house
in Rockford in April 1943. Fred Davis, in contrast, invested $3,750 in war
bonds in May 1943.

Records of Guilford Hope Grange meetings also reflected considerable
wartime activity in 1942 and 1943. In late 1942, the Grange was farming Wade
Hested's land while he was away in the service. The Grange also purchased
war bonds, donated to the Red Cross, entered a Victory Food Production
contest, and sent care packages to "our boys in the service."

Given the green light, farm production responded to the needs of war.
Murray Benedict described U.S. farm output during the war years as a "source
of wonder and gratification throughout the free world."[13] May's ledgers recorded a sharp shift in production toward soybeans and hogs, consistent
with war needs. And, as happened during World War I, when the shortage
of labor became severe in 1943, Elmo's wage bill dropped. It was simply too
difficult to find steady help, although Harold McLarty worked part-time
while also farming his father's land.

As farm labor became increasingly scarce, modernization on the farm
helped fill the gap. The adoption of tractors, corn pickers, and combines,
which had taken off in the late 1930s, continued, although farm machinery

was also rationed during the war. Even so, by 1945, there were eighty-five tractors for every hundred farms in Illinois—up from sixty tractors per hundred farms in 1940. (Nevertheless, May and Elmo bought a new horse in 1943.) Other new innovations, such as the self-tying field baler, introduced in 1941, caught on quickly. Mr. Matheson baled Elmo's hay that year with such a baler. Joanne Lyford, now nearly eleven, her three-year-old brother, and her new neighbor, Jacqueline Andersen, rode back from the hay field triumphantly on top of the stacked bales that summer. Increased use of chemical fertilizers and pesticides boosted yields. Rural electrification expanded; by the end of the war 45 percent of farms had access to central power, up from 25 percent in 1940.[14] Roads also continued to improve; Bell School Road was widened and black-topped in 1941.

The demands of the war effort sped up long-term trends. The population on farms fell, as did the number of farms, and farm size increased. The profitability of farming improved. With the maze of price supports, price controls, and subsidies in agriculture, government involvement on the farm became further entrenched. Farm lobbies traded promises of farm price support after the war for controls over farm price increases during the war. When farm machinery became more available again after the war, horses were finally abandoned on most farms, and the last of the old Golden Age threshing machines threshed their final shocks of grain.

May's Diaries End

By early 1944, the "power and might" of the U.S. economy and the courage of its sons and daughters in uniform had begun to turn the war around. The critical victory marking the beginning of the end of World War II, however, was the invasion of Western Europe at the beaches of Normandy by Allied forces on D-Day, June 6, 1944. The story told in May's diaries ends several months before that turning point. She died before the end of February.

Both May and Elmo were in better health in 1942 and 1943 than they were in 1941, Elmo in particular. Recorded medical expenses were relatively low. After their confinement in late 1941, they got out frequently to pay calls in 1942. They called on Belle Whittle several times, both before and after her mother and Elmo's sister, May Purdy, died in March in Tacoma, Washington, at the age of eighty-three. They often went into Rockford to pick up Annetta, who might spend the weekend or the night. (She had moved to a small house of her own in town.) They took another trip to Wichita in September; Annetta came along to help care for May. Later when the trees had turned, May and Elmo drove down to Moline to see Lee Fitch and his family. They also attended various Grange functions, including the traditional Halloween party at the old town hall. (The Guilford Hope Grange had recently purchased the hall as a meeting place.)

May's new wheelchair, purchased at the end of 1941, was rarely used. It was mentioned just twice in early 1942. May noted, "Elmo and I go to Dr.'s with wheelchair," and a few weeks later, the hired man "lower my wheelchair." On the other hand, no one remembers May using the wheelchair. Not Joanne Lyford, who turned thirteen years old in 1943 and came by regularly after school; Joanne also worked for May in late 1943. Not Harold McLarty, who worked for Elmo through much of 1943. (Harold remembered that Elmo did most of the cooking those days, however, and that he still enjoyed going out for ice cream.) Once he was healthy again, Elmo carried May to and from the automobile, just as he had throughout their marriage.

From May's 1944 diary.

After a gap of one year during 1943, May's diary resumes again on January 1, 1944, in Elmo's hand. He made brief notes for several days from May's perspective before she picked it up. Then they traded off a bit for a while. May noted the deaths of several neighbors and relatives. Elmo went to four funerals between January 22 and February 4. May went with him to the funerals of two Lyford-side relatives. Elmo was selling hay and straw to area stables; men from the stables came to retrieve it. May could have used more help in the house; Joanne Lyford helped out occasionally, and so did Mary Kleckner. May noted on February 2 that the "groundhog saw no shadow." Spring would be early.

May made her final diary entry on Sunday, February 13, 1944. It was a cold morning, and Elmo went to Rockford for the paper. Later in the day they both dropped off the wash before taking a short drive. May enjoyed the drive; she wrote, "Nice. My cold better."

But her cold was not so much better, and May's resistance was low by her seventieth year. The next entry was on February 19, when Elmo wrote, "May didn't feel very good. So I called Dr Edson. Said she didn't have any temp, but didn't like her breathing, said she might be developing pneumonia, said take her to the hospital where she could have care."

Finally on February 25, after several blank pages, Elmo penned the final entry:

Friday morning at a little past 12 o c
Dear sweet little May passed on and left me alone,
And so life will never seem quite the same, as we were kids, chums,
schoolmates, lovers (husband and wife) with never a quarrel, what hurt
one hurt the other.
The end,
E. M. Davis

EPILOGUE

Elmo lived more than a decade after May died, and life was not the same without her. He found himself unable to stay alone at the farm, so he moved to one of the houses he owned in Rockford. Beulah Heidenreich Otto and her family lived with him and took care of him. Beulah had grown up in the Guilford neighborhood and had worked for May during most of the 1920s. During the 1930s, both she and her husband had occasionally worked for May and Elmo. By the time May died, Beulah had a teenage daughter. Elmo gave the family the house they all lived in.

Elmo spent most of his time, however, out and about, dropping in on friends and relatives, catching a county fair or a farm sale, and keeping track of his farm and other real estate. The Lyford boys farmed his land for most of his remaining years, but Elmo was involved with all capital improvements to the property. He played cards with Annetta and spent many holidays and Sundays with Fred Davis and his family. He joined the Lyford family every year for a big Thanksgiving Day dinner with all of Starr's children and their children. He even did a little more traveling with his old bachelor friend, Willie Picken. Elmo died of pneumonia in 1955 at the age of eighty-one.

Annetta worked as a nurse until past the usual retirement age, and although she remained single through those years, she never lacked family life. After she retired at the age of sixty-eight, she finally married. The Lyford siblings who were still farming in 1940 spent their lives on the farm; so did Fred and Emma Davis and most other farmers in the area. These farm families all had children involved in 4-H and mothers active in Homemakers. Many of Starr's grandchildren and great-grandchildren have also been involved in farming or agriculture-related careers. Many of Elmo's young neighbors, including Willis Seele, Harold McLarty, and Jimmy Reid, also spent their lives farming the family farm. The many sons in the Kleckner family, however, found other careers while their father continued farming to a ripe age.

Elmo left the acreage that had been his father's to the daughters of Fred Davis, one of whom was my mother. When my mother married a Kansas farm boy (with an engineering degree), they decided to live on May and Elmo's farm. Although my father farmed the land (with the help of both my grandfathers and later my brothers), he worked full-time in Rockford as a structural engineer. My older brother has farmed full-time in central Kansas since the early 1980s. Some of the land he farms has been in my father's family since the late nineteenth century, and much of it he rents from elderly widows whose families have also been part of that farming community since those early years. Most all the other farmers in the area also belong to families with deep roots in the area. The successful ones farm much more land than their ancestors did.

Contrary to much of what we hear in the media, family farming is still the norm. As of the 2002 agricultural census, 99 percent of all farms were family owned, either by a single family, or a family partnership, or a family-held corporation. Family corporations represented only 3 percent of total farms, and family partnerships represented just 6 percent. These forms of family ownership also accounted for 94 percent of sales of farm products.

Most family farms are still small. Although the "average farm" has tripled in size since the Great Depression, 66 percent of all farms were smaller than 180 acres in 2002. Good roads and automobiles afford the majority of farmers today the opportunity to work both on the farm and off it, and many of them derive most of their income working off the farm. The USDA has estimated that off-farm income accounted for 85 percent of the income of the average farm household in 2000.[1] For many small farmers, the farm may be more of a hobby than a viable source of income.

Popular media often suggest that we should feel sorry for the small family farmer and scorn the large commercial farmer. But the reality is more complex. The 2002 agricultural census reported that 98 percent of farms in the largest-size category (over two thousand acres) were also family owned.[2] Either one or two operators managed 85 percent of these farms; a single operator managed fully half of them. Despite greater government involvement today, those that depend on large farms for their livelihood face risks and challenges similar to those faced by farm families in the first half of the twentieth century. Smaller farmers with less land, more diversified financial portfolios, and full-time jobs off the farm are more insulated from the ups and downs of the agricultural economy.

Farms today exhibit many variations along the spectrum of small to large. Some small farmers are wealthy, but others barely make ends meet. Some farmers farm aggressively on a small acreage; others produce relatively low output on much more land. The vast majority of U.S. farmland, however, is still commercially farmed under family ownership, as was the case throughout the late nineteenth and early twentieth centuries.

Nevertheless, times have clearly changed. Advances in technology have increased productivity and encouraged greater specialization in production on both small and large farms. The number of farms has been reduced to about one-third the 1940 figure, and the farm population has fallen to less than 2 percent of the total population. Indeed, the farm population is an increasingly difficult concept to define; many farm operators no longer live on their farms, and many who live on farms do not farm them. Increased specialization and the mere size of modern tractors and farm equipment have given modern farming an industrial quality. Few goods for home consumption are now produced on the farm. (Groceries and other goods are simply too cheap and convenient for this to make sense.) New technologies and the increased concentration of livestock operations have created serious environmental problems. Commercial farming is not what it was in the Golden Age of Agriculture.

Nor are farming communities what they once were. Many towns on the Great Plains are dying. The number of farm families is simply insufficient to sustain the businesses that once thrived, and few goods that farmers buy are now produced locally. Moreover, improved roads and automobiles allow rural families to travel longer distances for shopping, schools, and other services. Less isolated farming communities have been disoriented by the resultant suburban sprawl. The consolidation of rural schools has brought many benefits but has also contributed to the breakdown of rural communities. And American culture continues to provide many leisure-time alternatives to the visiting of friends and relatives that was so predominant in May and Elmo's time. All of us who have been touched by vibrant family farming communities mourn the loss of what once was. Perhaps it is only natural to look for someone to blame. Commercial farmers have become the scapegoats.

It is well beyond the scope of this study to analyze the wrenching change in agriculture since World War II,[3] but we don't advance our understanding of the present by denying the past. Commercial agriculture is not a post–World War II phenomenon. Commercial agriculture catapulted Chicago from obscurity to fame before the Civil War, when Chicago middlemen bought from and sold to the growing ranks of prosperous commercial farmers linked to Chicago by rail. In the mid- to late nineteenth century, commercial farmers bought not only plows and reapers but also a wide range of other farm implements and machines. The demand for such products provided the initial impetus for and the power behind the industrialization of the Midwest.

Agriculture was already big business when the twentieth century began. Companies such as International Harvester had grown into gigantic corporations, selling farm equipment to commercial farmers, and the Chicago meatpackers, who bought from farmers, had similar market clout. Then in the early years of the twentieth century many thousands of gasoline engines rolled out of midwestern factories onto farms in the Midwest and across the country. The commercial farmers who bought these grand engines soon became the fastest growing market for automobiles in the Golden Age of Agriculture.

The commercial farmers of the Golden Age in Guilford Township were financially savvy and market oriented. They switched crops when market incentives changed. They kept up with advances in technology and looked for ways to improve the productivity of their farms. Young farmers, in particular, succeeded or failed on the basis of their ability to manage large debts. A certain amount of good luck with market timing and weather conditions also played a role. The Golden Age of Agriculture was a lucky time to be a young farmer.

But the 1920s and the 1930s were just the opposite for farmers; those with large debts failed. Export demand evaporated by 1921 while farmers were still producing at expanded wartime levels. The ensuing farming depression of the 1920s drained the financial resources of commercial farmers as farming profits disappeared and land values plummeted. The weakened state of commercial agriculture in the 1920s may be among the more underappreciated factors behind the Great Depression of the 1930s.

The decidedly commercial nature of midwestern farming for a hundred years before World War II did not diminish the quality of community and family life in that region of the country. If Guilford is any indication, commercial farming prosperity enhanced family and community life. Golden Age mechanized agriculture encouraged farmers to work together. Rural organizations such as the Grange and Farm Bureau attracted progressive commercial farmers who were eager to make the most of their farming operation. Farm women were involved in their local women's auxiliary as well as in the Grange. Families actively participated in their local schools and churches.

The well-being, the resilience, and often the survival of any one individual depended on strong family and community connections. Together farmers weathered all kinds of crises and learned to respond to change. Through prosperity, depression, and two world wars, the community and families supported each other, and they seldom let each other down.

Appendixes

Aham Davis	Elmo's double first cousin; Fred Davis's father
Alice Lyford Richardson	May's widowed aunt; lived in Rockford
Almina Campbell Davis	Elmo's mother; born in Durand, northwest of Guilford; lived in Cherry Valley after Elmo married
Anna Rutz	worked for May in 1916
Annetta Lyford	elder daughter and oldest child of Starr Lyford
Augusta Lyford	May's unmarried aunt; lived in Rockford
Belle Purdy Whittle	Elmo's niece; daughter of May Purdy; married to Fred Whittle
Beulah Heidenreich	worked for May from 1921 to 1926 and in the 1930s
Beulah Johnson	worked for May during the Depression
Carrie Whittle Davis	married to Aham Davis; Fred Davis's mother
Charles Kleckner	original member of Elmo's machine company
Charley Johnson	worked for Elmo in 1915
Dan Davis	Elmo's uncle
Dudley Lyford	May's uncle; lived in Roscoe
Ed Fitch	son of German immigrants; married to Florence Davis
Elmo Davis	born in Guilford Township in 1873
Elsie Fitch	second daughter of Florence and Ed Fitch
Emil Carlson	worked for Elmo in 1916
Emily Brown Lyford	May's mother; came to Rockford in mid-1850s; graduated from Rockford Female Seminary
Emily Lyford	younger daughter of Starr Lyford
Emma Enders Davis	married to Fred Davis
Florence Davis Fitch	Elmo's cousin and Aham Davis's sister; married to Ed Fitch
Floyd Ralston	son of Mat Ralston; took Mat's place in machine company

Frank Davis	Elmo's cousin; dairyman
Frank Reid	member of Elmo's machine company as of 1913
Franklin Lyford	third son of Starr Lyford
Fred Davis	son of Aham and Carrie Davis
Fred Whittle	Carrie Whittle Davis's brother; married to Belle Purdy
George and Mary Andersen	tenants in May and Elmo's rental house in country as of 1941
George Brown	original member of Elmo's machine company
Harriet Campbell Davis	Elmo's aunt and Aham and Florence Davis's mother
Harry Shipe	worked for Elmo in 1934–35 and 1937
Howard Fitch	elder son of Florence and Ed Fitch
Hugh Reid	original member of Elmo's machine company
Jacob Davis	Elmo's uncle; Aham and Florence Davis's father
Joanne Lyford	daughter of Joe and Marian Lyford
Joe Lyford	eldest son of Starr Lyford; farmed his grandparents' farm
John Pratt	worked for Elmo from 1910 to 1914
Joseph Davis	Elmo's father; came to Guilford with parents in 1839 at age fourteen
Joseph Lyford	May's father; came to Winnebago County in 1842 at age three
Lee Fitch	younger son of Florence and Ed Fitch
Linna Pratt	worked for May during 1910–14
Lizzie Rutz	worked for May in 1915
Mabel Fitch	elder daughter of Florence and Ed Fitch
Maggie McFarland Lyford	married to Starr Lyford
Marian Pepper Lyford	married to Joe Lyford, eldest son of Starr
Marion Whittle	daughter of Fred and Belle Purdy Whittle
Marjorie Pepper Lyford	Marian Pepper Lyford's sister; married to Russell Lyford

Mary Pepper Kleckner	married to Charles Kleckner
Mat Ralston	original member of Elmo's machine company
Mattie Pratt	worked for May during 1910–14
May Lyford Davis	moved to Guilford Township as a child; married Elmo Davis on January 1, 1901
May Purdy	Elmo's half sister; Bertha Purdy Breckenridge and Belle Purdy Whittle's mother
Miss Froom	schoolteacher in 1908
Mitchel Breckenridge	member of Elmo's machine company as of 1913
Mr. Grow	handyman during 1910–14
Mr. and Mrs. (Ed) McLarty	lived in Lyford house after Joseph died and Emily moved in with May and Elmo
Mrs. Frigast	did wash for May from 1915 to 1920
Mrs. Pratt	worked for May during 1910–14; mother of John, Linna, and Mattie Pratt
Nettie McFarland	Maggie Lyford's sister
Ruby Miller	May's hired girl in 1908
Russell Lyford	fourth son of Starr Lyford
Sophronia Campbell Post	Elmo's aunt
Stanley Lyford	youngest son of Starr Lyford
Starr Lyford	May's brother
Walter Lyford	second son of Starr Lyford
Walter McFarland	Maggie Lyford's brother
Will Brockman	worked for Elmo from 1922 to 1924
Will Johnson	Elmo's hired man in 1908
Willis Seele	worked for Elmo from 1931 to 1933

APPENDIX B
Expenses, Income, and Net Farm Savings

This appendix is a modest revision and summary of the accounting system that May established and followed, with some adjustments, for forty-three years.

Farm and Household Expenses is an adjusted version of May's "General Expenses." All farm and household expenses, with the exception of wage help and groceries, are included in this category, whether capital expenses or maintenance expenses. Contracted services are also included: threshing, baling, custom corn husking, painting, wallpapering, and carpentry. Laundry expenses are under *Hired Help, Indoor.* Real estate taxes are included, but personal taxes, which began in the 1920s, and income taxes are not. From 1921 to 1931, May tracked her personal expenses separately in two small notebooks, and these expenses were added back into this category for those years. Loans and outside investments are not included; May typically recorded purchases of Liberty Loans, personal loans, purchase of stock, and so on, as expenses. She recorded the purchase of real estate and the building of two houses in 1937 and in 1940–41 in her "General Expenses" category. These have been removed, along with any other expenses that relate to outside investments. Finally, because the farm is essentially the same size through the course of the diaries until the purchase of eighty acres in 1941, the purchase of the eighty acres and other costs to put them in production are not included, and the income from the eighty acres is not included in farm income for the remaining three years.

Groceries and Butter follows May's account rather faithfully. Occasionally she put a quarter of beef in "General Expenses" rather than *Groceries.* Dinners in town usually went in "General Expenses." Until 1917, May and Elmo sold cream or milk and bought back butter from the dairy. They never sold butter.

Hired Help includes wages for labor that was hired on a monthly or weekly basis and wages for occasional daily help. As stated above, it includes payments for laundry, whether it was done at home with the help of the hired girl or whether it went out.

Total Expenses is the sum of the above three categories.

Farm Income represents primarily the gross income from produce sold. Any other payments for services or farm equipment in the ordinary course of farm activity are also included. Interest income, stock dividends, and income from real estate transactions or rental of houses are not included.

Net Farm Savings is the difference between *Farm Income* and *Total Expenses*. Except for the exclusion of income taxes and personal taxes from *Total Expenses,* this category essentially represents savings that later produced interest and outside investment income, or it represents the amount of outside income necessary to cover expenses. Income taxes were paid only in 1918–20 and 1943. Personal taxes were recorded beginning in 1924 but were not recorded consistently.

Year	Farm and Household Expenses	Groceries and Butter	Hired Help Outdoor	Hired Help Indoor	Total Expenses	Farm Income	Net Farm Savings
1901	1368.88	115.93	164.28	17.02	1666.11	1715.03	48.92
1902	859.12	129.85	182.16	29.76	1200.89	1900.08	699.19
1903	1591.60	135.02	189.00	65.54	1981.16	1982.74	1.58
1904	1758.20	150.61	224.90	72.10	2205.81	1946.98	−258.83
1905	1050.12	202.10	184.00	80.10	1516.32	1610.24	93.92
1906	1437.17	228.40	217.50	91.45	1974.52	2111.18	136.66
1907	1105.30	262.50	289.00	140.75	1797.55	1912.55	115.00
1908	1771.09	217.82	224.75	100.76	2314.42	2194.25	−120.17
1909	991.87	241.13	233.25	133.50	1599.75	1750.15	150.40
1910	1441.85	261.52	199.46	141.75	2044.58	2128.70	84.12
1911	1888.48	223.44	240.25	146.66	2498.83	2604.82	105.99
1912	1479.52	254.17	311.53	173.28	2218.50	2638.75	420.25
1913	1716.21	299.27	316.65	192.61	2524.74	3135.29	610.55
1914	1595.32	245.61	340.69	169.85	2351.47	2402.44	50.97
1915	1880.58	235.75	379.45	188.40	2684.18	2547.46	−136.72
1916	1910.56	378.46	359.25	202.69	2850.96	3490.95	639.99
1917	1422.94	334.14	246.60	167.85	2171.53	3285.17	1113.64
1918	1375.83	391.59	196.08	189.83	2153.33	5207.58	3054.25
1919	2673.62	406.20	162.50	170.94	3413.26	5552.37	2139.11
1920	2285.86	397.78	159.00	225.81	3068.45	4233.48	1165.03
1921	1859.30	362.07	242.55	302.25	2766.17	2795.48	29.31
1922	2484.47	362.48	285.25	367.85	3500.05	2352.40	−1147.65
1923	3403.05	364.24	301.25	366.55	4435.09	3164.23	−1270.86
1924	3241.47	328.38	246.25	366.60	4182.70	2692.17	−1490.53
1925	2463.68	330.45	278.34	319.50	3391.97	4059.10	667.13
1926	3196.96	319.72	81.65	223.83	3822.16	3954.64	132.48
1927	3178.87	396.78	350.87	221.00	4147.52	3500.93	−646.59
1928	4854.23	428.49	127.75	286.85	5697.32	3096.24	−2601.08
1929	4681.85	333.96	166.30	282.60	5464.71	4319.48	−1145.23
1930	3472.93	314.75	143.76	263.75	4195.19	2967.18	−1228.01
1931	3008.93	324.59	217.23	270.50	3821.25	2798.99	−1022.26
1932	2258.51	214.94	164.56	191.50	2829.51	1984.21	−845.30
1933	2247.00	253.76	204.40	158.10	2863.26	1698.95	−1164.31
1934	1965.19	283.59	217.20	169.50	2635.48	1919.34	−716.14

Year	Farm and Household Expenses	Groceries and Butter	Hired Help		Total Expenses	Farm Income	Net Farm Savings
			Outdoor	Indoor			
1935	3505.19	336.32	246.21	189.45	4277.17	3283.91	−993.26
1936	2905.56	342.37	194.16	250.30	3692.39	3466.59	−225.80
1937	2672.80	326.70	273.85	287.95	3561.30	2845.81	−715.49
1938	4871.64	338.32	350.60	305.11	5865.67	3204.96	−2660.71
1939	3285.26	338.06	401.50	265.47	4290.29	3322.53	−967.76
1940	3061.14	312.86	360.28	239.47	3973.75	3049.91	−923.84
1941	2999.24	381.03	322.71	399.42	4102.40	4164.73	62.33
1942	2989.36	391.61	336.30	294.55	4011.82	3061.12	−950.70
1943	2395.03	319.37	112.95	248.21	3075.56	3456.78	381.22
1944	NA	NA	NA	NA	NA	4818.89	NA

NA = no data available.

APPENDIX C
PRIMARY FULL-TIME OUTDOOR HELP

Year	Hired Help	Monthly Wage (in dollars)	Contract Length	Notes
1901	F. Hardy/C. Garrett	23/24	April 3–October 30	Hardy till July 18
1902	Charley Garrett	24	April 1–September 30	
1903	Thomas Lee	25	March 16–November 23	$22/month till June 16
1904	Thomas Lee	25	March 14–November 14	
1905	Vernie McFarland	20	March 6–November 15	
1906	O'Connors/Johnson	27/24	February 26–November 24	
1907	Geo DeMunn	28	February 25–December 14	
1908	Will Johnson	25	March 3–October 14	$20/month in March
1909	Smith/Peterson	28/28	March 2–November 15	Smith till June 15
1910	John Pratt	20	March 8–December 10	
1911	John Pratt	25	March 1–December 30	$10/month in December
1912	John Pratt	28	January 1–December 31	$10/month in January and February
1913	John Pratt	28	January 1–December 31	$10/month in January and February
1914	John Pratt	32	January 1–December 31	$12/month in January and February
1915	Charley Johnson	35	March 2–December 30	
1916	Emil Carlson	36	March 7–December 9	
1917	Carlson/Connelly	44/30	March 13–August 12	Carlson till war declared in April
1918	Osterberg/Henry M.	21/48	May 27–August 2	overlap in July, other day help
1919	Axel Holmnes	2–2.50/day	June–November	additional day help
1920	Carl Sell	65	June 21–August 14	day help: Walter at $2/day
1921	John McDowell	25	May 9–August 13	additional day help at $2–3/day
1922	Will Brockman	27.50	March 27–December 29	
1923	Will Brockman	30	January 28–November 28	

Year	Hired Help	Monthly Wage (in (dollars)	Contract Length	Notes
1924	Will Brockman	32	March 12–November 15	
1925	four different men	45/40/25/45	March 23–October 25	
1926	Craig	45	July 8–15	day help: Joe and Walter at $2–3/day
1927	Holmes/Sallee	60	March 21–August 20	
1928	Witold Powell	40	July 11–September 1	day help: Russell, H. Shipe, Stan
1929	George Minet	35	July 5–August 31	day help: Stan and Russell, Joe
1930	George Minet	35	June 23–August 30	day help: Russell, H. Shipe
1931	Willis Seele	35	June 22–November 15	
1932	Willis Seele	30	June 20–September 6	day help: various
1933	Willis Seele	30	June 12–October 28	
1934	Harry Shipe	28	April 5–November 17	
1935	Harry Shipe	30	April 1–November 27	
1936	Phil Snyder	25	April 15–September 5	
1937	Harry Shipe	40	April 5–November 20	
1938	Warren Graham	40	March 21–November 9	
1939	Red Pearson	40	February 1–November 15	
1940	Fred Crocker	50	March 13–January 31, 1941	wife helped May ($50 for both)
1941	Fillmore Brostad	60	April 7–September 9	wife helped May ($60 for both)
1942	Ed Brockman	35	January 8–October 15	$20/month till May 8; worked full-time at factory, too
1943	Harold McLarty	2.50/day		occasional day help, July–October

CROP SHARES OF TOTAL PRODUCTION
(IN PERCENTAGES), BY PERIOD

Years	Soybeans	Corn	Hay	Oats	Cattle	Hogs	Milk or Cream	Eggs	Poultry
1901–5	—	7.3	2.8	10.5	41.4	20.8	10.9	0.0	0.0
1906–10	—	20.6	9.0	14.6	18.7	22.8	5.3	0.0	—
1911–14	—	10.1	19.5	15.4	15.0	29.8	5.0	0.0	—
1915–20	—	3.9	20.2	14.7	12.4	32.4	5.1	0.4	0.1
1921–29	—	0.2	12.9	1.7	47.4	22.5	5.2	0.9	0.0
1930–34	0.0	0.1	3.3	0.1	68.7	13.9	2.2	1.0	0.0
1935–39	3.0	1.5	1.0	0.1	69.0	14.6	2.3	0.9	0.3
1940–44	11.5	22.8	7.8	2.1	16.7	26.3	1.5	0.7	0.3

— indicates none.
0.0 indicates production too minimal to register.

Notes

INTRODUCTION

1. For a more complete account of the early agricultural history of Winnebago County, see Carrie A. Meyer, *Founding Farmers: Roots of Agriculture and Industry in Northern Illinois* (Rockford, Ill.: Midway Village and Museum Center, 2005).

2. Some of May's diaries (1911–13, 1915, and 1938) were passed down to Stanley Wayne Lyford and were used with his permission. The diaries of Marian Lyford were used with permission from her daughter Janice Lyford Leitz.

3. See Roger Grant and L. Edward Purcell, eds., *Years of Struggle: The Farm Diary of Elmer G. Powers, 1931–1936* (Ames: Iowa State University Press, 1976); Pamela Riney-Kehrberg, ed., *Waiting on the Bounty: The Dust Bowl Diary of Mary Knackstedt Dyck (1884–1955)* (Iowa City: University of Iowa Press, 1999); and Laurel Thatcher Ulrich, *A Midwife's Tale: The Life of Martha Ballard, Based on Her Diary, 1785–1812* (New York: Alfred A. Knopf, 1990). In all these cases the authors of the diaries wrote longer and more reflective entries than did May.

4. Further details and references on the family histories of May and Elmo, those of their neighbors, and the local environment they grew up in can be found in Meyer, *Founding Farmers*.

5. Elmo kept farm accounts for 1892–1900.

6. See William Cronon, *Nature's Metropolis: Chicago and the Great West* (New York: W. W. Norton, 1991); and James E. Davis, *Frontier Illinois* (Bloomington: Indiana University Press, 1998), on the nineteenth-century growth and development of Chicago.

7. Farm values nearly doubled in *nominal* terms. For simplicity and consistency, all the data I refer to are in nominal terms; that is, they are not adjusted for inflation.

8. To help keep track of key family members as well as other main characters, see the cast of principal characters in Appendix A.

9. See Jon W. Lundin, *Rockford: An Illustrated History* (Tarzana, Calif.: American Historical Press, 1996), on the development of Rockford industry.

10. See Cronon, *Nature's Metropolis*, 132–42.

11. Guilford Hope Grange Secretarial Record (1871–73).

12. See Allan G. Bogue, *From Prairie to Cornbelt: Farming on the Illinois and Iowa Prairies in the Nineteenth Century* (Chicago: Quadrangle Books, 1963); David B.

Danbom, *Born in the Country: A History of Rural America* (Baltimore: Johns Hopkins University Press, 1995); and R. Douglas Hurt, *American Agriculture: A Brief History* (Ames: Iowa State University Press, 1994).

1. THE NEW CENTURY DAWNS, 1901–1910

1. Winnebago County plat maps supplement information from the diaries and community sources.

2. If it was recorded, that diary has not been found.

3. Unless noted otherwise, the national- and state-level data used in this work can be found in U.S. Bureau of the Census, *Historical Statistics of the United States, Colonial Times to 1970, Bicentennial Edition* (Washington, D.C.: U.S. Bureau of the Census, 1975). Series K has been used extensively for agricultural data, including farm vehicles; series D740 and D802–804, for manufacturing wages; series E40, 42, and 135, for wholesale prices, farm prices, and consumer prices; and series Q153, for motor vehicle registration. Data specific to Rockford or Winnebago County, such as this, and selected state-level data come from the census reports themselves.

4. Dwight Conrad, "Agriculture: Pioneers Break Prairie Sod," in *Sinnissippi Saga: A History of Rockford and Winnebago County, Illinois* (Rockford, Ill.: Winnebago County Illinois Sesquicentennial Committee, 1968), 396.

5. State-level data on the percentage of farms with certain facilities can be found in the annual statistical yearbooks compiled from the U.S. Bureau of Census reports. See also Ronald Kline, *Consumers in the Country: Technology and Social Change in Rural America* (Baltimore: Johns Hopkins University Press, 2000), 26–27.

6. John T. Schlebecker, *Whereby We Thrive: A History of American Farming, 1607–1972* (Ames: Iowa State University Press, 1975), is an excellent source on the history of farm machinery; so is C. H. Wendel, *Encyclopedia of American Farm Implements and Antiques* (Iola, Wis.: Krause Publications, 1997).

7. "The Farmer's Power Plant," *Literary Digest* (November 27, 1915), 1219–20. For further references, see Carrie A. Meyer, "Gas Engines on the Farm: The Forgotten Transition," George Mason University working paper, 2006.

8. C. H. Wendel, *American Gasoline Engines since 1872* (Sarasota, FL: Crestline Publishing, 1983), 315, 456.

9. Wendel catalogs these companies and their engines in *American Gasoline Engines since 1872*.

10. Willard F. Mueller and Leon Garoian, *Changes in the Market Structure of Grocery Retailing* (Madison: University of Wisconsin Press, 1961), 16.

11. See Oscar Edward Anderson, *Refrigeration in America: A History of a New Technology and Its Impact* (Princeton, N.J.: Princeton University Press, 1953), on the history of refrigeration in America.

12. Eric E. Lampard, *The Rise of the Dairy Industry in Wisconsin: A Study in Agricultural Change, 1820–1920* (Madison: State Historical Society of Wisconsin, 1963), compares the dairy industry in Wisconsin with that of northern Illinois.

13. Charles A. Church, *History of Winnebago County* (Chicago: Munsell Publishing Company, 1916), 1035.

14. Payments to carpenters are included in the capital costs. Smaller expenses for maintaining buildings and fences are not included as capital costs.

15. Part of the expense for equipment and horses is replacement cost, but this may be canceled out on Elmo's labor and that of his hired man on new capital.

16. See the table in Appendix B for a summary of gross farm income, expenses, and net savings. The tables in Appendixes C and D also provide supplementary data from May's ledgers on wages and contracts for farm labor and crop shares of total production by period.

17. U.S. price and commercial production data for specific farm products, like this for hogs, are taken from Harold Barger and Hans H. Landsberg, *American Agriculture, 1899–1939: A Study of Output, Employment, and Productivity* (New York: National Bureau of Economic Research, 1942), appendix table A-1.

2. The Glow of the Golden Age, 1910–1914

1. Pat Cunningham, *Rockford: Big Town, Little City* (Rockford, Ill.: Rockford Newspapers, Inc., 2000), 20.

2. Warren Kellogg, "Chronological History: Day by Day Happenings," in *Sinnissippi Saga*, 512; Lundin, *Rockford*, 9.

3. James J. Flink, *The Car Culture* (Cambridge, Mass.: MIT Press, 1975), 24.

4. John B. Rae, *The American Automobile Industry* (Boston: Twayne Publishers, 1984), 37–38, 180.

5. See Reynold M. Wik, *Henry Ford and Grass-Roots America* (Ann Arbor: University of Michigan Press, 1972), 20–23, on distribution systems.

6. Don Brown, *Alice Ramsey's Grand Adventure* (Boston: Houghton Mifflin, 1997).

7. Carl H. Scheele, *A Short History of the Mail Service* (Washington, D.C.: Smithsonian Institution Press, 1970), 136, 117.

8. See M. M. Musselman, *Get a Horse! The Story of the Automobile in America* (New York: J. B. Lippincott, 1950).

9. Flink, *The Automobile Age*, 169.

10. This refers to both horses and mules of three years and older. Eugene G. McKibben and R. Austin Griffin, *Changes in Farm Power and Equipment: Tractors, Trucks, and Automobiles*, National Research Project, Report no. A-9 (Philadelphia: Works Progress Administration, 1938), 62.

11. Harold Katz, *The Decline of Competition in the Automobile Industry, 1920–1940* (New York: Arno Press, 1977), 127.

12. Cunningham, *Rockford*, 19; Cherry Valley Bicentennial Commission, *Cherry Valley 1835–1976: Our Memories Are Warm* (Cherry Valley, Ill.: Cherry Valley Bicentennial Commission, 1976), 174.

13. LaVahn G. Hoh and William H. Rough, *Step Right Up! The Adventures of Circus in America* (White Hall, Va.: Betterway Publications, 1990); John Culhane, *The American Circus: An Illustrated History* (New York: Henry Holt, 1990).

14. John E. Tapia, *Circuit Chautauqua: From Rural Education to Popular Entertainment in Early Twentieth Century America* (Jefferson, N.C.: McFarland, 1997).

15. All of these magazines appear in May's expense records during the 1910–14 period.

16. See Derek Nelson, *American State Fair* (Osceola, Wis.: MBI Publishing, 1999), on early airplanes at state fairs.

17. Wendel, *Encyclopedia of American Farm Implements and Antiques,* 119. See also Robert H. Engle, "The Trends of Agriculture in the Chicago Region," Ph.D. diss., University of Chicago, 1941, 112.

18. See J. Sanford Rikoon, *Threshing in the Midwest, 1820–1940: A Study of Traditional Culture and Technological Change* (Bloomington: Indiana University Press, 1988).

19. Barger and Landsberg, *American Agriculture, 1899–1939,* 279.

20. May's farm ledgers account completely for produce sold and farm and household expenses, but records of the settlements of estates are not available, nor are such wealth transfers recorded consistently. During these years from 1911 to 1914, interest payments on personal loans are recorded but not bank interest, and there seems likely to have been some. Records of real estate transfers are also incomplete. Thus, the revisions of May's accounts, included in the table in Appendix B, exclude income from interest and off-farm sources. Nevertheless, partial information on such investments and income informs the narrative.

21. See Wayne D. Rasmussen, *Taking the University to the People: Seventy-five Years of Cooperative Extension* (Ames: Iowa University Press, 1989), on the Smith–Lever Act and early extension service; and see Church, *History of Winnebago County,* 930–31, and Conrad, "Agriculture," in *Sinnissippi Saga,* on its formation in Winnebago County.

22. Church, *History of Winnebago County,* 931–32, lists sixteen granges in Winnebago County as of 1916.

23. See Donald B. Marti, *Women of the Grange: Mutuality and Sisterhood in Rural America, 1866–1920* (New York: Greenwood Press, 1991).

24. Guilford Hope Grange Secretarial Record (1910–14).

25. Annetta's memories are recorded in two unpublished interviews: J. Otto, "Annetta May Lyford Clark," mimeo, no date; and Josephine Theo, "Interview with Annetta May Clark," audiotape, no date.

26. Kellogg, "Chronological History," 509; Cunningham, *Rockford,* 29.

27. See Edith Breckenridge, "History of the Guilford Gleaners," mimeo, 1993, for a history of the auxiliary.

28. Rockford Female Seminary became Rockford College in 1892.

3. THE GREAT WAR AND ITS AFTERMATH, 1914–1920

1. National Geographic, *Eyewitness to the 20th Century* (Washington, D.C.: National Geographic Society, 1999), 70–71; Jeremy Atack and Peter Passell, *A New Economic View of American History,* 2nd ed. (New York: W. W. Norton, 1994), 555; Jonathan Hughes and Louis P. Cain, *American Economic History,* 5th ed. (New York: Addison Wesley Longman, 1998), 428.

2. U.S. Bureau of the Census, *Historical Statistics,* series U324–326.

3. Lundin, *Rockford,* 111.

4. Southwest Missouri State University, Agricultural History Series, http://ag .smsu.edu/footm1.htm, http://ag.smsu.edu/footm4.htm, accessed June 25, 2002; USDA, Animal and Plant Health Inspection Service, www.aphis.usda.gov/oa/pubs/ fsfmd301.html, accessed June 25, 2002.

5. Church, *History of Winnebago County,* 932.

6. Kellogg, "Chronological History," in *Sinnissippi Saga,* 515.

7. *Rockford Morning Star,* April 3, 1917; National Geographic, *Eyewitness to the 20th Century,* 74.

8. George Soule, *Prosperity Decade, from War to Depression: 1917–1929* (1947; reprint, Armonk, N.Y.: M. E. Sharpe, 1975), 37–38.

9. *Rockford Morning Star,* June 15, 1917.

10. Daniel G. Harvey, *The Argyle Settlement in History and Story* (Evansville, Ind.: Whipporwill Publications, 1924; reprinted 1986), 109; Cunningham, *Rockford,* 37; Lundin, *Rockford,* 122; Kellogg, "Chronological History," 515.

11. The quote is from Cunningham, *Rockford,* 38. See also Harvey, *The Argyle Settlement in History and Story,* 109.

12. "Today in Weather History," www.weatherforyou.com; Soule, *Prosperity Decade,* 39.

13. Foster Rhea Dulles, *The American Red Cross: A History* (New York: Harper and Brothers, Publishers, 1950; reprint, Westport, Conn.: Greenwood Press, 1971), 155, 162.

14. See Murray R. Benedict, *Farm Policies of the United States, 1790–1950* (New York: Twentieth Century Fund, 1953), 162–66.

15. Benjamin H. Hibbard, *Effects of the Great War upon Agriculture in the United States and Great Britain* (1919; reprinted in *Readings in the Economic History of American Agriculture* [New York: Macmillan Company, 1925]), part 1, chapter 4, 511. See Rasmussen, *Taking the University to the People,* 88, on the rise of 4-H during the war. The 4-H name and clover symbol were used as coordinating forces during the war but were not universally recognized until 1924.

16. *Rockford Daily Register-Gazette,* October 4, 1918.

17. From an advertisement in the *Rockford Morning Star,* October 4, 1918.

18. *Rockford Daily Register-Gazette,* October 4, 1918.

19. Cunningham, *Rockford,* 39.

20. Francis M. Carroll and Franklin R. Raiter, *The Fires of Autumn: The Cloquet–Moose Lake Disaster of 1918* (St. Paul: Minnesota Historical Society, 1990).

21. Cunningham, *Rockford,* 38.

22. Ibid., 39; David Brown, "On the Trail of the 1918 Influenza Epidemic," *Washington Post,* February 27, 2001.

23. Cunningham, *Rockford,* 39.

24. Flink, *The Automobile Age,* 78; Rae, *The American Automobile Industry,* table 14.10; and Soule, *Prosperity Decade,* 17–18.

25. Rae, *The American Automobile Industry,* 38.

26. Flink, *The Automobile Age*, 121; National Geographic, *Eyewitness to the 20th Century*, 73.

27. Cunningham, *Rockford*, 41; see also Kellogg, "Chronological History," 516.

28. Benedict, *Farm Policies of the United States*, 168; Willard W. Cochrane, *The Development of American Agriculture: A Historical Analysis*, 2nd ed. (Minneapolis: University of Minnesota Press, 1993), 100.

4. Down on the Farm in the Roaring Twenties

1. Hughes and Cain, *American Economic History*, 444.

2. Atack and Passell, *A New Economic View of American History*, 575.

3. For consistency with other years, May's personal expenses are included in household expenses in the table in Appendix B.

4. Other farmers owned two cars for the same reason. See Michael L. Berger, *The Devil Wagon in God's Country: The Automobile and Social Change in Rural America, 1893–1929* (Hamden, Conn.: Archon Books, 1979), 52.

5. Hughes and Cain, *American Economic History*, 443.

6. Katz, *The Decline of Competition in the Automobile Industry*, 41, 54; Rae, *The American Automobile Industry*, table 14-1. The percentage of households with cars is calculated by dividing the number of registered autos by the number of households, but many households owned more than one car.

7. Michael E. Parrish, *Anxious Decades: America in Prosperity and Depression 1920–1941* (New York: W. W. Norton, 1992), 34, 41; Atack and Passell, *A New Economic View of American History*, 578.

8. Flink, *The Automobile Age*, 171; Benedict, *Farm Policies of the United States*, 187.

9. E. M. Dieffenbach and R. B. Gray, "The Development of the Tractor," in USDA, ed., *Yearbook of Agriculture, 1960: Power to Produce* (Washington, D.C.: U.S. Department of Agriculture, 1960), 33.

10. See Wayne G. Broehl Jr., *John Deere's Company: A History of Deere and Company and Its Times* (New York: Doubleday, 1984), 479, 489; and Sally H. Clarke, *Regulation and the Revolution in United States Farm Productivity* (New York: Cambridge University Press, 1994), 38. The number of tractor manufacturers fell from 186 in 1921 to 38 in 1930.

11. See Clarke, *Regulation and the Revolution in United States Farm Productivity*, 87–88; Robert E. Ankli, "Horses vs. Tractors on the Corn Belt," *Agricultural History* 54 (January 1980): 134–48; and Allan G. Bogue, "Changes in Mechanical and Plant Technology: The Corn Belt, 1910–1940," *Journal of Economic History* 43, no. 1 (March 1983): 1–25.

12. McKibben and Griffin, *Changes in Farm Power and Equipment*, table D-1.

13. Engle, "The Trends of Agriculture in the Chicago Region," 119.

14. Charles V. Piper and William J. Morse, *The Soybean* (New York: McGraw-Hill Book Company, 1923).

15. Cochrane, *The Development of American Agriculture*, 375–76.

16. Many of these sales were concentrated in 1922 and 1923 and later in 1928 and 1929. In the first two decades of the century, he went to only two or three per year.

17. This was according to economist Roger Babson; see Cunningham, *Rockford,* 53.

18. Woodward Governor Co., *The Woodward Way: A History of the Woodward Governor Company* (Rockford, Ill.: Tan Books and Publishers, 1997), 71; Cunningham, *Rockford,* 52.

19. Lundin, *Rockford,* 124.

20. Robert Heck, "Transportation: From Canoe to Jet," in *Sinnissippi Saga,* 131.

21. Berger, *The Devil Wagon in God's Country,* 62; National Geographic, *Eyewitness to the 20th Century,* 89.

22. National Geographic, *Eyewitness to the 20th Century,* 99; Soule, *Prosperity Decade,* 330; Kellogg, "Chronological History," in *Sinnissippi Saga,* 516.

23. Rockford Historical Society, "Remembering Guilford Township," mimeo, 1995, 10, 18–19.

24. At its height, the picnic attracted up to fifty thousand people. Conrad, "Agriculture," in *Sinnissippi Saga,* 395.

25. Emergency federal funds available for extension services during the war ran out in July 1919. See Rasmussen, *Taking the University to the People;* Winnebago County Farm Bureau, *75 Years of Service to Winnebago County Agriculture* (Rockford, Ill.: Winnebago County Farm Bureau, 1995).

26. Breckenridge, "History of the Guilford Gleaners."

27. "Bell School Historical Play," mimeo, 1969; Anne D. Meyer, "A History of Bell School," mimeo, 1969, 4.

28. Maureen Ogle, *All the Modern Conveniences: American Household Plumbing, 1840–1890* (Baltimore: Johns Hopkins University Press, 1996), 2–5; Katherine Jellison, *Entitled to Power: Farm Women and Technology, 1913–1963* (Chapel Hill: University of North Carolina Press, 1993), 34.

5. Depression, Drought, and the Next Generation, 1930–1934

1. Benedict, *Farm Policies of the United States,* 247.

2. The new iron and milking machine were noted in Marian Lyford's diary. Her diaries from 1930 to 1934 provide other details in this chapter; they were used with permission from Janice Lyford Leitz.

3. A rough estimate of farm profit yields about eight hundred dollars for 1929.

4. In this chapter and the next, May's descriptions of weather and crop yields are supplemented with county and state crop data from the USDA, National Agricultural Statistics Service, www.usda.gov:81/ipedb/ (accessed July 2, 2003); and with Rockford weather data from the National Climactic Data Center, www.ncdc.noaa.gov/cdo .html, cooperative station number 117375 (accessed June 22, 2003).

5. Frederick Lewis Allen, *Only Yesterday: An Informal History of the 1920s* (1931; reprint, New York: First Perennial Classics, 2000), 296, 300; Hughes and Cain, *American Economic History,* 461; Atack and Passell, *A New Economic View of History,* 588.

6. Work Projects Administration (WPA), *Rockford* (Rockford, Ill.: Graphic Arts Corporation, 1941), 109–12.

7. Benedict, *Farm Policies of the United States*, 240, 261–62; Allen, *Only Yesterday*, 299.

8. Robert McElvaine, *The Great Depression: America 1929–1941* (1984; reprint, New York: Times Books, 1993), 137; Atack and Passell, *A New Economic View of American History*, 607–8.

9. Benedict, *Farm Policies of the United States*, 247.

10. Ibid., 251.

11. Guilford Hope Grange Secretarial Record (1930).

12. Dixon Wecter, *The Age of the Great Depression 1929–1941* (New York: New Viewpoints, 1948), 28.

13. Ibid., 130.

14. Tax forms confirm that the "beach" acreage sold for $11,125 in 1929. A 1940 loan application of Fred's recorded twelve houses.

15. Cronon, *Nature's Metropolis*, 259.

16. Atack and Passell, *A New Economic View of History*, 613.

17. See WPA, *Rockford*, 103, 110–11, on Rockford bank failures.

18. Atack and Passell, *A New Economic View of History*, 583–88; Hughes and Cain, *American Economic History*, 460–65; Broadus Mitchell, *Depression Decade: From New Era through New Deal, 1929–1941* (1947; reprint, New York: Harper and Row, 1969), appendix tables; WPA, *Rockford*, 112.

19. Benedict, *Farm Policies of the United States*, 262–63.

20. Atack and Passell, *A New Economic View of History*, 575; Lee J. Alston, "Farm Foreclosures in the United States during the Interwar Period," *Journal of Economic History* 43, no. 3 (November 1983): 888, 894–96; Clarke, *Regulation and the Revolution in United States Farm Productivity*, 109–11.

21. Donald Worster, *Dust Bowl: The Southern Plains in the 1930s* (New York: Oxford University Press, 1979), 10–13.

22. John L. Shover, *Cornbelt Rebellion: The Farmers' Holiday Association* (Urbana: University of Illinois Press, 1965), 3–7.

23. T. H. Watkins, *The Great Depression* (New York: Little Brown and Company, 1993), 118–20.

24. U.S. Department of Agriculture (USDA), *Farm Employment and Wage Rates 1910–1990*, Statistical Bulletin no. 822 (Washington, D.C.: USDA National Agricultural Statistics Service, 1991), 93.

25. These milestones of Joanne's early months are from Marian's diaries.

26. Guilford Hope Grange Secretarial Record (1931–32).

27. Cabell Phillips, *From the Crash to the Blitz* (1969; reprint, New York: Fordham University Press, 2000), 71–72; Wecter, *The Age of the Great Depression*, 41–53; Benedict, *Farm Policies of the United States*, 273–74.

28. Cunningham, *Rockford*, 58.

29. Will Rogers, *Will Rogers' Daily Telegrams*, vol. 4: *The Roosevelt Years: 1933–1935*, edited by James M. Smallwood (Stillwater: Oklahoma State University Press, 1979), 122.

30. Hughes and Cain, *American Economic History,* 461.

31. Frederick Lewis Allen, *Since Yesterday: The 1930s in America* (1931; reprint, New York: First Perennial Library, 1986), 100.

32. Rogers's column began to run on the front page of the *Rockford Morning Star* in late 1930. On Rogers, see Peter C. Rollins, *Will Rogers: A Bio-bibliography* (Westport, Conn.: Greenwood Press, 1984), 161–72; and E. Paul Alworth, *Will Rogers* (New York: Twayne Publishers, 1974), 13–28.

33. Will Rogers, *The Autobiography of Will Rogers,* edited by Donald Day (Chicago: Peoples Book Club, 1949), 211.

34. As quoted in Donald Day, *Will Rogers: A Biography* (New York: David McKay Company, 1962), 250.

35. Rogers, *The Autobiography of Will Rogers,* 285.

36. Ibid., 313.

37. As quoted in Allen, *Since Yesterday,* 104–5.

38. *Rockford Morning Star,* March 10, 1933.

39. Allen, *Since Yesterday,* 106–7; Wecter, *The Age of the Great Depression,* 65–66.

40. As quoted in Wecter, *The Age of the Great Depression,* 67.

41. Benedict, *Farm Policies of the United States,* 280–84.

42. Ibid., 289; Allen, *Since Yesterday,* 123–26.

43. These two names were changed for privacy considerations.

44. Allen, *Since Yesterday,* 123.

45. R. Douglas Hurt, *The Dust Bowl: An Agricultural and Social History* (Chicago: Nelson–Hall Publishers, 1981), 33–34.

46. Rogers, *Will Rogers' Daily Telegrams,* vol. 4, 90.

47. Allen, *Since Yesterday,* 126–27, 162.

48. Theodore Saloutos, *The American Farmer and the New Deal* (Ames: Iowa State University Press, 1982), 72; Wecter, *The Age of the Great Depression,* 141–42.

49. It is Marian's diary, rather than May's, that reveals the strain on relationships.

50. Mitchell, *Depression Decade,* 202.

51. WPA, *Rockford,* 110; *Rockford Morning Star,* May 20, 1934.

52. D. A. FitzGerald, *Corn and Hogs under the Agricultural Adjustment Act* (Washington, D.C.: Brookings Institution, 1934), 57–59, 67.

53. Ibid., 76.

54. Engle, "The Trends of Agriculture in the Chicago Region," 121.

55. Saloutos, *The American Farmer and the New Deal,* 74.

6. Fits and Starts in the Late 1930s

1. WPA, *Rockford,* 112–13.

2. Mitchell, *Depression Decade,* appendix tables; Hughes and Cain, *American Economic History,* tables 24.1, 24.2.

3. Hughes and Cain, *American Economic History,* table 24.1.

4. *Rockford Morning Star,* August 17, 1935; December 10, 1936; May 7, 1937.

5. Hurt, *The Dust Bowl,* 3, 49; Worster, *Dust Bowl,* 15.

6. Schlebecker, *Whereby We Thrive*, 268–69.

7. Allen, *Since Yesterday*, 209, 281; Phillips, *From the Crash to the Blitz*, 319.

8. Benedict, *Farm Policies of the United States*, 314.

9. Ibid., 313.

10. Ibid., 314–15; Saloutos, *The American Farmer and the New Deal*, 265.

11. Saloutos, *The American Farmer and the New Deal*, 264; Benedict, *Farm Policies of the United States*, 354; Mitchell, *Depression Decade*, 198, 210.

12. Benedict, *Farm Policies of the United States*, 352–53; Sally Clarke, "New Deal Regulation and the Revolution in American Farm Productivity: A Case Study of the Diffusion of the Tractor in the Corn Belt, 1920–1940," *Journal of Economic History* 51, no. 1 (March 1991): 117; Alston, "Farm Foreclosures in the United States during the Interwar Period," 888.

13. Kellogg, "Chronological History," in *Sinnissippi Saga*, 518; Peter W. Colby and Paul Michael Green, "Voting Pattern in the 96 Downstate Counties," *Illinois Issues* (August 1978): 18.

14. Benedict, *Farm Policies of the United States*, 346.

15. Wecter, *The Age of the Great Depression*, 174.

16. Ibid., 175.

17. Phillips, *From the Crash to the Blitz*, 241.

18. Allen, *Since Yesterday*, 200–201.

19. Worster, *Dust Bowl*, 26, 31; Hurt, *The Dust Bowl*, 54–55.

20. Mitchell, *Depression Decade*, 200–201, 221; Allen, *Since Yesterday*, 253.

21. Broehl, *John Deere's Company*, 527.

22. McKibben and Griffin, *Changes in Farm Power and Equipment*, 13–14; Dieffenbach and Gray, "The Development of the Tractor," 35–36.

23. Anne Davis was born in 1933 and has no memory of her father owning horses. She does remember that he used a neighbor's horses one year to pick corn.

24. McKibben and Griffin, *Changes in Farm Power and Equipment*, appendix tables C-2, C-8. Of the 847 farms, 38 used two tractors and 2 used three or more tractors.

25. Bogue, "Changes in Mechanical and Plant Technology," 17; Clarke, *Regulation and the Revolution in United States Farm Productivity*, 171, 198.

26. Broehl, *John Deere's Company*, 541.

27. Mitchell, *Depression Decade*, 222; Schlebecker, *Whereby We Thrive*, 264; Clarke, *Regulation and the Revolution in United States Farm Productivity*, 167; Zvi Griliches, "Hybrid Corn and the Economics of Innovation," *Science* 132 (July 1960): 277–78.

28. Mitchell, *Depression Decade*, 225.

29. Robert T. Beall, "Rural Electrification," in USDA, ed., *Yearbook of Agriculture, 1940: Farmers in a Changing World* (Washington, D.C.: U.S. Department of Agriculture, 1940), 790–809, table 1.

30. Ibid., 796.

31. Interview with Harold McLarty.

32. Cochrane, *The Development of American Agriculture*, 375.

33. Clarke, *Regulation and the Revolution in United States Farm Productivity*, 168; Bogue, "Changes in Mechanical and Plant Technology," 6.

34. Eldon E. Shaw and John A. Hopkins, *Trends in Employment in Agriculture, 1909–36,* Report no. 8 (Philadelphia: WPA National Research Project, 1938), 20–23.

35. Harry's wages compare favorably with average U.S. farm wages, which also dropped 50 percent from 1929 to 1934 and then partly recovered. USDA, *Farm Employment and Wage Rates,* 93.

36. Benedict, *Farm Policies of the United States,* 353, 377, 450.

7. Another Great War Fuels Change

1. As quoted in Mitchell, *Depression Decade,* 372.

2. Felix Gilbert, *The End of the European Era, 1890 to the Present,* 2nd ed. (New York: W. W. Norton, 1979), 339.

3. As quoted in National Geographic, *Eyewitness to the 20th Century,* 174.

4. Roosevelt coined the phrase in December 1940. See Gilbert, *The End of the European Era,* 344.

5. As quoted in Hughes and Cain, *American Economic History,* 503. See also Peter Fearon, *War, Prosperity and Depression: The U.S. Economy 1917–45* (Lawrence: University Press of Kansas, 1987), 262–64.

6. WPA, *Rockford,* 115–16.

7. Watkins, *The Great Depression,* 343; Cunningham, *Rockford,* 71; WPA, *Rockford,* 116.

8. Anthony S. Campagna, *U.S. National Economic Policy 1917–1985* (New York: Praeger Publishers, 1987), 161; Hughes and Cain, *American Economic History,* 461, 465, 503–4.

9. Wecter, *The Age of the Great Depression,* 316; National Geographic, *Eyewitness to the 20th Century,* 177; *Rockford Morning Star,* Second Extra, December 7, 1941.

10. Hughes and Cain, *American Economic History,* 504–5, table 26.1; Fearon, *War, Prosperity and Depression,* 278, table 16.3.

11. Hughes and Cain, *American Economic History,* 506–11.

12. Benedict, *Farm Policies of the United States,* 417.

13. Ibid., 401.

14. Beall, "Rural Electrification," table 1; John H. Rixse Jr., "Electricity Comes to Farms," in USDA, ed., *Yearbook of Agriculture, 1960: Power to Produce,* 69.

Epilogue

1. Bruce L. Gardner, *American Agriculture in the Twentieth Century* (Cambridge, Mass.: Harvard University Press, 2002), 71.

2. Among the largest farms, 20 percent were owned by family partnerships and 13 percent by family corporations.

3. For two analyses with different perspectives, see Gardner, *American Agriculture in the Twentieth Century;* and Jane Adams, *The Transformation of Rural Life: Southern Illinois, 1890–1990* (Chapel Hill: University of North Carolina Press, 1994).

Index

CARRIE A. MEYER grew up on a farm in Illinois and served as a Peace Corps volunteer before completing her Ph.D. in economics at the University of Illinois. She has published two previous books, *The Economics and Politics of NGOs in Latin America* and *Land Reform in Latin America: The Dominican Case*. She teaches economics at George Mason University.